The

Palestinian

Correspondent

Paul Bulkley

They Believe what They wish to Believe!

Wise Owl sighed and asked.

" Why unhappy Man are your beliefs so often based on ignorance, greed, and prejudice, when contentment is found in Understanding, Equity, and Compassion.? "

The Palestinian Correspondent

1948 Nakba (Catastrophe) Events

Month	Attacked Districts	Attacked Towns	Attacked Villages	Attacked Inhabitants	Expelled Inhabitants
December 47	6	1	16	96,000	7,000
January 48	9	2	33	133,000	8,100
February	9	2	44	133,200	2,700
March	9	1	48	123,000	9,350
April	10	4	143	319,000	147,200
May	13	6	188	279,000	243,400
Mid/End May	British Mandate and Troop Departure				
Mid/End May	Entry of Arab League (small number poorly organized)				
June	9	2	50	82,000	34,500
July	11	3	102	201,500	168,000
Aug/September	2	-	3	4,000	800
October	7	3	71	115,400	93,400
November	4	-	11	11,000	11,000

Note: During this twelve month period about 725 thousand individuals were expelled from towns and villages in Palestine. These refugees lacking security, food, habitation were forced to flee considerable distances to neighboring countries and West Bank often without transportation subject to hostility, aggression, and the extreme heat of the mid Summer.

The Monthly Reports include records of individuals massacred. These records are limited reflecting the difficulty and confusion of recording unfortunate inhabitants blown up in their homes, the many killed on the streets and highways , and those who died due to stress, injuries, exposure, lack of food and secure habitation.. Experts consider that 13 to 20 thousand died..

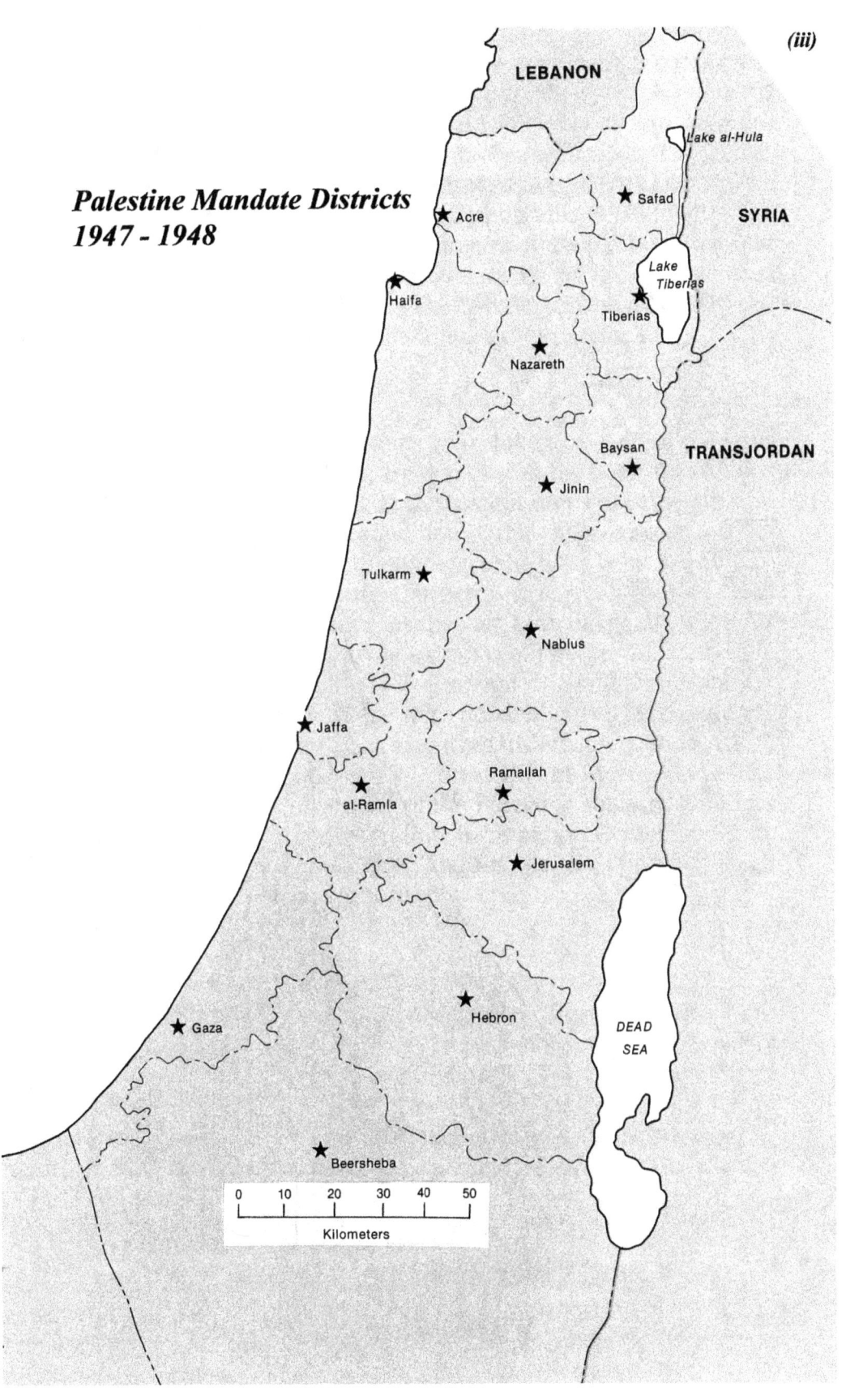

Palestine Mandate Districts
1947 - 1948

(iii)

LEBANON

★ Acre

★ Safad

SYRIA

Lake al-Hula

★ Haifa

Lake Tiberias

★ Tiberias

★ Nazareth

Baysan
★

TRANSJORDAN

★ Jinin

Tulkarm ★

★ Nablus

★ Jaffa

Ramallah
★

★ al-Ramla

★ Jerusalem

★ Hebron

DEAD SEA

★ Gaza

★ Beersheba

0   10   20   30   40   50

Kilometers

Recommended References

The Ethnic Cleansing of Palestine (llan Pappe)

All that Remains (Walid Khalidi)

Origins of the Arab-Israeli Wars (Ritchie Ovendale)

Gertrude Bell - Queen of the Desert (Janet Wallach)

$$$$$$$$$$$

All Profit derived from the sale of this Novel to be given to the Children of Gaza.

Introduction

I gaze at my manuscript, and shake my head. The subject of my novel - the records of events during the year of 1948. How often I have deliberated and procrastinated over the past sixty years. And yet it is still not published. The reason I regret is unacceptable. My change of heart - the continuing persecution that has made Palestine a prison for the past 60 years; the numerous books filling the shelves of American Universities claiming that the events never happened completely contrary to my observations. Finally the persistent Zionist propaganda in newspapers.

Inevitably the question arises. Are these authors correct and I wrong? Certainly it is a matter that requires an explanation because it addressed a major human catastrophe. And if all these authors are correct, one has to ask who was responsible 1948 for the 600,000 to 700,000 individuals who fled Palestine; who committed the raping and killing of 10,000 to 20,000 Arabs, who demolished 500 to 600 Muslim villages now piles of rubble with Hebrew names, and who stole all the real and personal property of these unfortunate Arabs. Finally despite the United Nation Resolutions, and the passing of 60 years, why have none of the 600,000 to 700,000 Arabs returned to their country , repossessed their stolen real estate and bank deposits, and compensated for the terrible harm caused to them.

The Arabs of Palestine describe 1948 as "Nakba" *The Catastrophe*. Incredibly a hostile group of people and their descendants of that time deny that such a happening ever occurred. And for the past 60 years have invested considerable effort in concealing every vestige of evidence that Palestinian Arabs ever existed.

I recollect the times that I have discussed this tragedy with strangers, mentioned some of my memories, and noted their coolness and hostility to my recollections. Apparently I was the cause of their unhappiness. I am reminded of Josephine Tey's significant book " *Richard III* " and her recollections.

The basic theme of Josephine Tey's book was the unproved accusation that Richard III was responsible for the murder of two young boys, his nephews, in the Tower of London. Even to this modern day, Richard's hideous crime is claimed by many. There is no evidence, and yet the belief of that accusation persists! And although historical texts clearly absolved the unfortunate ruler of the terrible crime, the opinion of guilt has persisted to this day!.

Josephine Tey sums up the problem through a character in her novel, an actress friend of the main character, and writes:

" It's an odd thing but you tell someone the true facts of a mythical tale they are indignant not with the facts but with you. They don't want to have their ideas upset. It rouses some vague uneasiness in them, I think, and they resent it. So they reject it and refuse to think about it. If

they were merely indifferent it would be natural and understandable. But it is much stronger than that, much more positive. They are annoyed. Very odd is it not? "

It was certainly most thought provoking. Later in her novel, another character explained the phenomena which he described as *"Classic Tonypandery ", and* gave a number of examples of individuals unwilling to accept the truth:

" In Scotland the Scots, still celebrate the drowning of two women Covenanters claimed to have died for their faith. In fact the Covenanters were a branch of thugs, little different to the Irish IRA, and the claimed drowning never occurred. Yet this very moment you can see their gravestones recording their fictitious deaths. "

Unfortunately and sadly, there are so many examples of untrue claims and denials in these modern times. Just consider the disgraceful criminal charges that persisted against the unfortunate and brilliant Robert Oppenheimer. And of course the many lies directed at the unfortunate Palestinian Arabs by the media and Washington.

I scratch my head. People are so strange. Their beliefs defy common sense, and yet their conduct is evidence of their nature, weakness, and often guilt. ***They believe what they wish to believe!*** No wonder there is so much prejudice and hate. People not only do not understand others, they are determined not to understand. Fifty years of wars in numerous countries since the Second World War is evidence that the people of the USA still have little understanding of others, and without thought permit millions to be killed with the convenient and fabricated excuse that the fighting and killing is for a good and sound democratic cause.

Of course if the nation is saturated with erroneous books of prejudice, the media full of mindless bias, and Washington politically dishonest, obviously it creates a difficulty for anyone to have an informed opinion.

" What is the Truth?" It would appear a simple question, but is it? For example visit any law court, and listen to the witnesses of an accident. Often the evidence given will contradict the evidence of others. *What was the Truth?"* All witnesses would consider themselves responsible intelligent sincere citizens, and possibly would be puzzled to note the contrary evidence given.

The problem is that our minds are tainted with prejudice and incorrect recollections that inevitably blend into our immediate impressions. Naturally you consider that your impressions as a witness is not subject to prejudice and incorrect recollections - however are we reasonable to assume that the other witnesses were wrong and you are right.?

It is a troublesome question because so often many of us are wrong.

Let us consider my manuscript which contains my memories and reports of events over a twelve month period. The memories and observations were of an independent observer with no political or material connections with the people of that time. There was *" No axe to grind"* And yet there are millions in the year 2008 who subscribe to beliefs and happenings totally foreign to my records.

" What was the Truth?"

It is my hope that this manuscript will assist the reader to determine the *Truth.* The *Truth* or a close understanding of the *facts* is desirable in order to have an informed opinion not subject to prejudice. Currently the world is in such a mess caused by a singular lack of compassion, understanding, equity, and an unwillingness to strive for a better future for all - rather than one's selfish future!. Hopefully after you have read this book, you will examine the many books and public documents that relate to the happenings of 1948. And then question why the US taxpayer subscribes billions of dollars annually to a terrorist state, and permits dishonest authors line University shelves with their propaganda.

I, like most people, have difficulty envisioning large numbers. We are subjected to millions, billions, and now trillions. Such statistics have little meaning. However to portray the current subject in a meaningful and human perspective, consider the enormity of five hundred thousand refugees, within a short 12 months, fleeing from death and torture in a country far smaller than most American states, and a little larger than a British county. If that five hundred thousand formed a single line, that line would be over one hundred miles in length!. And everyone of those unfortunate individuals would be trudging 50 to 200 miles in 100F - 140 F heat lacking food, water, habitation, and safety., subject to hostility and vicious attacks..

Before you commence reading, examine and remember the names of individuals listed below who were involved directly or indirectly with the 1948 departure of 600,000 to 700,000 people to foreign countries and prison camps. How and why they departed is for you to decide. Was the departure voluntary or caused by force. The death, torture, rape of possibly 10,000 to 20,000, the looting and theft of all personal property, the theft of all buildings and land throughout the country, and the complete demolition of hundreds of villages are all matters for you to decide.

Individuals responsible for Nabka included:

Yigal Allon	*Head of Palmach commanded forces East and South*
Zvl Ayalon	*Deputy to Galili - commanded forces Central Front*
Shimon Avidan	*Led forces South*
Menachem Begin	*Leader of Irgun/Stern/Haganah, created laws for the control of Arabs*
Yitzhak Ben-Zvi	*Zionist leader and political historian.*
Moshe Carmel	*CommanderNorthernFront.for Galiliee forces*

Moshe Dayan	*Military Commander*
Ezra Danin	*Syrian Jew - Senior Intelligence*
Dan Even	*Commander forces coastal plain*
Abba Eban	*Ambassador at U.N. "disclaimed all responsibility"*
Yehoshua Globerman	*Commander Haganah (assassinated 1947)*
Israel Galili	*Head of High Command*
David Ben-Gurion	*Zionist leader and master planner of Plan Dalat*
Isar Harel	*Head Intelligence Mossad and Shabak*
David Horovitz	*Committee for Arab Affairs.*
Moshe Kalman	*Deputy Commander of the Palmach - operations in North*
Sasha Goldberg	*Purchased and Manufactured Flame Throwers*
Ephraim Katzir	*Headed biological warfare - gasses caused blindness*
Tuvia Lishanski	*Information collector Arab villages.*
Gad Machnes	*Orientalist-DirectorGeneral Israel Ministry for Minorities.*
Golda Meir	*Senior Zionist Leader.*
Yossefi Nachmani	*Close aid to Yossef Weitz.*
Yehoshua Palmon	*Secondi to Danin - trained with British Commando.*
Yitzhak Pundak	*Assisted Shimon Avidan - forces in the South.*
Yohanan Ratner	*Strategic adviser to Ben-Gurion.*
Yitzhak Rabin	*Head of Harel Brigade. Second in command to Yigal Allon*
Eliyahu Sasson	*Syrian Jew - consultant adviser*
Reuven Shiloah	*Aid to Sasson - Orientalist*
Moshe Sharett	*ForeignMinister, head political department Jewish Agency*
Pacti Sela	*Intelligence*
Ariel Sharon	*Commando officer - Bersheba district*
Yaacov Shimoni	*German Jew Orientalist - Information gatherer*
Bechor Shitrit	*Minister of Minorities*
Yitzhak Sadeh	*Head of Armoured Units., Palmach.*
Shlomo Shamir	*Senior Officer representing Ben-Gurion.*
Dr Yaacov Taho	*German Jew who planned Jewish Colonization early yrs*
Yossef Weitz	*Head Settlement Department Jewish National Fund*
Yigael Yadin	*Head operations, acting chief Haganah and Israel Army*
Tuvia Zishanski	*Information gatherer-planned Arab evictions*

It is thought provoking that so many of these individuals would eventually become Prime Ministers, Foreign Ministers, and senior Army Officers of their Terrorist State. And significantly omitted from the list   are the many thousand individuals in Kibbutz Settlements. who also participated in the crimes of Nakba.

In Israel, there is a complete denial of the Ethnic Cleansing of Palestine between 1945 and the current time , the destruction of so many towns and villages in Palestine, the murder, rape, assault, the expulsion of the whole defenseless Palestine population , and the theft of all personal and real estate property.

Yet there is a mountain of evidence recording the crimes of Ben-Gurion, the Jewish Haganah, the Palmach, the Irgun and Stern Gangs, the armed Brigades, and the approval of the Jewish people. For sixty years there has been a complete denial*, and the United Nations Resolution 194 demanding that the Palestinian people be permitted to return and reclaim their property has been openly ignored since 1948.*

Sadly I recollect meeting 2006 a woman in Fort Collins Colorado, her insistence of the great innocent Israel, and the absolute hate in her eyes when I mentioned the suffering of defenseless Palestinians whom she described as scum. And what really is deplorable is the complete ignorance of the people of America and Britain. The acceptance of fabricated explanations and excuses of this illegal Terrorist State that   are accepted without thought or concern.

In the Western World so often the virtues of Democracy are claimed without the realisation that the very virtues that we value are not enjoyed at all! We permit ourselves to be completely brain washed with lies, distortions and fabrications,   enter into War after War, cause the death of possibly 20 million directly or indirectly over the past sixty years, support terrorist organizations, and have successfully destroyed our freedom, respect, and economy.

We have permitted Washington and London to advise us with phony reasons, fabricated wars, and created a bankrupt economy that is based on aggression. This explains why an American President has shoes thrown at him - the greatest of insults in the Middle East - sadly only people elsewhere in the World are prepared to think, analyse, and identify real criminals.

The people of the Middle East are very much aware of the problems caused through Western Interference in their countries. Over the past one hundred years an unacceptable problem has been Western political and military interference in the affairs of countries such as Iraq, Iran, Syria, Egypt, Saudi Arabia, Lebanon, and Palestine. Millions have died, and numerous economies and lives destroyed.

An excellent example is the political and military support of the Zionist Terrorist State of Israel. Taxpayers have been shelling out billions of dollars annually for decades supporting a Jewish Terrorist State that was illegally formed in Palestine, its people responsible for aggressive attacks against the defenseless Palestinian Arabs.

It is incredible that the criminals responsible for the Ethnic Cleansing of Palestine in 1948, and their descendants for the past 60 years, have persisted to claim, and are permitted to claim, that this horrific happening never occurred! And it is incredible that this terrorist State continues to persecute and kill Palestinian Arabs - in 2006 over one hundred Palestinians were killed every month. And in 2009 already the horrific attack and callous killing of thousands of innocent Arabs in Gaza.

In this novel the reader, regardless of his beliefs, is obligated to analyse the facts as claimed by various individuals Jewish, Arab, and British. The wise reader will delve into past records - they exist. For example David Ben Gurion, first prime minister of the State of Israel the prime promoter of the Zionist State, reveals his thinking, his planning, and his joy ridding the country of Arabs, the pleasure of walking down the streets of Lifta, where only Jews could be seen.

Read his diaries, his letters, his speeches, consider the terms and the implications of Master Plan Dalet (The Ethnic Cleansing of Palestine). And then relate it to the recorded attacks and destruction by Zionist thugs of hundreds and hundreds of villages which now exist as scattered rubble and Hebrew names.

And it is important to understand the history and nature of the Arab, their passivity and lack of action, inability to work together- their apathy and unwillingness to retaliate and permit Zionist Thugs such as Yitzhak Rabin (another future Israeli Prime Minister) to commit the most horrific atrocities. Their willingness to blame United Nations and the British for their woes. If the United Nations and the British are partly to blame for the catastrophe as claimed,   you have to ask for what reason?

And the dismal performance of the Arab League made up of so many nearby Middle East countries. David Ben Gurion claimed that his Jewish people were facing a Second Holocaust (through the actions of the Arab League) during the six months after the UN Resolution 181 Partition of Palestine November 1947. And yet the records indicate that the Arab League never entered Palestine during that six months, and finally entered after the departure of the British troops in May 1948! What was the truth?

Paul Blackberry, a young Englishman, the main character of this novel, had a conventional public school education, and might be considered a typical example of a brain washed individual who firmly believes Great Britain is the greatest country in the world, and that its people possess all the virtues of a great society. The native people of the many Colonies were the fortunate beneficiaries of this great nation!

He receives a letter from Palestine mid 1947 from a rugby football friend Roger Standish enquiring if he might be interested in being employed by a Jerusalem Information Service. Excited he accepts, and within a short time flies to Beirut (Lebanon). At the hotel he receives mysterious instructions whereby he would be met by a driver name Ahmad Al-Husseini. Considerable secrecy is demanded, and their departure took place early morning whilst still dark.

Despite the secrecy, they are followed on the main coastal road from the Lebanon border to Tel Aviv. Ahmad skillfully eludes his followers in Tel Aviv. Finally he delivered Paul Blackberry to Jerusalem and introduced to Ibrahim Shiqaqi the business owner of the Information Service. The first few months Paul became acclimatized to Palestine, and given a general education addressing current events.

November 1947 he is advised that he will now act as a Palestinian Correspondent, and work in the Jaffa office under Roger Standish. His duties would include recording current events throughout the many districts of Palestine, and preparing every month a summarized report. Ibrahim would examine the reports, and forward the information to an English Newspaper in London.

The purpose of this Information is to refute the Zionist Propaganda fed to international readers, and to educate readers of the plight of the Palestinian Arab who has not provoked the horrific aggression of the Zionist troops.

David Ben Gurion is advised that his propaganda in International Papers is being damaged by an independent Information Source operating in Palestine. Whilst he has been busy proclaiming the forthcoming Second Holocaust of his fellow people, he has in fact been building and planning an enormous powerful military force, and with the aid of fellow criminals has prepared Plan Dalet - "The Ethnic Cleansing of Palestine"

The Zionist leader is well aware that if conflicting reports continue advising brutal attacks of his troops and the expulsion of hundreds of thousands, International Zionist support would be withdrawn. Thus Issar Harel Head of Jewish Intelligence is instructed to catch and destroy this Information Service.

Throughout the 12 months of 1948, Paul Blackberry continues to prepare reports. He and other members of his group suffer persecution and death as the Mossad relentlessly search throughout Palestine. He is very fortunate at the end of the year to be aided in his escape from Palestine by the mysterious Ahmad Al- Husseini.

At the end of this novel, the Reader is obligated to question what was the Truth? Remember that Blackberry like every character in this novel is likely to suffer from this human failing

"We Believe what we want to Believe"

Your task as a reader is to determine the cause of the 1948 Nakba "The Catastrophe", the claimed expulsion of 800,000, and that despite United Nations Resolutions demanding the 800,000 be permitted to return to Palestine and reclaim all their land and property, these people have not been allowed to return over the past sixty years.

You, as a reader, should study the many books written about the subject. You will discover that the authors of these texts contradict and refute the claims of others. It is obvious that many of author claims are untrue or are serious distortions of the truth. What is the Truth? And why the lies and distortions?

It is vital for your future well being, and of your children, that you understand the truth.

Ethnic Cleansing is a crime regardless of the reputation of national political leaders who were initially responsible. And regardless of the reputation of national political leaders who currently support a Terrorist State.

Ethnic cleansing is a crime regardless that the event took place sixty years ago.

And Ethnic cleansing is a crime despite the protestations of those who support a Terrorist State and insist:

"We Believe what we want to Believe"

When you read of the unfortunate horrific conditions of the Palestinians in Gaza, a concentration camp of 1.5 million Arabs, the despair of people persecuted for sixty years, you will immediately identify the criminal claims of newspaper writers who blame the unfortunate Palestinian Arabs for all their troubles.

*Remember that such writers are classic examples of " **We Believe what we want to Believe".** Their agenda through prejudice and hate condemns innocent people. What is far more important, the crimes of the Zionist Jews demands a public admittance of guilt, and a restoration and compensation of all the terrible wrongs committed against the Palestinian Arab.*

A Letter is Delivered, London 1947

Our second home was in Wimbledon SW 19, part of Greater London, about 10 miles southwest of Westminster. Our previous home was flattened by a German V1. The records of that time describe a solitary V1 that chugged over Wimbledon late at night complete with its lethal bomb. It was not particularly high, its red exhaust evident, and it continued chugging a further three miles to Putney. The engine finally cut out as designed by its engineers. However the engineers had not allowed for the contrariness of their weapon which decided that it wanted nothing to do with Putney, and glided back to Wimbledon. There was very little left of the old home, and no doubt what remained was very puzzling to my white rabbit *"Blanco"* who was found hopping around the ruins the following morning.

The Second World War years were no doubt heart breaking for my parents and others. For the young it was a time of excitement and change. Bombs fell everywhere, whole streets demolished. At night the searchlights, the crack and thunder of anti aircraft guns, the constant rattle of shrapnel beating down onto streets like a severe storm, and the heavy drone of overhead bombers. I was a typical London school boy and excited.

It all started on a Sunday morning. I remember Mother and Father huddled around our quaint ugly wireless, as Chamberlain explained that Hitler had ignored prior international agreements. England was obligated to comply to agreements resulting from Hitler's aggression. Mother cried - she understood - so many died in the First World War. Father looked very serious. I simply remembered. the Sunday scene detached.

Chamberlain subsequently was chastised for having had faith in Hitler and his promises. But knowing the fickle public, there is no doubt he would have been blamed for the war if he had no faith in Hitler. He just could not win, and one suspected, listening to the tired tone of his voice, that he knew he was in a difficult political trap.

And then Churchill took over as a national hero - a man responsible for the death of millions in the First World War - further evidence how ridiculous people can be. One matter is certain. If these wretched politicians were expected to lead their people into the front lines of their declared wars, there would be no further wars.

But then why pick on politicians the absurd invention of the human race. The typical voter simply votes through a sense of greed, not the interests of his fellow people. What hope is there when reasoning for political support is limited to merely *I'm Labour, I'm Conservative, I'm Republican, or I'm Democrat.* And in response to being asked the cause of the country's demise. they simply roll their eyes in apparent despair, and with a resigned voice declare *" Well. What can you do?"*

Well. Enough of that negative talk. There is an old saying of the North of England *"There now't so strange as folk".* So very true.

But who cares at the exciting age of twenty. Wimbledon in my eyes was an exciting place. I had been persuaded to take up the profession of Quantity Surveying which seemed a highly praiseworthy endeavour. My time was invested fully in work, study, and sport. Every spare conceivable minute was employed playing rugby, football, and cricket. What else could one desire?

London admittedly was drab. But thinking back, nothing has improved over the past 70 years, and plenty has deteriorated. Public transport was reliable, speedy, and cheap. There was no need for that deplorable smelly and inconvenient car. Mail was delivered three times a day - a letter posted in the morning would be delivered later that day.   Streets were quiet and safe. At the very young age of eight, my younger brothers and sister were entrusted in my care on busy streets and what would now be considered extremely spooky alleys. Everyone was safe.

Time was slowly changing although probably none of us was aware of the changes. Young men need to be occupied, entertained, and the like, otherwise they get into mischief. Somehow I persuaded a doubtful Mother and probably a very thoughtful and concerned Father that a successful busy young man needed transportation superior to public transport. I proposed a Arial 500 motor cycle.. I was now fully occupied. Any romantic thoughts of a young lady who faithfully watched my participation in cricket and rugby, remained fortunately for her simply romantic thoughts.

Every working day I traveled to Bloomsbury Square employed as an assistant in a Quantity Surveyor's office. Every night I studied for my professional examinations. The profession demanded skills in construction cost management and contract law which held my interest, although the profession was in fact very different to the reckless claims of an oblivious French School Master. Regardless I was well occupied.

Gradually I became increasingly aware of the frustration of a country virtually bankrupt. For example a mere lean to roof to the side of the house - a few sheets of corrugated iron, and a few lengths of timber - demanded permits and material cost limits. So much for the dreams of a potential builder!

That was life in 1947 - it was the same for just about everyone. And in fairness we knew no better. For example Monday was washday for just about every household in England. For the unfortunate woman washday was a momentous back breaking affair. Most households had a large number of children, and the kitchen sink, the scrubbing board, the hand operated mangle, and the clothes line, were the implements for   a very hard days work .

And if the weather was overcast and rain, the poor woman would stare through her Kitchen window at her day's washing hanging on the clothes line, knowing full well that Tuesday she would have to repeat washing the wet laundry now covered with London soot. Unfortunate Mother shrugged, and her eldest son, after an hour operating the mangle, cursed. There would be plenty to do on Tuesday - hopefully the rain would desist.

Tuesday morning I helped Mother collect the soaked laundry off the clothes line - how she managed to handle those heavy loads is beyond my understanding. Likewise the considerable effort needed to operated the hand operated mangle. Late morning our work was complete, and the sun glimmered through the clouds. Washing machines and dryers at that time were as rare as owning a castle. The laundry machine was Mother!

We had a Pye television set given to us by grandfather. It was a modest affair but quite unique because few possessed such a thing. Television was in its infancy and much of the entertainment consisted of monotonous cricket matches that lasted 4 to 6 days, Horse Racing, Football and Rugby matches, and the Brains Trust. All would take up many hours of viewing time. My attention that Tuesday was watching an utterly boring cricket match from the Dining Room table, when Mother entered.

"Letter for you Dear"

I looked at a small envelope with some surprise. I had not anticipated any communication. What took my intense interest was the postage stamp - The British Mandate of Palestine! I used to collect postage stamps increasing Dad's collection, and was well acquainted with the stamps of the Middle East. Although a very common stamp green in color, this did not dispel both curiosity and excitement. I wondered

" Who could have written to me?"

One of the Bedser twins finally bowled out a stubborn and uninspiring batsman. No doubt half of England woke up now aware of a change, but that change did not deter my interest in the letter. The writing was firm and well set out. The writer an old friend Roger Standish, a fellow rugby player of considerable skill.

"Dear Paul,

I am writing from Jerusalem, and am employed as a Correspondent for a small company that collects information for sources throughout the world. It is well respected, and specialises in matters that are pertinent to the Arab people.

Reason for this letter is that the company requires assistance. Someone of professional nature, educated, reliable, and with plenty of energy.

I thought you would be the perfect candidate. The owner has agreed to pay for your air fare provided that you agree to remain employed with the business for at least six months. You will be adequately compensated. Life here is very interesting, very different to Wimbledon and London, and I suspect that you will thoroughly enjoy yourself. Living in Palestine will be an experience that you will never forget.

Please respond immediately by telegram if interested. You will be required to arrive by air

before the end of the month. Travel arrangements will be made for you to travel via Beirut Lebanon.

Best Wishes,

Roger

I imagine that blood rushed to my head reading this exciting invitation. Already I knew I had to go. But there were certain hurdles to be surmounted. I needed a passport and health documents. Perhaps the greatest hurdle was Mother. She was an Ashton, a past Suffragette who chained herself to Westminster railings, and had been congratulated by Prime Minister Lloyd George. And she possessed those firm steel blue eyes dominated by a common sense based on years of troubles. Always she possessed an anxiety about her children - particularly her eldest!

Times were changing. Dinner no longer was consumed in the middle of the day. The War put a stop to that with both parents employed. We had our mid day meals at school, and the main meal dinner in the evening. So there we were seated around the small Oak Kitchen table - Father, Mother, Ralph, Katherine, Clive, Charles, and I. The event remains in my mind - the meal consisted of lamb chops, mint sauce, mashed potatoes, brussel sprouts, and probably a mix of beans, peas, and carrots. Mother firmly believed that good health was reliant on at least three vegetables with each meal. She was no doubt right because we rarely were the cause of medical bills.

I had decided my strategy, and would make my announcement to Father. Although a fine musician and teacher, I cannot recollect ever his dictating on any matter of consequence. Or perhaps he dictated so softly, one was unaware of being dictated. Anyhow he had no need to dictate because Mother made up for any lack of response from Father.

" Say Dad. Guess what. Just received letter from Roger Standish. He is in Palestine"

Dad had his usual serious countenance.

"Well Well Fancy Roger going there. What did he have to say?"

His mind at that moment was on a second helping of vegetables - there was no waste in our household. But that thought was distracted by my reply.

" He has offered me a post with a company in Jerusalem that specialises in collecting information of national events "

Mother immediately suffered anxiety.

" Paul. What about your exams?   Is it safe?"

" No problem " I declared without thought

" I can take the examination in December rather than in July. It will be a fantastic experience, and very beneficial for my profession "

How can children tell such down right distortions of the truth to their loving parents is beyond my comprehension. And my reasoning came to me in a flash. It was just as well no reputable representative of my profession was present, because he would have been very curious to learn how this proposed experience would have anything to do with Quantity Surveying.

Mother's face dropped. The pain of losing her eldest to some strange country that could not compare to France and Germany that she knew as a young woman was very disturbing. Despite her lack of knowledge, she possessed that strange female sense that the Middle East was not exactly as secure and safe as her France and Germany.

Her eldest son, like all eldest sons, was patently dishonest reassuring her that there was no problem.

" Mum - this will be a great experience and education for my Quantity Surveying "

Poor mother. She looked doubtful and downcast. Fortunately she had no meaningful response, and luckily she did not question what this experience and education consisted of. Her eldest would not have had the faintest idea.

She possessed two important ingredients in life - common sense and caution. She was an Ashton - successful commercial men who recognized the wisdom in investing in land; also the wisdom of making astute marriages that increased their property port-folios. Basically the complete opposite to the irresponsible Blackberrys. Admittedly the Blackberrys for a thousand years had resorted their mental skills in education, the law, justice, music and similar occupations, but the investment in property was a formality singularly lacking in their resume and also in their wallets.

Anyhow Mother was no fool. She well knew that *" A Rolling Stone gathers no Moss "*, an opinion that all wise British women held. Their men were so incredibly irresponsible.

Poor Mother. Her heart had sank as she accepted my bland assurances. Those anxious eyes that had suffered five children, the London Blitz, the bombing and loss of her home and possessions. And now her eldest was exposing himself to a foreign country of which she knew very little, and suspected the worst.

Father reassured her.

"Charlotte. This will be a wonderful experience and education. And Paul will be back before the end of the year"

I rose from the table, and placed my arms around her.

"Mum. It will be a great experience. And you will get a letter from me once a week"

Mother quietly accepted the situation. Gradually some hope and optimism returned to her breast, and eventually my journey was accepted. I sat by her side. Jean, my black and white cat. who turned up scratching at the door during one of the worst London Blitz raids, jumped onto my lap, and immediately commenced to needle purring with contentment. So it was approved.

With excitement I sent a telegram to Roger Standish, and within a week I had notification that all my travel arrangements had been made. A British Passport and the necessary health documents seemed to involve innumerable journeys and consultations visiting many obscure places in the north of London. Finally I was ready. Despite the excitement of London and Wimbledon, my journey to the mysterious Middle East now absorbed all my interest.

The Die is Set

Mathew Paris, a wise and observant monk of the 1200s, was busy recording his observations of that time. It was rather significant that the French, according to Mathew, looked over the Channel with both apprehension and contempt. The British were aggressive, ignorant, always warring, and constantly drunk!

800 Years later one might be forgiven if one thought little has changed!

Of course the Normans could be blamed for this unfortunate opinion, but the records would suggest that the nature and character of the British existed well before William the Conqueror and his very aggressive Scandinavians decided to take over England.. Perhaps William and his comrades simply perpetuated that opinion through their fondness of violence and drinking.

Certainly one can refer to the Crusades which Blackberry and many others thought of with pride and admiration. That thinking unfortunately is the product of national history and ignorance. In fact the Crusaders constituted of gangs of unruly Normans crossing Europe fighting, raping, stealing, and whatever. And if they managed to get to their destination, they then attacked the local Arab people on behalf of their Great White god who apparently did not approve of the Muslim God.

Perhaps the most significant feature of British History over the past eight hundred years is that the local real estate agent is correct when he claims the finest investment is real estate. The British never recovered from the Norman real estate take over in 1066. Those canny Normans and their descendents gradually traded in their castles and became owners of extensive real estate holdings, directors of factories, breweries, banks, importers and exporters, and capitalized on the available cheap British labor. The British vented their disappointment and frustration in pubs, the law courts, prisons, and heavy drinking.

Modern Britain remains unchanged. Admitted the inhabitants are permitted to possess the unnecessary car, the absurd freezer, and possess the right to sign up for another meaningless war. But otherwise the status continues with the same people controlling the money strings, demanding astronomical interest rates, and ensuring commerce is a monopoly in nature and fact. The guy in the street continues to be screwed by those canny Normans, and the British continue to drink.

Friday and Saturday nights are excellent examples of this British penchant for drinking. A stranger might be forgiven imagining that he is approaching hell when walking along the pavements of any town or city. Numerous locals celebrate within and without, raucous music only fit for imbeciles, the screams and shouts of men and women, the disturbances with excessive customers thrown out, and general obscenities.

One might shrug - why be concerned - it is of their making. That is true. Unfortunately when a country has extensive rights over foreign countries, the inhabitants of such countries are exposed to the bad habits, the ignorance and prejudice of the Colonists, and suffer accordingly.

Fortunately Paul Blackberry, despite a public school education, was well aware of his ignorance of Palestine, and sat down to rectify that fault. First he examined a map. To his surprise, he discovered that the country was really a narrow sliver 40 to 75 miles across set between the Mediterranean and the countries of Syria and Jordan. From Galilee in the north adjoining Lebanon and Syria, to Aqaba in the south set at the top of the Red Sea - a distance of about 240 miles. The area of the country similar to a large British County, and perhaps about 25% the size of Washington State USA.

The topography of the land dominated by a central spine of hills and low mountains, with plains adjoining the Mediterranean and the River Jordan. Although arid in nature with limestone rocks, the rural areas could be quite productive in agriculture provided water was available. In general the plains were rich in agriculture - cereals, orchards, vineyards, and many of the hills were productive.

Transportation road and rail was evident in the plains and valleys, with connections between the major towns and cities, and the two ports of Haifa and Jaffa on the Mediterranean coast.

The population under two million of which 67% were Arab and 33% Jewish. Since the end of the Second World War, the population of Jews had increased considerably due to immigrants from Europe. About 60% of the Arabs lived in rural areas employed in agriculture, and 40% in the towns. The Jews had little interest in agriculture, and in general attracted to commercial activities in the towns.

The Arabs were native people of Palestine, and a small number of Jews could claim a similar right. About 95% of Palestine land was owned by the Arabs, the balance by the Jews.

The British held the Mandate of Palestine, and provided administration, security, law and justice over the past thirty years. There was talk of the country becoming two States - one Arab and one Jewish - but it appeared to be only talk that had continued endlessly for thirty years.

Historically man has been active in the Middle East for many thousands of years. Mesopotamia, the modern Iraq, has possessed extremely intelligent civilizations, and so much of their learning has filtered into and adopted by European nations. Even areas that now appear hostile to life such as the Negev Desert had flourishing populations. At Napheeba, for example, there is plentiful evidence of water courses, dams, and structures of an earlier time.

No doubt Palestine, and in particular Lebanon, can attribute a busy past due to being at the crossroads of the East and the West. Beirut was a terminus for traders arriving by ship from Europe or arriving by caravan via the Silk Roads from China and other eastern countries.

Jerusalem, capital of Palestine, is the religious center for so many beliefs, possesses churches representing the Eastern Orthodox, Armenians, Franciscans, Coptics, Greek Orthodox, Jews, Syrian Orthodox, Ethiopians, Roman Catholics, and many many more all celebrating the life and death of Christ. Later arrivals included the Russian Orthodox, Anglicans, and Lutherans. To absorb the formalities and beliefs of these many groups is a mind boggling task.

But perhaps far more important, and yet to be mentioned are the people of the Middle East. Well before the advent of Christ, there were many Semitic nations - the Amonites, Arameans, Canannites, and Hebrews- who had inhabited the land, but were rapidly replaced by the Arab complete with his unifying description of the One God, and the message of an unknown prophet Mohammed of Mecca. The Muslims had arrived.

It is interesting to understand that the Muslims did not arrive as religious fanatics. Unfortunately the Jews decided to resist Islam, and the prophet Mohammed prudently advised his followers to pray facing Mecca rather than Jerusalem. It was the Jewish practices that he repudiated, not their religion.

Whatever one's belief, there is plenty of religious controversy and intolerance. And no mention has been made of the Crusaders and their aggressive activities, or of the cruel Ottomans in more recent time.

One would imagine that with all these problems that the people of Palestine would be anxious to live in peace and harmony, the Arabs mainly in agriculture, and the Jews in commerce. However that has not been possible due to the Zionist Jews in the USA and Britain desiring a Jewish State. Initially the promoters considered various places including Uganda in Africa.. Then an independent state in Palestine became their passion irregardless of the fact that the majority of people in Palestine were Arab who owned 95% of the land.

1917 Balfour (British Foreign Minister) declared the desirability of a Jewish State in Palestine, and during the next 30 years there were a number of proposals partitioning the country into two states. Never was the approval of the Arab people ever requested, and never was any concern expressed in the eventuality that the Arabs did not approve of the proposal if adopted.

Despite the British Mandate of Palestine, the records suggest little interest or sympathy for the Arab people. And the proposal to partition the country continued.

Paul shook his head and thought

"These wretched religions and their crazy followers. Thank goodness I am not involved!"

He thought back of his memories of the Anglican Church - those interminable hours kneeling wishing so often that the priest would hurry up and end his boring prayers. It was a church that was forever praying for the troops to fight the good fight and knock the daylights out of every unfortunate individual now termed an enemy. Despite the obvious fact that troops on both sides were supposed to be Christians, apparently God was on our side, and it was just tough luck for our chosen enemy to whom God has no compassion or sympathy.

One was for ever singing hymns in memory of the dead. The church bells tolled gloomily reminding one of the dead rather than the living. And of course this absurd and inequitable state of affairs applied just as much in the USA. God was always on their side.

Paul absorbed all this information in some form or fashion. The handicap of being British is to actually comprehend reality We have a background of being "top dog" for hundreds of years, and accustomed to stare at maps of the world that are splattered with crimson representing an enormous empire. The problem of being "top dog" is that one tends to assume that all others are just an ignorant lot, and that lot need to educate themselves and emulate the British way. This unfortunate attitude discourages any British citizen from studying and understanding foreigners, and encourages prejudice and ignorance.

Despite Paul Blackberry's education, it is quite clear that he suffered from the handicap of all his fellow people. Even with some humility, it was very difficult for him to admit that he was not superior to all foreigners.

Paul examined his air ticket just received in the mail from Roger Standish.

"British Overseas Airways Corporation Flight 12 departure 9.30am Heathrow Monday July 12th 1947"

Mother and Father were impressed. No one in the family had ever traveled in a plane. Apprehensively Mother asked if a parachute would be available, which raised a great laugh by the family experts but did not resolve her anxiety. Father turned to Mother

" Charlotte - a parachute is not required. These modern planes do not crash"

It was just as well that Dad's expertise was music rather than aeronautical matters.

Time passed by rapidly. Uncle Arthur's old suitcase was packed, unpacked, and repacked. Despite my limited wardrobe, and my one and only suit worn for the journey, there was no difficulty exceeding the Economy class weight limit of 44lbs.

It is strange - I cannot remember how we traveled to Heathrow. Probably we took the train to Victoria, and then coach from Victoria Coach Terminal or possibly BOAC's departure lounge at Victoria.. Regardless my only memory is boarding the Hermes, a four engine passenger plane. A BOAC bus conveyed us to the plane which appeared to stand alone far far away from the Terminal. As I entered the plane, I looked back and could see a small solitary group waving farewell.. What a contrast to modern times with Concourses so long I sometimes wonder why the passenger uses a plane - he might as well walk the rest of the way!

The Hermes seemed to take an eternity checking all four engines, and shuddered as each engine was revved to maximum revolutions. Finally the plane took off. How times have changed. Flying at that time was so respectable and civilized. Everyone dressed well, considerate of others, and spoke in a refined manner. The air hostesses attractive and smart in their BOAC uniforms. It was truly a delight to travel by air. No doubt many of us were not exactly executive class, but we certainly gave that impression. And no doubt many of us anticipated an attractive future which would elevate us to that executive class.

Cautiously we would reveal to our fellow passengers our destination, our future work, and our hopes. Possibly a little exaggerated, we were excited and optimistic. Likewise we learnt a little of our fellow passengers.

There was time to relax - the plane simply droned on and on, and occasionally the plane's captain would describe some topographical feature far below. Mid day the Swiss Alps appeared on our left with many peaks as high or higher than our plane., and eventually we landed at Rome.

My memory of the Rome/Beirut leg is poor. I was tired, and I realized that the knowledgeable traveler would choose a seat on the left hand side of the cabin, and avoid the afternoon sun. My composure shaken although hopefully not revealed after the plane struck an air pocket. My fears increased noting an alarming flutter of the wing, a red hot exhaust, and some strange unexpected sounds. The perils of the inexperienced traveler are innumerable. Fortunately the air hostesses remained calm, and I irresponsibly left the perils of flight in their capable hands.

Finally we arrived at Beirut late evening, and I was exhausted. My only memory of the airport were the many strange faces, a wide variety of clothing and languages. What a pity that I was so tired. Beirut stands at the crossroads of the West and the East. For thousands of years the centre of commercial activity with merchants of all nationalities seeking business.

Probably the most significant people were the Christian war lords - the Chamouns, the Franjiehs, and the Germayals - all ruthless in war and diplomacy. Beirut was a place of political, military, and commercial undertakings that was the backbone of Lebanon's success, and the domination of foreign affairs.

In 1947 Beirut was described as the *Paris of Lebanon* reflecting the wealth and quality of successful businesses. Like Elizabethville, often called the *Paris of Belgian Congo* , both suffered similar fates in later years through instability and wars.

Little is remembered of the journey in the hotel car north bound on the coastal road to the West Beirut Commodore Hotel. Late night, I staggered into my hotel room, and finally sitting on the bed edge, I wearily looked around with little comprehension.

Shortly I was aware of a strange rustle - something sliding. I looked around, and to my surprise realized that someone had slid a letter under the door. The sight of the letter did not immediately register. Then I thought .

"How very odd"

Wearily I dragged myself to the door. The letter was a personal communication from Roger Standish. Within were specific   instructions.

"Dear Paul,

Welcome to Palestine. Our driver will pick you up in the square at the rear of the hotel 4.00am tomorrow morning. Important. Do not advise hotel staff of this arrangement. And most important mention not a word to anyone. Leave your luggage in the hotel room. We will collect later. The driver's name is Ahmad Al-Husseini. He will identify himself with his name. Please identify yourself by name, and remain in the shadows of the Mosque entrance.

Look forward to seeing you.

Roger Standish."

The unexpected letter and its rather mysterious instructions were a puzzle, but certainly did not dampen my excitement. Needless to say I did not sleep well that night. Soon after mid night, I had a hot bath, washed, shaved, and dressed. All my belongings were packed ready for the arranged collection.

Quietly a lone figure made his way from the Commodore Hotel, walked to the back of the building, and patiently waited in the shadows of the Square. The air warm, humid, and still. All was quiet. Patiently standing back from the Square close to the Mosque entrance, I remained expectant and waiting. A church bell struck four hours.

Within moments I was wondering *" Where is my driver?"*

It was so quiet and still. Suddenly a small car appeared without warning or noise. The driver beckoned to me. In a clear whisper he announced

" I am seeking a traveler from England"

I responded with the obvious *" Are you the driver to take me to Jerusalem?"*

He nodded, and demanded in an officious manner *" Your name sir"*

"Paul Blackberry"

" Welcome to Palestine Mr Blackberry. My name is Ahmad Al-Husseini. I am your driver"

He was of slight build, perhaps 30-40 years of age, a narrow intense face with a distinct Arab appearance. The passenger door was open, and I made myself comfortable seated next to Ahmad. Quietly we departed leaving the Square to its ghosts and memories.

My driver pointed to a map in the glove compartment.

" As you are a stranger, examine this map. We will take the coastal road past the Shuf Mountains, and will pass through the coastal towns of Samour, Sidon, Tyre, and Naqoura. The distance to the border is about 50   miles.

An after thought came to his mind, and he asked rather anxiously.

" Your travel and health documents are all in order?"

I nodded *" No problem with Lebanon Immigration"*

Rather grim, his response.

" Might be a bit different at the border"

"Why?"

"We are living in difficult times. Why I do not truly understand. Regardless truly difficult."

The early rising morning sun breached the hills as we approached the border post. The Customs and Immigration on the Palestinian side was manned by British personnel.   I was shown a list of items that were subject to tax, and shook my head.

" Any alcohol? Any pets?"

I shook my head.

Immigration, was it my imagination, was not exactly pleased to view a citizen from the Olde Country. Stiffly the man asked.

" What is the purpose of your visit Mr Blackberry?"

My explanation was very grudgingly accepted, my work permit carefully scrutinized, and reluctantly I was permitted into Palestine. But before we left I received a telling remark.

" Listen Mate - get yourself involved in any trouble, and you are out. Understood!"

" What kind of trouble?"

Grimly Immigration responded

" Any kind of trouble Mr Blackberry. Don't forget"

The engine of the Morris Minor was restarted, and with some relief we commenced our journey to Jerusalem.

" Gee" I complained

"What a reception. That was not a friendly welcome"

Ahmad shrugged and explained.

" We live in very difficult times. There are people who wish to take our land and possessions from us. And these criminals are supported by special interest groups in Britain, USA, and I believe Russia. My people are simple rural workers reliant on agriculture, and their ancestors have been here for thousands of years.

All we desire is peace and to be left to our work on the land. But others wish to steal our land and possessions through aggressive means. Unfortunately my people are not particularly aggressive, and the country appears to be full of spies, informers, and the like."

Rather undiplomatic, I responded strongly

" You have got to fight for your rights"

Briefly he looked across, and eventually he gloomily remarked

"Yes, perhaps you are right"

Was it my imagination that the driver studied me with increased interest? I examined Ahmad carefully. Perhaps he was older - 40 to 45 lean, with intelligent eyes and a determined mouth. A man accustomed to making decisions - no doubt prudent, secure, and confident. I had difficulty imagining that he made a living by merely driving.

As we continued on the coastal road, the heat of the Middle East Summer became evident and exhausting. Eventually one becomes accustomed to the heat. However after a life time in London damp and cool, the heat, the intensity of the sun, and the glare against white buildings proved trying. The road dusty, uneven, potholes, and subject to innumerable obstacles. Arabs with their herds of goats and sheep, donkeys and camels with loads of baggage, ancient trucks belching blue black smoke, British troops and their transport, and was it my imagination that many individuals eyed me with suspicion.

According to the map, the road from the border to Jaffa was about 80 miles, and from Jaffa to

Jerusalem about 35 miles. The roads were mainly level, the central hills set back east about 20 miles from the coast. The scenes peaceful and pastoral. One could imagine that little had changed over the past 2000 years. Stone structures were softened with Beeches, Cedars, Palm and Olive trees, and when a village was set on a slope stone terraces often would be prominent with ancient retaining walls.

Ahmad was friendly, and pointed out many features of Palestine which were rapidly forgotten. I was too tired, in a strange country, and much was a blur. A touching memory were the young Arabs tending their flocks waving as we passed by. One definite impression was that in the rural areas, all inhabitants were Arabs, whilst in the towns there was a mix of Jews and Arabs.

Villages were a visual mix of houses and hovels, structures of rock, clay, and mud, and a notable lack of vegetation. Possibly the lack of vegetation was due to a lifetime of working in the fields, and yet one would imagine that the quality of life could be well improved with ample trees and plants around the dwellings. There seemed to be a lack of regularity in planning and design with little concern of aesthetics and compatibility; and yet the product of individual thought was evident.

Market squares, domed mosques, the occasional school and administrative building, and graveyards offered relief to the mix of dwellings. The public scene of activity around village wells, the common sight of groups of Arabs huddled in absorbed discussion, and individuals with the unique ability to crouch low and remain rested.

The towns presented a more conventional appearance with commercial structures in the business centers, larger market squares, a greater variety of mosques and churches, and significantly a general separation of residential neighborhoods defining Arab from Jew. The busy ports of Haifa and Jaffa demonstrated their importance by having much larger populations ranging from 75,000 to 100,000.

Initially the car windows were closed for comfort preventing the entry of dust, insects, and noise. But as the morning progressed, it became increasingly hot and uncomfortable, and the windows were partially opened for fresh cool air. But then the dust and insects crept in. There was no ideal solution, and eventually the interior was red with dust.

South of Haifa, I noted curiously another Morris Minor, a station wagon, about one hundred yards behind. The Morris Minor was perhaps the most successful design made by the British. An excellent engine, consumption of 40mpg, and a well built body had my admiration, and it was unfortunate that Nuffield did not have the intelligence to retain that early design.

Anyhow the vehicle held my interest, and I realized that I had in fact seen that car back at the border post. I turned to Ahmad

" I never thought I would see so many British cars. We have a Morris Minor behind us that has followed us for the past 35 miles"

Ahmad expressionless nodded saying nothing. However his eyes seemed to harden a little, his mouth tighten, as he briefly stared at the rear mirror. About three miles further on, he abruptly turned off the coast road, entered a small village, and without explanation parked the car behind a Cedar set back from the entry road. I glanced curiously at Ahmad for an explanation. Steadfastly he observed the entry road.

A few moments later the Morris station wagon entered the village, and passed by slowly. The occupants heavy set individuals were clearly seeking something or someone. Were they seeking us? Within moments Ahmad took off at quite a speed for Tel Aviv.

I looked at Ahmad demanding an explanation. Grimly Ahmad drove on without comment. I looked back. Was it my imagination that the station wagon was still behind us. Within ten minutes there was no question that we were being followed.

" That station wagon is behind us again"

Ahmad nodded, and said nothing. I sensed his tenseness, and in turn my alarm. As we approached Tel Aviv, Ahmad ignored the Jerusalem road destination sign, and headed into the city centre.

"Slight change to our plans. We need to lose our followers"

Rapidly he entered neighborhood alleys and twisted tracks, finally lost our followers, and turned into the gated opening of a court yard adjoining a general store. Ahmad immediately parked the car, and called to the janitor to close the gate quickly. Turning he smiled sadly.

All is well - we will continue to Jerusalem this evening"

Bewildered I blurted

" What is going on? Who are those people?"

He shook his head, shrugged, and signaled he would explain in a few moments. Rapidly he strode over to the Store Owner standing stolidly at the back entrance door appraised of our presence. Ahmad greeted the man and spoke urgently. He in turn simply nodded, a man who required little explanation.

I looked around. The dusty stone walled courtyard and its solid gated entrance suggested centuries of security and peace. What had just happened seemed both incredible and unreal.

The store keeper gazed at me and continued to be non committal. A decision was made.

" I will send one of my men to Ibrahim and appraise him of the situation. It is far too risky using the phone. They are eaves dropping all the time"

His eyes were firm and hard as he made a further decision..

" You cannot leave before this evening at the earliest. Please ask your friend inside"

Ahmad beckoned to me, and we entered the dark cool interior of the store. The store owner Haidah Abd Al-Shafi was of medium height, muscular, with some evidence of increased weight reflecting his age. Initially the man might not draw attention - his appearance similar to thousands. But examination of his dark thin face revealed a man of determination, strong will, and the confidence of a sound mind and body. He turned to me.

" I understand that you are English, and a good friend of Roger Standish. I welcome you to our unfortunate country. Please be seated, and I will arrange a meal for you. You will excuse me. I have some urgent business that requires my attention"

He then addressed Ahmad.

" Ahmad. Let us go the office. "

I had hoped for an explanation. Ahmad was adamant. Roger Standish would explain Abruptly he left the room with Haidah.

Later in the afternoon Ahmad provided me with some information about Tel-Aviv which was a commercial business center with a predominantly Jewish community. Adjoining Tel-Aviv was the ancient port city of Jaffa with a large Arab population. Ahmad explained.

" Tel-Aviv is the first Hebrew city set by the Mediterranean, and described by many as the "White City". No doubt the title reflected the large influx of new Jewish immigrants from Europe and Russia. Its existence indicative that the inhabitants desired to separate themselves from the indigenous people of Jaffa.

Despite Jewish claims and denials, Tel-Aviv possessed much native Palestinian architecture reflecting its historical past. Regardless recent Jewish immigrants in particular have insisted in dissociating themselves from the larger Palestinian population.

Unfortunately this attitude has encouraged evidence of extreme thinking resulting in the notorious Red House where Ben Gurion had formulated Zionist policies, and the equally notorious and aggressive Haganah and its head quarters located close to the sea on Yarken Street in the north of Tel Aviv."

The driver's advise of Tel-Aviv seemed depressing. What hope was there of understanding with such hostility. I asked

" What is the solution?"

" We pray for peace but ----------------" He did not complete his words, turned away, and shrugged.

That evening, it was decided to depart. Dusk rapidly transformed itself to pitch black darkness and we prepared for the 35 mile journey to Jerusalem. The main road rose and fell through the hills with increasing numbers of villages set on both sides of the highway. As we approached Jerusalem, the capital of Palestine, residential communities and neighborhoods appeared with increasing density. Whilst evidence of villages was minimal due to lack of street lighting, one was occasionally aware of the denser communities with   street lights.

Finally our car approached the ancient city within its 400 year old Ottoman walls. A city divided into four quarters - Christian, Muslim, Armenian, and Jewish. And adjoining the Muslim Quarter the large imposing Courtyard the Al-Haram Al-Sharif (*The Noble Sanctuary*) that included he Dome of the Rock and the Al-Aqsa Mosque.

Ahmad spoke of some outstanding features, but the darkness made it difficult to comprehend their relevance in the close suburbs of Jerusalem. Then suddenly we passed through Jaffa Gate set in the city wall, and immediately we were driving down David Street with the Armenian Quarter on our right, and the Christian Quarter on our left. At the intersection with Khan es-Zeid, we turned left, and traveled northwards to Via Dolorosa, and entered the Muslim Quarter.

Where ever one looked, there were churches and mosques, buildings of all shapes and sizes, roofs flat, sloping, and domed, with construction in general of stone. And a general sense of a lack of conformity in building design and layout. Unlike conventional cities, the normal grid of streets was replaced by numerous narrow and twisting alleys that did not appear to claim any obvious purpose.

Without any warning, Ahmad turned off down a narrow lane. We had arrived.

Ibrahim Shiqaqi's Business

" What did I expect? "

Bluntly I had no idea. True I regularly purchased the Daily Telegraph which was considered a highly respectable newspaper free of the vulgar sensational news common in other British papers. The sports columns were excellent, and Mother was entertained by studying announcements which might or might not apply to known acquaintances.

However little was known of the newspaper business, its manufacture and distribution, and its methodology collecting reliable information throughout the world. True I had some vague idea that enormous spinning rolling presses spat out innumerable copies of the paper daily, that somehow the latest editions were circulated to all newspaper vendors, and presumably the editor was the recipient of many letters, telegrams, cables, and phone calls advising the latest news.

Anything in my mind relating to the newspaper industry was based on suspect films and rumours. The reporter always a hero subject to innumerable difficulties, hostile conditions, criminal organizations, always overcame adversity, and won his girl. The editor, the subject of timetable pressures and often the problems created by his team of reporters, generally had a very worried countenance, and one had the impression that there were many jobs far more attractive for sane intelligent ambitious young men. Quite possibly the ability to spell also gave the editor's occupation an unfavorable reputation.

Ahmad and I entered the premises of Ibrahim Shiqaqi late that night free of our presumed pursuers. Close to the entrance was a small counter and reception desk. At the rear there were two small unlit rooms. We were expected. A small slight man approached us. His suit was worn but well cut. He had the air of an alert college professor. His face lined and tired, his eyes dark brown steady and alert, a high forehead, a firm chin, portrayed an individual decisive, competent, a decision maker, and an appearance that suggested he had a mission in life..

He smiled at me, offered his hand, and invited me in.

" Mr Blackberry - it is a great pleasure to make your acquaintance. My name is Ibrahim Shiqaqi, and I am the proprietor of Filastine Al- Hurriyah. We specialise in providing news information of Palestinian events to our customers throughout the world. Your friend Roger Standish is currently on assignment.

Welcome to Palestine. "

Seated he provided me with a small brochure containing advise of his business, and then asked to be excused for a few moments in order to speak to Ahmad Al-Husseini The two men closeted quietly together.

" What happened ? " asked a rather anxious Ibrahim.

" There should not have been any problem "

Ahmad grimly nodded.

" There should have been no problems but there certainly were problems. Somehow they knew I was conveying Blackberry to Jerusalem. We were tailed south of the Lebanon border. And as you know, we managed to lose them in Tel-Aviv "

Ibrahim listened intently trying to ascertain the implications of the recent events..

"How could they have known Ahmad? Were you seen delivering that note at the hotel? "

The driver shook his head

" Very very doubtful. I took considerable care - no one saw me "

" Are you really certain - they have spies, informers, confidents everywhere "

Ahmad agreed but rejected that idea.

" I have thought much about this matter. One idea is that they intercepted Standish's letter to Blackberry, or perhaps someone in the airline reservations office reported Blackberry's forthcoming itinerary to Palestine, and they checked who had made the reservations. Of course possibly we are over rating their ability to glean information. "

Al-Shiqaqi buried his face into his hands, and strived to resolve a very dangerous state of affairs. If Ahmad was correct, everyone was in danger including the business. But perhaps the explanation was much simpler.

" What happened at the border crossing? "

" Well the British made an unnecessary fuss but allowed us through. Now that is a point. I wonder if that wretched sergeant advised them of Blackberry. Because our trackers turned up soon after passing through. Yes. That might be the explanation "

Ibrahim sighed. He liked the appearance of this new visitor who probably would be ideal assisting him in Jerusalem. But the risks were too great. His planned arrangements would have to be scrapped. The young man would have to be employed elsewhere with no immediate connection with his office. With some luck, any association of this young man with Jerusalem could be avoided.

As he returned to his office, he realized that more had to be done immediately. He went back to

Ahmad, and quietly gave him further instructions.

"Ahmad. This is urgent. Just in case Standish's letter was intercepted, we need to change all current methodology in making communications immediately."

Ahmad realized the implications, and agreed that he would attend to the changes immediately. The situation was very difficult.

Ibrahim returned, and smiled wearily at me.

" You must be terribly tired. First you shall have a sound rest and recover from your journey. I propose that you stay at my daughter's home. Later this week you may study some papers addressing our activities and our interest in events in Palestine of the past and present.

I would like you to gradually absorb Palestine. Arrive at your own conclusions what makes us tick. A fresh mind is always of value. I will be interested to learn of your thoughts."

He was correct. I was completely washed out. Within an hour I was in a strange bed dreaming of hostile cars manned by unknown thugs chasing after me   throughout the highways of Palestine.

My baggage was delivered the following day. Gradually I became accustomed to my strange setting. Ibrahim kept me well supplied with texts addressing Palestine, and rapidly I realized that many years of study would be necessary to understand the complex history and activities of its inhabitants.

The information service proprietor proved quite a demanding task master who realized the importance of understanding a complex subject. At the end of the week, I was submitted to a crucial test.

" What is your general impression of the current relationship of the people of this country, and what does it portend for the future of this country"

Ibrahim sat at the table facing me with hands clasped waiting expectantly.

What was my gut impression. What an interesting way to combine the loads of information presented to me and my recent observations. It all resolved around people. Irregardless of a nation's material wealth, the future success of any nation is its people, their nature, and their character. I took a deep breath and presented my thoughts.

"Palestine has two major populations - Arab and Jew. Both Arab and Jew have lived side by side for thousands of years. Until the advent of the Second World War the Jewish population

represented a small proportion of the total population, was mainly involved in commercial activities, whilst the Arab activity was mainly rural agricultural. Neither party actively interfered with each other, and were mainly passive in nature accepting the administration of the British Mandate.

This state of affairs changed radically after the Second World War with the Jewish Zionists demanding a Jewish State, and some demanding the extreme aggressive exclusion of all who did not share their beliefs. This unsatisfactory demand was exacerbated by Zionist extremists in America and England who sought this mythical independent State, first considered Uganda, and finally chose Palestine producing all kinds of illogical reasons to support their claim.

This claim finally formulated the idea of partitioning Palestine into two States - one for the Arabs and one for the Jews. Zionists in America and England persuaded governing authorities, and finally United Nations to pass a Resolution - The Partition of Palestine. Despite the fact that 95% of the land of Palestine is owned by the Arabs, no one appears to have given any consideration in obtaining the approval of the Palestinian Arabs, and no one has given any thought what will happen if the Arabs disapproved of the idea.

Bluntly I share the opinion of Gertrude Bell's forecast thirty years ago that any proposal of partitioning the land would be a total disaster.

Now since the Second World War end, an enormous number of Jewish immigrants have entered Palestine, many under the pretext of the future Jewish State, who have nothing in common with the native Arab people. They have little or no possessions, and their presence is irresponsible in a poor country like Palestine.

The separation of the Arab people and the Jewish people whilst living together amicably under one State is possible - it is little different to the separation of the working man and the rich in England - on the opposite side of the coin to live together with one side venting aggressive claims, and the other side owning 95% of the land and expected to accept and share land with this aggressive group is extremely troubling. And the British Administration's indifference to this trouble making is of considerable concern because they are responsible for law and order.

Finally the nature and character of the Palestinian Arab, probably in fact all Arabs of all Middle East countries is troubling."

Ibrahim's eyebrows shot up, and he interjected.

" Explain what troubles you Paul"

What was it that troubled me about the Arab. I realized that I was treading into dangerous waters and could easily upset Ibrahim. Regardless I decided it was necessary to be honest, and not hide behind the curtains.

" *Rightly or wrongly the history of the Middle East, particularly the past 300-400 years has been highlighted by intrigue, treachery, lack of faith in others, deceit, religious persecution, tribal hostilities, family enmities, and other disagreeable features.*

Decisions, agreements, and policies are rarely maintained - nearly always they are subject to immediate material interests. No doubt the oppression of the Ottoman Empire has contributed to the problem.

It is just about impossible to guarantee any long term agreement despite people having a common god and religion. And yet for the people of any nation to succeed, they must work together for a common cause. And they must be positive rather than passive"

Ibrahim pondered over my thoughts, and smiled rather sadly.

" *Paul. You are very astute. You have my congratulations. Now what I would like you to do is consider the rise and fall of every nation on this planet over the past four thousand years.*

I suspect that every nation, and that includes Britain, and eventually USA, have suffered similar fates, and that in every case similar failings and causes can be discovered."

Later that day he placed his hand on my shoulder.

"Paul. You will become bored staying with an old man. I propose that we visit my daughter Ghada. She has a nice home nearby, and will be delighted to have your company. There you can continue your studies, and become acquainted with the Old City."

Ghada's Guide to Jerusalem

With due respect to Ibrahim, life in lovely Ghada's home was wonderful. I was welcomed without reservation, treated as if I was a favorite son, and within hours I felt I had always known Ghada. She provided me with a spacious bedroom complete with a table where I could study. She fed me as if I had starved all my life, and her kind advise never forgotten.

" That is enough study Paul. I think you should commence discovering the Old City of Jerusalem"

Ghada was always so excited about her temporary visitor. Probably my company was a great change in her life. This morning she sat down opposite me at the dining table full of curiosity and interest. I explained how I proposed to discover the city.

" I would like to see as much as possible"

" That is a formidable task"   She frowned

" Wait. I have a map that may simplify your exploring"

From a kitchen drawer, she pulled out a worn map that illustrated the major quarters of the old city - Muslim, Christian, Armenian, and Jewish - and included the largest religious feature *" Al-Haram Al-Sharif"* - the Muslim Dome of the Rock, the El Aqsa Mosque, and the Antonia Fortress.

Ghada explained

" The Old city is enclosed within the 400 year old Turkish walls. In every quarter you will discover religious shrines, monuments, and mosques. Really it is a city of religions!"

She observed my incredulous look,   smiled sadly, and bitterly murmured.

" Yes. A city of religions. A city in which there is always strife, discrimination, and unhappiness. A city controlled by criminals and bigots. "

I observed her distressed countenance reflecting her unhappy thoughts. But then   her face brightened, as only a woman can, remembering her courtesy as a host.

" There now - enough of that talk. The great danger for you, is spending too much time staring at religious features. Allow me to list a number of topics. I will have a list ready for you when you return this evening"

Her spontaneous kindness and hospitality was very touching. Perhaps I could assist her in some way.

" Ghada. Can I do some shopping for you - say some fruit, vegetables, or whatever?"

Initially the young woman shook her head rejecting my offer. Then she realized that a little shopping would be a great experience and education for me.

" Why yes - you can purchase some dates and figs in the Muslim market"

She showed me the location of the market which was not far from the house.

" Now" she announced with a mischievous smile.

" You will order the fruit in our Palestinian language. You will be respected despite your lack of knowledge of our language"

She wrote on a sheet of paper - *"dert"* *"Thamra"*(date) , - *"fig"* (fig), - *"Zitun"* (Olives), - *" Kafin, Kifaya"* (Enough), - *" Kam "* (How Much).

" Pronounce the words" she commanded.

I pronounced the words very clumsily, and she burst out laughing.

" Listen to me"

A typical Britisher glumly listened. My ability to tackle a foreign language was deplorable. Regardless I gritted my teeth, and tried to imitate Ghada.

Eventually Ghada declared.

" Very good. We will make you a great Palestinian yet"

A further thought crossed her mind

" Have you enough cash?"

" I have plenty of UK cash - can I use it?"

" No problem in the large markets. I will give you a bag. Here is the current exchange rate for UK currency. The currency exchange offices will not be as generous, and probably you will be better off visiting a British bank. Foreign currencies fluctuate so it is difficult to make any recommendation"

I listened to her carefully. It would take some time to become accustomed to local conditions. I decided to tackle the shopping experience immediately; then commence my exploration of the city. Whilst on my shopping spree, Ghada declared she would prepare some mid day snacks .

Finding the market was not difficult. However my negotiation with an old Arab store keeper proved a disaster. He did not understand my pronunciation, and I was obliged to merely pointing,

And despite my knowledge of cost, my acquisition proved extremely costly.

I felt certain that he was taking advantage of my inability to communicate. However that is the penalty of ignorance. Already I was determined that I would return again better prepared and demand a reasonable price.

Regardless of my costly transaction, Ghada was touched by my first venture in the market. My mid day snacks were ready packed in a bag. I had the map, and was ready to leave.

" *Now*" she instructed " *I suggest that you discover the Muslim Quarter first. Do not rush.. There is an awful lot to see*"

Her face then frowned with a further thought, and spoke with some concern

" *Paul. There is little to worry but please do not draw attention to yourself. There are people everywhere who spy, inform, and report. You are a stranger and British. You are an individual liable to be recorded if observed. Remain close to tourists viewing the wonders of this city.*"

With that important warning stressed, she gave further thought of my proposed survey.

" *By all means view the major tourist sights. But remember that mosques and monuments tell little of its people. Let me give you some ideas.*"

She made herself comfortable at the table, and continued.

" *My people are basically pastoral, their lives dependant on the land. Their existence subject to the availability of water and favorable weather. Most are poor, own few possessions, lack resources for bad times, and really live from day to day. Poverty is a way of life, and needs inevitably reduced to the minimum.*

Try and forget European standards of which you are accustomed. Observe the people in the street. Probably you will see groups of men huddled in intense discussion, small groups engrossed in backgammon and other board games, and the single individual perhaps lying flat on his back, his head swathed in the age old protection of the Kaffiyeh, relaxed taking a rest.

In contrast you may observe the rather grim appearance of Jews in their somber and

depressing black, their behavior and attitude suggesting a lack of humor, compassion, and understanding.

Arab women are significant in their typical Palestinian clothes of long muslin or floral dresses with ample muslin scarves. Their presence often absent from the street scene, their place and duties mainly in the home. Normally they are veiled in strict adherence to Muslim orthodoxy.

Their children play in the street like all children in poor parts of the world. They are happy unaware that they lack material possessions. Many will be seen wearing school uniforms. No doubt all will wear Western clothing when they grow up.

Arab beggars are to be seen everywhere. Many suffer the handicap of blindness, deafness, crippled limbs, and other faults. You will observe for example blind men crouched on street pavements, with their upturned palms as an invitation for the Muslim devout to perform their religious duty of almsgiving, and you will see many individuals drop coins into those patient waiting hands.

The relationship of Arab and Jew is disappointing. Some will communicate with each other, but indifference reigns.

Poverty breeds commercial activities that are very labor intensive. Everywhere you will see men carrying enormous loads of every conceivable item, particularly in narrow twisting lanes and alleys inaccessible to vehicles.

And of course rural life dominates many individuals with their small flocks of sheep, goats, and donkeys for hauling heavy loads. I strongly suggest Paul that you visit the ancient Sheep Market on Friday. It is located set against the north east stone city wall where many ancient graveyards exist. There, from the hills, shepherds bring their sheep to the market well before dawn, a practice that has been repeated for thousands of years. By dawn the market is already busy. Men bargain in the buying and the selling of animals. Watch the trader experts inspect their long eared sheep, and their children with attentive eyes delegated to watch over their father's flock. By late morning all is quiet again, and new owners may be seen guiding their newly purchased sheep heading again for the hills.

When you stroll along the Old City streets, examine the scenes of the many cafes, their customers often sheltered from the sun by louvered shutters perhaps reading newspapers or holding intensive conversations oblivious of the café's Spartan surrounding. And often you will see the solitary Arab smoking his narghide (water pipe) deep in contemplation. Local tobacco is commonly available, and occasionally mixed with Hashish that presumably soothes the mind.

I think such observations will improve your understanding of the Palestinian Arab, an understanding that strangers to this country do not have. My people are looked down by their cousins in the Middle East through ignorance and prejudice. And I fear a similar thought applies to many other countries. Examine the record of so many Palestinians who have achieved professional excellence in the law, engineering, the sciences, architecture, and many other activities.

My people are not simple minded as some may suggest. Consider the history of this area. All major features of modern civilization in the West originated from the people of Mesopotamia. Examine the bright eyes of modern children. All that is needed is the correct encouragement. It is unfortunate that the British have only partly provided the necessary momentum.

Ghada rose and went to the Kitchen to make some coffee, and left me with much to think about. When she returned, she warned me.

" Do not be misled by hostile critical thoughts presented by those who desire dissension."

Her warning was well noted. There always appeared to be disturbing elements in the Middle East, and in particular Palestine. But it seemed to me that the Palestinian should not be passive, and should take care of negative situations. It was important to understand the nature and purpose of critical thoughts.

" So much you say is true" I confirmed

"However remember the success of any society is subject to its own ability to work together free of unnecessary and destructive dissension. There has to be co-ordination and a common desire for the good of all, and not subject to personal dislikes of proposed leaders. Without good will, no amount of support from outside nations can resolve and create a content and meaningful nation."

She smiled to herself, and murmured.

"Paul - you are old for your age. We all have failings, often unaware of them, and sadly often unwilling to resolve them"

During the following week, I visited markets, squares, streets, narrow lanes of the Muslim Quarter all contained within the ancient stone walls of the city and of course the stone walls of the *Al-Haram Al-Sharif. (The Noble Sanctuary)*

But initially I was obliged to undertake my second commercial transaction with a Palestinian market stall vendor. I dreaded the exercise but it had to be accomplished.. What a disaster. First I cautiously appraised products, prices, and the stall owners. Finally a stall was chosen. The stall owner glanced at me, and no doubt that glance had already summed up how that customer would be handled. He stared hard waiting for the order.

Nervously I pointed at a fine pile of dates, and gave my order. *" Dates - one pound please"*
The stall owner responded   firmly *"Two pound"*. Uncertain of his pronunciation, I simply nodded.
The stall holder also nodded as if all was understood, and busily selected and weighed the dates. He
looked at me for any further order.

I then requested *" Figs - one pound please"* My pronunciation did not sound like Ghada. The
owner screwed his face impatiently. *" Figs"* he demanded. I meekly pointed at the figs, and with an
exasperated look, I was finally served.

He held out his hand to receive payment. My calculation roughly assumed   a total cost of about 60
piastres. I commenced to hand out what I thought was adequate. *" More. More."* demanded the man
impatiently. Meekly I finally parted with another 40 piastres. Already I sensed that I had been taken
advantage but accepted again that was the penalty of ignorance. With a rather red face I departed,
and returned to Ghada's house, and related my second transaction in Palestine.

Ghada shrieked with laughter. But then she was indignant.

"All those Arab vendors in the Old City are rogues. He really took advantage of you."

She shook her head, then thanked me for the kind gift - her thanks more than compensated my
embarrassment. Kind lovely Ghada.

" Oh dear" my instructor teased

" I thought my student was very bright"

I promised to improve. She kindly taught me a few more words, and gradually my education
progressed. Ghada's suggestion that I study the people rather than monuments was excellent. For
days I wandered around the Muslim Quarter absorbing all that I could see, and slowly I captured a
sense of Arab life in the Old City.

Poverty definitely was a way of life for many. And yet despite that handicap, their life seemed quite
vibrant free of our many material considerations. The children excited and gay not weighed down
with dreams of possessions. Likewise young men were animated and skilled at sport not
encumbered by the absurd demands of American sports gear, and certainly not spoilt by the
unhealthy concept of win or nothing. The young ladies demure and attractive adopting Western
dress and retaining their conventional Arab head scarf. And they appeared well aware of the failings
of their western cousins making an unnecessary spectacle of themselves to attract their men folk.

Arab women in Palestine commonly have 5-6 children, their first born perhaps at the young age of
16-17. I sensed that the Islam religion and its conventions dominated   their married life, thinking,

and   behavior. They appeared content and accepted, or perhaps resigned, to their lives. No doubt their men folk were just as troublesome, irresponsible, unpredictable, unreliable as their Christian brothers of the West. Anyhow the women tended to remain in the background out of sight set in the shadows of buildings and courtyards.

What of the men? Whether the Arab was a shopkeeper, employee, craftsman, or one of the hundreds or possibly thousands of vendors wandering the streets and alleys, all were searching for the gullible tourist. In general all were masters of their lives, reliant on their skills, cunning, quickness of brain, in order to survive. One has the impression that they are obligated to be both sophisticated and simple, thoughtful and impulsive. All opposites that have to fit the mold of the moment.

Like the conventional country scene, the city is one of many worlds - the morning, the afternoon, the evening, and night. All times need to be experienced To improve one's impression of city life, wander down the main streets of Khan el-Zeit, Via Dolorosa, El Wad, Street of the Chain, and others. Always, but in particular the late afternoon and early evening, people are seated at coffee shops with cups of coffee balanced in front of them. All are relaxed occupied in the talk of the day. Others find pleasure playing back gammon, chess, and other board games surrounded by watchers. Small groups stand huddled head garbed with a fez, a tasseled fez dating from Ottoman times many years past, or the Arab Kaffiyeh, and all held to discussions of the latest scandal or whatever.

I envy their apparent enjoyment in each other's company - modern artificial entertainment is not important or desired. What might surprise some, and yet knowledge of history would dispel that thought, is that the Palestinian Arab possesses a wide variety of faces. Thus evidence of the Crusaders (red hair and blue eyes), African (their conventional negroid heritage), and an amazing variety of what would be claimed conventional Arab stock. Regardless the important endeavor of all is commercial, their customer the gullible religious tourist, and their product for sale talismans and the general trivia   of the many religions.

As I wander around the neighborhoods, I become aware of schools, institutes, libraries, foreign and missionary institutions. Much has been created and built by the British encouraging Arab education. Occasionally I observe an open door. Peering through often reveals a bare interior. Few Arabs have many possessions as evidence of their wealth. And behind these doors are house courtyards with overhanging   vaults and arches.

I become more aware of others, not Arab, dark and somber, who do not seem to participate in the street gatherings. Many are similar in appearance with wide brimmed black hats and whiskered countenances. They make their way down streets indifferent and clearly separate. They seem to lack humor and compassion, and I wonder what kind of religion and what kind of man is so intolerant of others.

I am reminded of the despised money lenders of Europe of the Middle Ages. It is both strange and thought provoking to realise that many of these people are newcomers, immigrants from Europe since the end of the Second World War, who presumably suffered inequity, intolerance, lack of compassion and worst. Hopefully these newcomers do not possess the same fault imposing inequity, intolerance, and lack of compassion of others.

Many of the men wear the black robes of Eastern Europe - black shoes, black stockings, black coats ankle length, and the black wide rimmed hat. Their women with shaved heads wigged and head scarves. Their religious beliefs, extreme to many, is their prerogative, but potentially worrisome coupled with present extreme Zionist thinking.

Later in the week I continued my survey of the Muslim Quarter. I stepped outside Ghada's house early morning, and looked around. What a higgly piggly conglomeration of buildings. Little appears to conform. All was unique with little compatibility. Stone walls so often out of plumb and crooked, constructed of stones of every shape and size. Windows and entrance doors in general set deep in walls softened by shadow. Finally roofs of every design, shape, and material. Roofs of stone, clay and cement tile, corrugated iron, and sheet metal. The uniqueness of structural design and material complemented by non conforming locations, and of different ages. Neighboring properties might differ by many centuries.

The air is cool and pleasant. The extreme heat of the day has yet to come. From the neighborhood mosque minaret the imams can be heard calling and beseeching all to prayer and rejoice. The scene the many crooked and narrow streets complemented by leaning buildings, substantial overhanging arches with structures above, the irregular stone paving and steps, and ramps for delivery hand carts.

The general color cream red sand of the local stone, and the mellowness of the ages. Arab houses lean against each other separated at places with dusty courtyards and high stone walls. Every building could tell a story - so much of the past and the present. The aspect of buildings, walls, paved alleys has a character that is so human. Unlike western development which reflects the Industrial world, here there are no vehicles. The planning is anchored to the past, and now difficult for change. Even the transportation of goods and materials is handled by porters and donkeys all carrying immense loads.

Entrance doors butt immediately to the sidewalk - few buildings are set back. There is a sense of closeness to the outside street. Voices can be heard within and without. Occasionally an open door reveals an interior commonly devoid of possessions. And then you realise another striking difference - where are the women. Muslim women tend in general to remain in contentment in the shadows occupied with their household and family obligations whilst their men work from early dawn to late sunset.

One is very much struck by the numerous shops, often so very small, set between the cafes, and the thousands of vendors. It is a reminder that tourism is a major business in the Old City.

Every stranger and foreigner a potential customer to be offered the typical tourist rubbish that will remind the naive visitor of his visit to Jerusalem for many years.. And for those with more money than common sense, there are the dealers of antiquities.

I gaze at the groups of men huddled in intense discussion. I note the mischievous and sly smile, the chuckle. What could they be discussing? They certainly do not have the rather grim humorless countenances of their Jewish neighbors. One cannot deny that the Arab provides much of the color and the variety of the Middle East. And the cafes were an important part of Jerusalem life where Arabs just talked and talked.

At the far east end of Via Dolorosa is St Stephen's Gate, also known as Lion's Gate. Close by the garden of the White Fathers, the Pond of Bethesda, and the Church of St Anne. The church 800 to 900 years old is a solemn reminder of austerity. Saladin the great Muslim converted the church into a religious school when he seized Jerusalem back from the Crusaders 1188. In more recent times, the 18th Century, the Ottoman governor housed his horses within the church. Finally Napoleon III gave the building to the White Fathers who restored the church back into its former glory.

Mid day was rapidly approaching, and I was becoming increasingly aware of the heat. I decided to cool seated in the shade of the gardens, and eat Ghada's lunch. I look around, and realised that I am staring at a small meeting hall. Within the instructor was addressing a class which was just ending. The subject *Introduction to Economic Planning,*

The subject fascinated me. So rarely do business enterprises truly plan wisely, and so often their decisions are a disaster. I mentioned this to a thin studious man who smiled, and remarked.

" Young man - you will eventually learn that the human race is not wise - and commonly causes so many unnecessary problems. Man rarely learns - through greed he simply acts"

I explained my interest in *Design Economics* as it applied to Construction Cost Planning and Cost Management. And the unfortunate fact that very few construction companies invested adequate thought at the planning phase.

The lecturer nodded thoughtfully.

" Regret there is very very little planning anywhere. Selfish interests and greed eliminates the possibility of unbiased planning. I see you have your lunch. May I join you?"

We retired to the shade of the gardens, and the elderly man pulled out some wrapped sandwiches from his brief case, and continued with his thoughts. His name was Gerald Cuthbertson. Perhaps prudently he queried with courtesy my name and   background, and cautiously asked.

" British? Jew?"

My advise presumably guided him an appropriate avenue to discuss any future subject. Anyhow I thought it a great opportunity to ascertain his thinking about a problem that seemed to need a lot of planning.

" Gerald. Here is a planning problem, or so it appears. How will this advertised large increase of Jewish immigrants be employed? Palestine is basically a poor agricultural country - the potential of the employment of many poor European immigrants seems slight."

Did I sense a trace of irony and sarcasm.

" No problem they will all get immediate employment in the Haganah, Palmach, Irgun and Stern gangs. And remember that the Zionists claim that they desire a truly Jewish State, and will not employ Arabs. Thus there is theoretically potential for employment although no doubt economic greed will overcome the desire of Jewish employees when cheaper Arab labor is available."

That explanation might or might not resolve the problem. Regardless these European immigrants were poor, and they were entering a very poor country. Was that sound planning?

Gerald agreed that his response was not adequate, and stressed.

" Well Paul - I don't think that it will be a long term problem. I have no doubt that the Zionists plan to look after their own at the expense of the local Arab population. The Zionists are well organized, disciplined, and ruthless. I am sure that they have invested plenty of thought and planning to cover their future."

I looked doubtfully at him.

Exasperated Gerald exploded with irritation.

" My friend. Just consider the enormous skill and perseverance of the Zionists over the past thirty years. Basically the Zionist conspiracy is an excellent example of long term planning. It demonstrates what a determined unscrupulous group of people can achieve exerting enormous criminal pressures on dishonest and corrupt politicians and national leaders. Extremely harmful national policies have been created.

First one commences in the 19th Century with the writings of Disraeli, Britain's Prime Minister, and later in the century the thoughts of Theodor Herzl who desired to emulate the success of Cecil Rhodes in Africa, and during the first half of the 20th Century the persistent diplomatic force of Chaim Weizmann favoring Palestine.

It is absolutely remarkable how the Zionist infiltrated British political leadership, and indoctrinated notable leaders such as Balfour, Lloyd George, Churchill, Chamberlain, Ramsay MacDonald, Gilbert Clayton, Ronald Storrs, Henry MacMahon, Leopold Amery, Robert Cecil, and so many others.

And of course Arthur Balfour's declaration 1917 favoring a Jewish National Home in Palestine was a major coupe that has resulted in thirty years of grief in the Middle East."

I interjected trying to soften the guilt of Britain.

" But Gerald. It is in the hands of United Nations to determine Palestine's future."

The lecturer sadly gazed at his ignorant pupil, and shook his head.

" My dear Paul. The future of Palestine has been in the hands of Britain for thirty years, and all that has been achieved is a repetition of ideas   that have been dominated by Zionist thinking. Any unbiased planner would identify immediately the problem, recognise the natural rights of the Arabs in Palestine, and check mate the grave danger of Zionist thinking and their crazy ideas.

Now we are discussing planning, and the Zionists are truly experts. When it was clear that the British were incapable of taking any action that would meet the approval of the Zionists, they astutely switched to the USA realizing that their success could be achieved by getting the USA to pressure the British who were rapidly becoming economically bankrupt.

That planning decision was brilliant. In the USA there were 4.6 million Jews of which about 150,000 were Zionists. That number acting as a voting block basically black mailed and bribed USA politicians to make favorable Zionist announcements and resolutions at times of national elections. Thus Woodrow Wilson, Franklin Roosevelt, and Harry Truman all succumbed to Zionist pressures, and allowed the fate of national issues and politics dominate the international scene of Palestine.

Zionists such as Rabbi Stephen Wise, Lewis Braneis (Supreme Court Justice), Felix Frankfurter (Harvard University), Henry Morganthau (Secretary Treasury), Harry Stimson (Secretary War), Sumner Wells, and many others had successfully infiltrated Washington by the 1940s.

Thus by 1940 the membership of the American Palestine Committee included two thirds (66%) of the Senate, 200 members of the House of Representatives, the leaders of both major parties, and leading labor organizations.

By 1944 and 1945 both Roosevelt and Truman recognized the Jewish natural home in Palestine - and for both it was an Election Year!

And I have no doubt that now the decision is in the hands of the United Nations, that our Zionist friends will exert their muscle on the U.N members."

Gerald stopped to consume the rest of his lunch, and apologized for dominating the discussion. I was fascinated listening to this learned lecturer. His final sandwich eaten, he completed his talk, and stressed its importance with the following observation:

" Now Paul. What is so very significant is the diabolical and astute planning of the Zionists. In both Britain and the USA, the demands and claims of the Zionists changed continuously. Immediately any approach appeared to have little hope of success, they would immediately switch to another approach presented often to different individuals. And of course their methodology whereby politicians were forced to acquiesce to their Zionist interests was a dominant and beneficial feature that identified and understood the corruption of political thinking.

It is a classic example that the claimed democratic process of determining national and international policies can be completely undemocratic, and most certainly not in the interest of the electorate, and only in the interest of scoundrels and criminals.

And of course it is so sad the wisdom of Mahatme Gandhi was ignored:

Mahatme Gandhi 1947 *was very specific when addressing the proposed U.N Partition.*

*" The Arabs could choose - not be forced, but choose - to give the Jews refuge, and it would have been a great generosity. **The Jews did not have a right to the lands; It was the Arabs' decision to make, and they chose not to give the Jews land."***

When Gandhi was asked what would be the most acceptable solution to the Palestine Problem, he declared:

*" **The abandonment wholly by the Jews of terrorism and other forms of violence"***

Gerald examined his watch, realized that he had an immediate appointment, shook my hand, suggested that we should meet again, and rapidly departed.

What would be my next destination? I decided that it had to be the imposing *Al-Haram Al-Sharif.(The Noble Sanctuary)*

The Mamelukes built mosques and schools around the Dome of Rock way back in the past. Then the Muslims captured Jerusalem in the year 638. It is of interest to realise that many Muslims throughout the world do not speak Arabic, yet the Qur'an is written in Arabic. Also it may be a surprise to learn that the Arabs re -consecrated the site of a Jewish Temple, and built the Dome of the Rock over.

During earlier times the Middle East was controlled by the Emperor of Byzantium and the Persian King of Kings both of whom received advise sent in the name of an unknown prophet Muhammad of Mecca that they should renounce their idolatrous religion. Presumably the message was not taken seriously, a serious mistake, because within fifty years the Persian   power had vanished, and the Muslims were at the walls of Constantinople.

The Arabs did not arrive as religious fanatics. In fact Muhammad was identified as the last of the great biblical seers which the Koran recognise with great reverence. Initially the Prophet's followers were instructed to pray facing Jerusalem. However when the Jews resisted Islam, it was decided to pray looking towards Mecca. The Jewish religion was not rejected by the Muslims; it was the Jewish practices that were considered objectionable.

The Muslim entry into Jerusalem in AD 638 was quite peaceful and with their guarantee the gates were opened. And their attitude continued to be lenient evident in modern times of a large Orthodox and Armenian presence. Much tradition is centered upon the Rock, and many remarkable claims apply.

However despite such claims one might attribute commercial thinking for the erection of the Dome of the Rock which took place fifty years later. The Caliph in Damascus was subject to anti caliph thinking in Mecca, and the purpose of the Dome of Rock was to direct future pilgrimages, currently at   Mecca, to Jerusalem.

Regardless the Dome of Rock is a remarkable work of art created by architects and craftsmen who were not Muslim. And Muslim tradition is centered upon the Rock - the foundation stone of the world. It is here, so it is believed, that Mohammad made his visit to Heaven.

From the Muslim Quarter and its shaded streets, I approached the sanctuary over an enormous stone paved courtyard, very much aware of the bright sun, and pass by a number of small buildings complete with domes and arches. It is claimed that the proportions of this gigantic court yard was determined by Herod 2000 years past. Around its perimeter are patched walls and reconstructed colonnades and medieval minarets, with named gated entrances that lead into the city - *Gate of Darkness, Gate of Iron, Gate Beautiful, Gate of Absolution, and Gate of Tribes.*

The Dome of the Rock demands one's attention. Although not a Muslim design, the Dome's classical proportions have an Islamic face. The entrances have been set out oriented to the compass. The façade is decorated all over with geometric designs, mosaics, and tiles, covered with verse from the Koran, and free of images.. The formal patterns symbolize the harmony of Allah's presence. Octagonal on plan complete with a golden cupola, it is the world center.

Steps rise on all sides ascending to the platform. Around the entrance elderly *hajjis* stand who have made the pilgrimage to Mecca. Some seem disheartened sensing that their religion is subject to hostility and rejection, and claim that Islam never rejects the prophets of the Christians and Jews.

I enter the building. Within is a treasure trove of art from many cultures. Perhaps the most striking masterpiece is the inner face of the dome, the creation of 14th Century artists from India. My mind is overloaded with visions as I leave.

At the south end of the Courtyard the Aqsa Mosque stands with its striking silver dome. I imagine that Islam should meet the needs of current lives. Common sense is found in the Koran

" You may only pay back transgressors to the degree of the hurt. However if you forgive God will reward you"

Believers are encouraged to be good and limit their aggressiveness.

Many are praying in the mosque kneeling with hands behind, and foreheads to the floor. It is said that Moslems never lose sight of God's greatness. A thought provoking claim that appears to be contrary to the thinking of their Christian cousins.

I felt tired not accustomed to the strength and glare of the sun. I wandered back across the court yard and approached the Antonia Fortress. Amazing to learn that this fortress was built by Herod. Then followed impossible governors that eventually caused a revolt by the Jews. The whole of Judea revolted, and Jew fought Jew. The Romans returned, and the Jewish community sought the safety of the Antonia Fortress. Titus prudently let them starve. It is said that 115,000 corpses were carried out beyond the gates of the city.

I climb the stairs of the fortress, and from the top look down over the Muslim Quarter. What an amazing sight of buildings of all shapes and sizes complete with their courtyards. With some surprise I note the many domed roofs of stone construction, the construction of which would defeat many an European builder. What a complex higgly piggly gathering of buildings.

I wonder *" Did everyone have a detailed knowledge of their property boundaries?"* I decide that it must be a nightmare for land surveyors.

It is now mid afternoon and I have a headache. I staggered back to Ghada's house, and finally recover within its shade. My dear host eyed me anxiously as she handed me a cup of coffee.

" Take this aspirin and rest" she ordered.

I closed my eyes and relaxed.

" What a wonderful day"

Later I thought.

" I am no doubt another visitor entrapped by the mysteries of the Middle East"

After the evening meal, I advised Ghada that I now planned to visit the Christian and Jewish Quarters. She raised her eyebrows, and teased me

" Already tired of the Muslim Quarter?"

I grinned and denied my disinterest

" No No. not at all. I just want to see the other Quarters and make a comparison. I am curious to see what the Crusaders and the Jews have accomplished over the past thousand years."

She pondered over my decision, and finally capitulated.

" Well if you must, take great care of yourself, and don't believe a word that they say. And by the way set aside a day for Ahmad."

The Old City

According to my map, the Old City was about one square mile in area with a compact community of 25,000 within its ancient Turkish walls. What would be my itinerary tomorrow?

I decided to commence early in the day like everyone else, and take advantage of the cool early hours. My first destination the Church of the Holy Sepulchre in the Christian Quarter. I advised Ghada of my intentions, and that I would leave at dawn.

" Would that be in order?" I asked rather anxiously

Ghada approved remarking that leaving at dawn would be wise.

When I woke, no light had entered my room from the outside street. Rapidly I washed and dressed, and quietly descended to the living room below. Rather guiltily I realised that dear dear Ghada had preceded me, my breakfast was neatly laid out on the Kitchen table, and also a packed lunch for my mid day meal.

She seemed rather anxious and concerned.

" Remember Paul - remain in the background where ever possible. Father's business could be in jeopardy if anyone realises any possible connection between you and him. Please return early because Ahmad will be visiting here tomorrow"

Possessing the confidence of the young and the inexperienced, I brushed aside Ghada's concerns.

" Don't worry. And thank you very much for breakfast and lunch"

With a smile and a wave of confidence, I departed to commence my survey. Standing close to the Antonia Fortress towering high above, I heard the early calls to prayer from the local mosque minaret's. Musically the haunting calls once heard cannot be forgotten.

" God is Great, God is Great.
There is no God but God.
And Mohammed is the prophet of God.
God is Great, God is Great"

Everyone is called to pray.

The route to the Church of the Holy Sepulchre was the same route claimed for Christ on his way to Calvary, and is marked by the fourteen Stations of the Cross. Close by on Via Dolorosa is the Convent of the Sisters of Zion where, according to the sisters, Christ was condemned to death. The Jews supposedly accused Jesus outside the Judgment Hall.

The Church of the Holy Sepulchre was sited on Via Dolorosa a few hundred yards distant. Crossing the main intersecting street of Khan es-Zeit, I was now in the Christian Quarter, and rapidly approached the Church which, it is claimed, was built over the spot where Jesus was buried.

The Church consists of a multitude of structures, domes, and irregular roofs that enclose a conglomeration of chapels, holy places, and monuments. And what might seem remarkable, various parts of the Church are claimed by six different sects.

A community of about 11,000 Christian Arabs live in the neighborhood, their residences in general superior to the homes of the Muslim Quarter. Despite the early hour, citizens recognise the wisdom of commencing work early prior to the heat of midday. Already Via Dolorosa and the side streets are filled with monks, priests, Arab vendors, Arabs with their loaded donkeys, and the inevitable Jewish tourists and their guides.

In general the Christian Quarter appears more wealthy than the Muslim Quarter. The shopkeepers possibly more slick in their selling techniques. Regardless the customer is the same gullible tourist.

Entering the Church, one is bewildered. The Franciscans, the Eastern Orthodox, the Armenians, the Coptics, the Syrians, and the Greek Orthodox all insist on their presence. Thus the interior consists of a remarkable depository of faith and mementos, and accordingly very confusing. The real purpose of the Church completely lost through a sad lack of unity.

So often the various sects would endeavor to drown out their competition with singing, chants, bells, and distract the ritual of others. And of course, deeply opposed, the Greek and Roman Catholic would insist in their beliefs.

I watched an occasional Palestinian Christian Arab enter. She raised her palms in her gesture of prayer, and departed. In a sense she only suggested a feeling of peace and acceptance. I departed thankfully, questioning the sanity of the human race.

Outside a British army truck was delayed by a donkey load that had fallen on the road. Instead of patiently waiting or assisting the donkey owner, the driver berated the unfortunate man.

" Get your bloody donkey out of the way, you damn idiot"

Physically handicapped, the donkey owner struggled, and received further unnecessary and unkind remarks. Finally order was restored, the truck and donkey continued their way, and I crossed the street.

" Was that confrontation necessary?"

It is precisely events of that nature that can only cause unnecessary ill will. What right has a British truck driver to berate a local citizen who is supposed to be provided with administration, justice, and order by the soldier's country.. No doubt the truck driver, if questioned, would acknowledge his error. But one is obliged to ask why a truck driver even thinks he has the authority to be so un civil.

An explanation might suggest a society that has power, an authority that creates a singular lack of understanding and compassion of others. When power and money is the model for success, the individual becomes selfish and callous. It is an attitude that encourages sick individuals to ill treat others and become killers. But was that the only explanation?

I wandered down Christian Street, crossed David Street, and entered the Armenian Quarter. With Jaffa Gate and the Citadel on my right, I continued to the Church of St James. In my mind, unlike the Christian church just visited, this Armenian church fulfilled its purpose. The church was enormous, opulent in fine carpets, wall tiles, and numerous hanging lamps, preserved and supported in unity for over 1500 years.

According to the Armenians, the Church of St James is sited over the body of St James, brother of Christ, who was buried at this spot during the 4th Century. Armenian monks dressed in their dark pointed hoods pass by in contemplation, and bells chime providing an enchantment that seems to reflect this ancient Quarter.

Seated outside the Church of St James, I ate my lunch, and watched the people pass by. The basic occupation of the Armenians is Jewelry, and this activity is an Old City exception actually producing works of value and beauty. Groups of young boys well dressed in their dark school uniforms wait - all have handsome features, clean, and attractive. Such a contrast to the frequent garish ill dressed tourist and the uncouth loud voice.

An army corporal was seated on the bench and eyed me curiously.

"You're a Brit?"

I nodded and grinned.

" You are definitely a Brit?"

He accepted that status without dispute.

" Where you from mate?"

" London. What about you?"

"Chipping Norton"

I laughed, and responded with a question..

" You know how many pubs there are in Chipping Norton?"

I examined the soldier as he gave my question some thought. About my build and age, slight, scrawny, probably quite wiry but did not appear particularly healthy. It was a tricky question, and eventually he admitted that his number was just an estimate,

" Say about thirty?"

" You are totally wrong - there were one hundred and sixty nine pubs in 1943-1945"

"Go'arn. Can't be that number. How do you know anyhow?"

" Because I went on Harvest Camps during the War, and I was advised that was the number. It was amazing the number of one room pubs that sold hard cider - stuff that guaranteed you would be laid out flat"

His rather depressed face lit up with the thought of his home town - or was it simply being laid out flat!.

" Fancy you knowing me old town. Anything else you remember?"

" Beetroot sandwiches and carrots. There was nothing else to eat. Carrots were supposed to be good for eyesight and many other things. After the War the doctors realized that eating too much carrot was in fact bad for you. Anyhow we were all well and fit.

Another thing I remember were the Poles. I think they all belonged to a local fighter squadron. It was rumored that the whole lot were crazy. Regardless the local girls appear to have been attracted to their craziness to the irritation of some of the locals."

The soldier bent over knees set out wide and gazed at the sidewalk in lost thought, and sadly muttered.

" Bloody Hell. How I wish I was there now."

He was clearly quite fed up. I asked the obvious.

" Don't you like it here?"

He looked at me as if I was crazy.

" You kidding mate! This is the lousiest dump I have ever known. We are supposed to be here to provide administration, security, law, and order. And yet we are despised by the Arab

population and hated by the bloody Jewish population.

There are no pubs, no fish and chip shops, and nothing to do   except try and avoid being killed."

" Killed?"

The Oxfordshire man spat on the pavement contemptuously.

" You a visitor?"

" Arrived couple weeks ago"

He examined me more carefully, presumably decided that my explanation was correct, and sniffed.

" Listen mate. You take great care. Them Jews have armed forces known as the Haganah,, commando types known as the Palmach, vicious gangs named the Irgun and Stern, and other unbelievably cruel characters which operate all over Palestine, and have no respect for life or for the law.

Here are a few terrible happening in recent years:

1944-1945: Our police headquarters was blown up, and seven British police murdered.

1946:   Six British soldiers murdered. Nine British officers kidnapped and flogged.
They blew up a wing of the King David Hotel which housed the British Army headquarters, and killed ninety one of our men.

1947: The Jerusalem Officers Club was attacked, and twenty solders killed.
Two British Sergeants were hung, and their bodies booby trapped.

Every single individual in them Stern and Irgun gangs should be shot - they have no respect for life at all.

And here we are - supposed to provide security, law, and order, and act impartially - and yet we are despised and hated."

I tried to sympathise and suggest the brighter side of the coin.

" Well. What about the Arabs. They seem an interesting group of people. Perhaps once these Jewish gangs are put in their place, life here may improve"

The Corporal realized that he was dealing with a half wit, and laughed bitterly.

" Look. Put on your thinking cap chum. Them interesting group of Arabs just despise us. They have no guts, always whining expecting others to help them, and rarely grateful. If they had any gumption, they would not permit them Jews to push them around. They are treacherous to each other - just a big bunch of disloyal and deceitful characters that refuse to work together.

And finally get this in your blooming woolly head. Our British politicians are a bunch of complete idiots incapable of making a sound decision about anything. They just keep on changing their so called minds. It is so obvious that the Arabs and the Jews, particularly them Zionist Jews, will never share Palestine in peace. And to be fair why should the Arabs permit them Jews to come into the country. These suggestions of partitioning the country or expecting the Arabs and Jews to live in harmony is lunacy."

I had upset the corporal with my ignorance. He rose, his demeanor could be adequately described as *"pissed off",* and he departed shaking his head.

I have three to four hours to view the Jewish Quarter if I depart immediately. With regret I leave, walk along a street adjoining the south city wall, pass by Zion Gate, and finally enter the Jewish Quarter.

Standing by the city wall gazing around, endeavoring to determine my location in the Old City, I suddenly sense that I was being watched. Two men were huddled on the far side of the street. One had noted my presence, and what seemed with some urgency drew his companion's attention to me. Immediately both turned their backs to me - what now were they discussing?

It did not seem possible that I was identified - and yet why their interest? Rapidly I went down a side street, entered the heart of the Jewish Quarter, and finally made my way to the Street of the Chain - a continuation of David Street. Apprehensively I look back, but there was no evidence to be of concern.

The Jewish people, like the Arab people, are difficult to define. Some are deeply pacifist, and do not accept the extreme thinking of the Zionists. Their dress is a reminder of the seriousness of their varied beliefs, their education, devoted to waiting, learning, and self correction. Others, often newcomers from Europe and Russia, demonstrate a curious claim to their faith completely contrary to their behavior.

Their thinking is secular, aggressive and uncharitable; an unhappy sense of indifference of others. True there are many that desire peace and friendship, but unfortunately such peace and friendship lacks equity dominated by greed, and any proposed agreement far too one sided to ever be acceptable.

Their appearance, as already mentioned, is often featured with the somber black, bearded countenances, their wide brimmed hats. But how depressing. Immediately it suggests narrow extreme beliefs and adherence to inflexible education. Of course the failings and conclusions could be incorrect. One has only to be reminded of the typical American scene, the carousing with wild women, gambling, crime, and whatever to realise that one has to think carefully before making any critical conclusion.

However one cannot avoid the fear that such extreme religious emphasis on questionable historic events can only create intolerance and a lack of intelligent thought. It can become the product of intolerant leaders and followers with activities that common sense would define unacceptable.

I stand close to the Wailing Wall which adjoins the huge court yard of the Dome of the Rock. One legend claims that when Solomon erected the Temple, he instructed the beggars to erect the Wall. And when the Temple was destroyed by the Angels, they decided that the Wall, the work of the poor, should never be destroyed.. Often the site of the Wall is vacant and silent, and one wonders at the thinking of American Jews who travel many thousand of miles, and consider the kissing of the Wall so important.

Regardless it is considered the holiest of holy places - the work of King Herod. And in the crevices of the massive limestone block wall often may be seen written prayers tucked into the joints. It is believed that these prayers will be carried direct to God. And with sincere devotion, devout Jews may be seen facing the wall with head bowed studying their prayer book.

From the wall, I strolled down to Dung Gate located in the city wall, and there made my first exit of the ancient Old City. I did not have to walk far. Here I face Mount Ophel which is steeped in ancient history. It is here that David made the capital of an united Israel. Nearby is the Pool of Siloam connected to the Spring of Gihon through Hezekiah's tunnel.

Historically the Israelites, a group of Semitic tribes about 1000 BC began to believe in a God, a moral being, who offered a guide to his followers. Just and incorruptible, two major religions developed - Christianity and Islam.

It is claimed that the Israelites wandered into the Sinai Desert, although I understand that T.E. Lawrence never found any evidence to support that claim. Anyhow the twelve tribes realized the need to unite in order to survive against the Philistines. Hostile Jebusites, whose capital at that time was Jerusalem, presented a problem. David, a warrior king, laid siege, and finally captured the place. It is the manner of his success that is of interest.

The Jebusites had wisely channeled the waters of Gihon Spring deep into the hill of Ophel. There they constructed a vertical shaft (a well), and thus water supplies were guaranteed for the besieged. But what they never foresaw was David's strategy. He sent his men along the channel tunnel, and entered the Jebusite capital unsuspected through the vertical shaft (the well).

This tunnel and shaft was remarkable engineering for that early time. In later years (8th Century), King Hezekiah, threatened by the Assyrian invasion, extended the tunnel from under Mount Ophel into the city. More great engineering.

The sun was dropping down in the west - it was time for a very tired visitor to return home.

Ghada was full of news of the day. After I described my exploits, she reminded me that Ahmad would arrive 9.00am Wednesday. I made a note, and then recollected the strange incident when the two individuals noted my presence in the Jewish Quarter.

Ghada's face dropped with anxiety.

" Paul - you had better stop discovering the city - this can be a very dangerous place. Please believe me"

Ahmad Al-Husseini 's Brief

Every Wednesday I received a blue airmail letter from Mother; and every week Mother expected to receive an air letter from her eldest. Already I had adopted the habit of visiting the Jerusalem post office mid week, and collect what was often my one and only communication in my private post box. Ghada cautiously advised me the wisdom of having a private post box, and avoid any connection with her father.

Mother was quite unique. Unlike so many, her regular letters were full of information, and rarely did she ever repeat herself. Perhaps England was unique - one could guarantee a national economic disaster at least once a month, everyone was fleeing the poor country, and Clement Atlee and Ernest Bevin were the only stable pillars supporting Socialism, Nationalization, and whatever whilst Winston Churchill retired   smoking his cigar and painting farm houses and local cows.

And of course there were the neighbors, local scandals real or imagined, and the Wimbledon Borough News that often filled one page or more. However Mother had seen some upsetting headlines in the Telegraph in connection with the Middle East - the fact that the Suez Canal did not flow through Palestine was irrelevant.   Her concern was the danger faced by her eldest.

The first matter of real concern were these immoral Sheiks with 30 to 50 wives each. There they were - all 30 to 50 with just their mysterious eyes revealed to the world. How can any civilized individual know what was going on with 30 to 50 sets of eyes peeping at you! But what really disturbed Mother was the Sheik - blood thirsty evil faced character with the habit of cutting off heads with his wicked curved scimitar. She was uncertain how often heads were cut off, but regardless she warned me to avoid these people.   Don't stick out your neck!

The next matter of real concern developed from her meeting Mrs Potter at the Wimbledon Public Library. Admittedly Mrs Potter was not an expert on Palestine but then who is? Mrs Potter's poor husband, before he passed away,   had been in the army stationed in India and Palestine. Mother was assured that Mr Potter shook his head gravely (while he was alive) when the subject of the desolate Palestinian desert was discussed. There was no water, no pubs, in fact nothing except wild unlawful Bedouins so cruel. Life in the desert according to Mr Potter was not worth a farthing - and all those Bedouins did was steal cattle and women. And what was so shocking they never washed! One sensed that Mr Potter was still shaking his head!

And finally Mother had come to the conclusion that I should consider returning as soon as possible. She had just read a newspaper editorial by Abe Goldburg. He assured the reader that all Arabs are dishonest, unreliable, and not fit for modern society. He asked *"How can any society survive with such dreadful people?"*   And apparently he wrote paragraph after paragraph describing the unfortunate Jewish settlements (Kibbutz) subject to attacks by these terrible Arabs who had no pity for these poor unfortunate Holocaust survivors. Palestine was clearly a pail of worms.

Ahmad sat at the table complete with papers and documents for referral. I sat opposite, and my education commenced. The driver stressed that the purpose of this meeting was to provide me with an understanding of modern Palestine history, and the significance of events in recent years. He suggested that I make notes because there was   much to be covered.

"The Muslim Arab and the Jew have co-existed in the area known as Palestine for thousands of years. The activities and interests in general differ. The Muslim Arab rural with agricultural interests, normally peaceful and not overly aggressive. The Palestinian Jew urban with commercial interests, and materially aggressive.

In general both groups have remained indifferent of each other.

In 1917, the Turkish rule ended and driven out. The British were given the Mandate of the State Palestine providing general administration, security, law, and justice. Unfortunately the British, encouraged by Zionists declared that the Jewish people should be permitted to have their own State within the Palestinian Mandate. It was a very curious declaration because the Palestinian Arab was never consulted, and if consulted no doubt would have opposed the proposal.

At that time the Palestinian Arab had resided in Palestine historically for thousands of years, and owned 95% of the land. The Jewish people at that time were a small minority, possibly owned 5% of the land, and resided mainly in Jerusalem, Haifa, and Jaffa. Balfour Foreign Minister for the British having ignored the national rights of the Arabs, then declared that the rights of the Arabs socially, politically, and property should be observed!

The world Zionist Organization thereafter pursued an aggressive policy designed to claim most or all of Palestine for its future Israel State, and made the point of claiming the cities, ports, and most fertile areas. For the past 30 years, various Partition Plans were proposed, in particular the years of 1937 and 1938. Now in 1947 the United Nations are rumored to make an announcement"

Ahmad shuffled his papers, found a map of Palestine depicting the proposed Partition, and placed it in front of me.

" Now bear in mind that about 95% of the land is owned by Arabs and perhaps 5% by Jews.. Consider the inequity and the implications of United Nations determining the future status of Palestine   against the wishes of the Arab people..

Consider the inequity of this proposal even if you ignore the rights of the indigenous Palestinian Arab. Over 50% of the country to be in the Jewish State.- all   the prime fertile plains, the two major ports, the major rail and road transportation systems, and water sources.. And the Arab people are left with landlocked hills and mountains without any meaningful access to the world.

I interjected.

" But that is totally unfair. It will cause a lot of unhappiness and strife. "

Ahmad did not respond. He just tapped his pencil, and shuffled his papers. Finally he declared

" Well Paul - you are right. Terrible events have taken place over the past thirty years all over Palestine. And terrible events continue - it is a horrible trend"

Ibrahim's man then continued.

"Yes. It is unbelievable that such injustice has taken place by the most powerful countries and respected institutions in the world that all proclaim democracy. But of much greater concern has been the ever increasing malice, hate, aggression of the Jews without any provocation by my people.

Over the past 15 years, the Irgun gang, founded in 1931 by the Zionists with the purpose of supporting militancy against the Arab population, has increased its aggression and persecution throughout Palestine. Arms smuggling was discovered as early as 1935 in Jaffa. In 1938 the Irgun killed 119Palestinians. Since the Second World War, with the ever increasing numbers of immigrant thugs from Germany, Romania, and Poland, it is suspected that these strangers support the Irgun entirely. "

" Wait" I demanded

" How can this occur with possibly one hundred thousand British troops stationed in the Palestinian Mandate, and Britain's responsibility to provide administration and security. That kind of criminal activity would not be permitted. "

He shook his head

" You do not understand Paul. We have every reason to consider the British with mixed thoughts. Their acts so contrary, sometimes in our interest, other times very much against. Any protest has been treated with brutality, our leaders expelled from this country. And every act relating to this proposed partition has never been in our interest. Just examine the many records of Palestinian persecution. One might be forgiven having the impression that the British considered my people as second class citizens. Just consider the British encouragement of the immigration of European Jews to our country. "

I stared at Ahmad unwilling to hear such unfavorable comments of my country.

" Are you really certain about your claims? "

" Definitely" Ahmad sat back, and sipped his coffee.. He leaned forward, and stressed.

" Of course it is unbelievable that major countries and institutions should propose such inequities. Imagine if United Nations proposed that the Cockneys of London should be given 50% of England without consulting anyone. Imagine a proposal that recommends some extreme religious group in New York be given half the States of USA without consulting anyone!"

I thought over Ahmad's remarks. *" It just could not happen, and yet that appears to be the fate of the Palestinian Arab; not to be consulted or considered despite living in their country for so many centuries"*

I shook my head in disbelief

"It seems incredible that such an unjust decision could have been made"

The driver's face flushed, placed both hands firmly on the table edge, then leaned back in his chair, and gloomily declared.

" That is not the worst news"

" What do you mean?"

" We have learnt that Ben Gurion has held a number of meetings in Tel Aviv with Zionist leaders. They plan to seize the whole country from the Palestinian people"

" How can they?" I scornfully demanded. Ahmad really was exaggerating.

" Simply through force and aggression they plan to seize everything"

" That is absolutely absurd. This is 1947. The British Army is here, and the British are responsible for the welfare of all in this country. It just cannot happen."

"Well Paul - you are a civilized intelligent individual, and you have a right to imagine that such a crime is not possible. However understand that Ben Gurion is backed and financed by the World Zionist Organisation. Now he has the support of tens of thousands of murderous thugs from Europe who are eager to steal our property. The British currently are not interested in our welfare. It is rumored that they will soon give up their Mandate.

And there is a very powerful Zionist political group in Washington that has, through bribery, the backing of many US politicians. The general public, because of the Holocaust, have an international sympathy for the Jewish refugee. No one is anxious to confront the immigrants and the proposed State."

I pondered over Ahmad's warning, and continued to resist. *" How could it be possible"*

With doubt I suggested again that it would not, could not, happen. The Jews had suffered terribly in Europe by the Germans a mere three to four years earlier. It seemed inconceivable that such individuals would now emulate the actions of the German Gestapo.

Ahmad responded

" Of course in a world full of intelligent compassionate people, it is inconceivable. But this world is full of individuals who are materialistic, lack all compassion and understanding, and will destroy and kill to have their own way. And there are also hundreds of millions, although not actively participating, will sit back, watch, and even approve through their prejudice."

I examined my notes, then turned and stared outside the window into the peaceful courtyard. What Ahmad was saying was a serious reminder that behind the façade of peace and concord, are the seeds of hate and destruction. I imagine my face revealed disappointment, inexperience, and concern.

" What we need to do is to identify the root of the problem. The truth has to be accepted, however unacceptable, otherwise nothing is ever resolved. Remember that the Palestinian Arabs and Jews have lived side by side for thousands of years. There have been differences but in general have survived with respect of human dignity of all. And yet I fear that the orthodox Palestinian Jews will permit the Irgun and other terrorist groups to operate with impunity without meaningful protest. And finally these very people will probably support the terrorists, and steal from us."

I protested.

" Come off it Ahmad. These Jews may have different interests to the Arabs, but they will never descend to the levels of barbarians and worse."

Glumly Ahmad accepted my protest, and quietly replied

" Paul - we will see"

Later Ahmad returned for further discussions, and my knowledge increased. First he discussed the main urban centres in Palestine, and provided information regarding population, general activities, transportation, and highways.

" The total population of Palestine is about 1,900,000 of which 1,300,000 are Arabs. Jerusalem has the largest population of about 200,000 with about 60% Arabs. Within the districts. Jaffa has a population of about 100,000,   about   30% Arab. Haifa has a population of perhaps 100,000, about 55% Arab. All other districts are mainly Arab.

The towns of Acra, Safad, Tiberias, Nazareth. Baysan. Jinin. Nablus, Tulkam, Ramallah, El-Ramla, Hebron, Beersheba, and Gaza   have 20,000 maximum, and predominantly Arab.

What is very significant is that there are 700 to 1000 villages throughout Palestine with populations from 100 to about 5,000 which accommodate the main Arab population. In the Negev there are about 90,000 Bedouin.

The problem is that despite the Arabs having a larger population, there is no leadership. Important leaders have been expelled from the country by the British, and are unable to return. And to make matters worse, the Jews are capitalizing from years of planning and information gathering. Now they have spies, informers, collaborators in every urban town and modest village. The Jews possess more information about us and our affairs than we do!"

The discussion ended with Ahmad's announcement.

" Tomorrow we will leave Jerusalem, and I will take you to Roger Standish. We will leave at dawn so please ensure that all your belongings are packed. We must not delay."

Sadly I advised Ghada that I was leaving early in the morning. She nodded in a businesslike manner

" Your breakfast will be on the table early - eat everything. I do not want my guest to starve."

Her brave smile had a tinge of sadness. I, in turn, had a lump in my throat. I would miss Ghada very much.

Later that day Ibrahim visited his daughter's house, and advised me of his proposed business arrangements for me.

" Paul. Briefly this is your job if you are prepared to undertake the stress and risk. Roger Standish will advise you of your assignments, and you will be expected to prepare Reports on a regular and timely basis.

Your employment and your assignments are not known to anyone other than myself, Ahmad, and Roger Standish. Your life and our lives will be in jeopardy if your employment and assignments are made known.

Your work will demand ingenuity, sound decisions, prudence, and courage. This country is full of informers, spies, collaborators and the like, and you must remain aware of that danger at all times.

Your job will be to record events as they transpire throughout Palestine, and in particular acts of aggression by hostile thugs, the Irgun and Stern Gangs, and others, their methodology, their plans or probable plans. No doubt you will record wholesale destruction, perhaps death, and the expelling of innocent people. Only time will tell.

Remember that the Palestinian Arab is in general of a pacific nature and desires peace. Many

no doubt will arrange truces with these thugs, and no doubt many will regret those understandings. Their desire for peace is praiseworthy, but is no cure when organized armed thugs take over determined to destroy and kill."

Ibrahim smiled sadly, and placed his hands on my shoulder.

" I am so pleased that you are here. I have great confidence in you and of your undertaking - you will be our Palestinian Correspondent"

The Impending Storm

Excited I was awake well before dawn, washed and shaved, and quietly stepped downstairs with my baggage. To my surprise, Ghada and Ahmad were seated at the table. Clearly they had no intention of being the cause of any delay.

I greeted both, sat down, and had a fine breakfast. Ghada was solemn, and not very talkative. Soon it was time to leave. Conscious of Ghada's despondency, I gave her a brave smile.

" Ghada - you have been so very kind. I will miss you very much"

With eyes downcast, I gave her a little gift. It was very trivial, but I hoped she would appreciate the thought. I was disturbed to note her tears.

" Cheer up Ghada - I will see you soon"

It was one of many assurances that might prove incorrect.

Ahmad drove carefully down Via Dolorosa, passed the Church of the Holy Sepulchre, continued to the New Gate located in the northwest corner of the Christian Quarter, and immediately beyond the Old City wall, turned left and headed down the main street to the west and Jaffa.

I turned and addressed Ahmad.

" I have some knowledge of the Old City, but certainly know little of the New City and the suburbs adjoining it"

He accepted my declaration without comment, and seemed to have other matters on his mind. Eventually he responded flatly - his words depressing.

"I have no doubt you will eventually learn more than you might wish"

No more was said. We continued heading for the coast for about 20 miles. He then made a curious remark which in fact proved of considerable value.

"Remember Paul the location of the sun - it will advise you of the direction that you are traveling. You are a stranger, and will be visiting strange places. It can be important to understand which way you are facing. As you no doubt appreciate, when the sun is in your eyes in the afternoon, you are facing west."

His advise could be of value that truly applied to a city dweller. Rarely does one equate the location of the sun in London - that is if the sun can be seen. Now the early sun from the east illuminated buildings of the suburbs and villages on the hill slopes each side of the main highway.

Occasionally street signs indicated that we were approaching Tel Aviv and Jaffa. I asked the obvious question.

" Where are we going?"

Ahmad was not particularly communicative, and his answer rather tantalizing and obvious.

" We are going to Roger Standish"

No more was said.

We passed through crowded high districts of Tel Aviv, and then drove down hill to Jaffa. Tel Aviv was predominantly Jewish with commercial interests. Jaffa had a large Arab population, was an ancient port city, and was the supplier of Jaffa oranges so well favored in England.

Suddenly we were on the sea front - a curved coastline that faced the Mediterranean Sea. That early morning, the sea shore and the water was so inviting. And then we turned onto King Faisal Street. Everywhere the presence of British police and British troops with grim faces, suspicion, perhaps indifference, and possibly hostility. Few reminded me of the security and community concern of the English bobby.

Jaffa with a population of 100,000 was very much an Arab city. The streets filled with Arabs young and old. Many fine old established residences could be seen that displayed long time stability and pride. Architectural facades were varied as if there was no established design, and yet the scene was very much of a unique Muslim character. Commercial buildings stood firm separated by the occasional institutional structure and Mosques.

And there were the ever present cafes and coffee shops, small shops, vendors, and the usual groups of Arabs huddled in extreme discussion. One rapidly accepted the claim that Palestine was very much an Arab populated country.

Ahmad, for ever cautious, anxiously scanned his rear mirror a number of times, and seemed satisfied. Abruptly he turned off the main street, entered a narrow lane, and before I comprehended either location or direction, another quick turn, and we were parked within a quiet courtyard, and a solid gate closed behind us.

Ahmad quietly gave instructions to the Arab servant in the Courtyard. Rapidly he entered the building. And within moments Roger Standish walked out to greet us.

The last time I saw Roger was during the previous rugby season in London. About 5'8" in height, modest in build and fit, he was rather like myself. What always intrigued me about Roger, was his uncanny ability to understand my next move on the rugby field without any form of communication. Despite the choice of direction, the wide variation of speed, all determined by the action, the location, and the puzzlement of the opposing defense, I could always rely on Roger running at the correct place to receive that all important pass. If I was questioned my action in attack, and my methodology creating that unexpected opening for Roger, I would be unable to explain the movement and action that takes place in split seconds. And I suspect that Roger in turn would be lost for an explanation. Roger was certainly unique.

I had no doubt that Roger was quite intelligent. The immediate impression a man of reliability, loyalty, confidentiality, and common sense. Nine months later, here he was, very much tanned by the Mediterranean sun, but otherwise the same old Roger.

I clambered out of Ahmad's car, warm and dusty, and shook hands. Roger led me into a quiet cool room, and immediately asked to be excused - he needed to talk to Ahmad.

Outside, Ahmad expressionless, coolly eyed Roger who asked.

" Everything in order?"

" I think so - we were not followed . We need to take great care - he was seen by two men in the Jewish Quarter some time back - but I do not think there is any significant reason to be concerned. But I want to stress that we have to be very very careful. The forthcoming United Nation's Referendum and its recommended Partition will occur soon so rumors claim. As you may imagine, there will be ever increased hostility and aggression from our friends"

Standish nodded, tightened his mouth, and wondered if any news would ever be good news.

" Are you returning now?"

Ahmad nodded. He went to the trunk of the car, and took out my baggage.

With some concern Roger said.

" Take good care of yourself Ahmad, and thank you very much for your assistance. Hope to see you soon."

The two men shook hands, the courtyard street gate opened for a few moments, and the car departed.

Roger entered the building, and sat down by me, and grinned cheerfully.

"Paul - it is wonderful having you here. Welcome to Palestine. Now you know very little about

our company and our activities. Currently I do not wish to confuse you until you are better acquainted with this country and its inhabitants. Gradually I will introduce you to some of the country's current problems, and our desire to resolve them if that is possible."

Roger stretched himself, dwelt over his initial statement, and decided the importance of a warning.

" I had better be frank with you. Please understand that we are all living in very dangerous times. Our specialty is the accurate recording of current events. The population two thirds Arab has been subjected increasingly to hostile groups who wish to partition the country. They are merciless and extremely well organized and financed. Currently world thought and opinion is subject to propaganda, and there is little sympathy for the Arab people who are being subject to unprovoked aggression..

The purpose of our business is to record and provide the truth of current events, such information being forwarded to independent papers throughout the world. We are a small company, handicapped by few employees, lack financial resources, and subject to continuous observation, hostility, and worse. At all times, we must take great care, be prudent, and remain in the shadows."

I wondered if all this warning was really necessary. Really if I was not listening to Roger, I would imagine similar talk from some spy just arrived outside from the Cold! Yet already I had hints and warnings from Ibrahim, Ahmad, and Ghada. Caution was required.

" Well Roger. You certainly make my involvement sound both mysterious and dangerous. When do I start?"

Roger laughed mischievously, and thumped the table with approval.

" That is what I like to hear. You have already started. Now remember one very important matter. We are the hunters of information, but in turn we will be the hunted. Our friends are unscrupulous, possess no pity, and have the cunning of criminals. They may not be able to identify us, yet always they will suspect of our existence. And finally they are everywhere.!"

I was shown my bedroom which in fact was Roger's - we would be sharing. Later Roger addressed my immediate needs.

" First you will be paid adequate compensation to cover your work and expenses. All payments will be in cash - this will avoid any immediate connection with the company. You have your work permit - welcome aboard.

There is no medical insurance and no national health. If ill we will arrange for medical attention. Your mailing address is Iron Casting and Design, Box 1842 Jaffa. Any mail received will be collected and delivered to you. Laundry is undertaken in this building. You will be provided with all necessary transport. Currently I want you to accompany me as we travel around the country. You can assist me, and at the same time I can familiarise you with both the country and its people. I expect that within two to three months, you will be quite independent, and will not require my guidance"

To be independent within two to three months! I certainly would have my work cut out to achieve that status. Modestly I asked.

"You think so?"

Roger nodded.

" Have a good rest - see you at dinner this evening. I plan to start our travels tomorrow morning. Just bring along minimal needs - two spare shirts and underclothes. I will provide you with a file and draft paper for your records. I think the best move is for you to prepare your records similar to my record keeping. Every month we will need to summarise our records, and send them to Ibrahim."

For the next three months Roger Standish and I traveled from north to south, and from west to east. In general we visited the principal district towns and large villages with populations ranging from 5,000 to 50,000. There were sixteen districts, and in most districts the Palestinian Arab was in the majority - 85% to 100% of the population. A few such as Tiberias, Ramla, Baysan, and Jerusalem were 60%-80%, whilst the two port city districts of Haifa 55% and Jaffa 30%.

Initially it was difficult to identify significant features - every town seemed to have similar buildings and squares. But gradually, I became aware of unique features, and the memory of specific mosques, police stations, schools, and the occasional industrial development registered. And of course in every town I was introduced to strangers who were well acquainted with Roger Standish, and some were a great source of information. Any friend of their admired Roger was accordingly their friend, and their latest news would be made available whenever I might visit.

The months passed by - September, October, November. Was it my imagination that everyone was becoming graver with greater anxiety, due to the ever increasing hostility of the Jewish community. We were back in Jaffa when we learnt of United Nations Resolution 181 at end of November which proposed the Partition of Palestine into two States based on the recommendations of their special committee UNSCOP on Palestine. It was declared that the two proposed States would be bound together Federation like through economic unity. And the city of Jerusalem would be a separate entity administered by the United Nations.

It is remarkable that United Nations never took any consideration of the majority population of Palestinian Arabs who owned 95% of all land. How it expected such an inequitable decision be accepted is beyond comprehension. To imagine that the Jewish minority population that owned a mere 5% of the country's land should be given over half of Palestine, the best rural land, the two major ports, the main transportation rail and road systems! It was inconceivable.

Roger Standish held out a copy of the Resolution with a grim face.

" This is a terrible disaster. The Zionists have been given over half of Palestine. The basic rights of the Palestinian Arabs has been ignored. It will be utter hell because the British Mandate will end early 1948."

I stared at the documents and wondered.

" What did it all mean?" .

I was well aware that the Palestinian Arabs had few leaders - all had been expelled from the country by the British. My general impression was that the Arabs would tend to avoid trouble and hope to be left in peace in the rural areas. 60% - 70% lived in rural villages - perhaps 700 to 1000 villages with populations ranging from 250 to 5000. All these villages isolated, desiring to be left in peace, would be helpless attacked by aggressive forces and thugs.

" You know Roger - I suspect we will have plenty of news gathering. The British administration responsible for security law, and order, appears to be very loath to be involved, and probably will wash their hands of its obligations. And I cannot imagine the Arabs organizing any meaningful resistance."

Standish drummed his fingers on the wood table trying to envisage the implications of the U.N Resolution, and what would happen. He buried his face in his hands, elbows on the table, and tried to comprehend the future. Finally he looked up

" Paul. We have a lot of work facing us. We may be subject to considerable danger. Are you willing?"

I nodded little comprehending what I was facing. British education demands common decency, and playing to reasonable and civilized rules. I knew nothing of what I would have to contend with.

For the next few weeks we visited some of the small villages surrounding the Jaffa area. It was convenient being close to our home office if any disaster might happen. In general the villages had much in common. Dependant on agriculture, their living standards were reliant on everyone, young and old, to work every day of the year. Homes often so poor little better than hovels, with no electricity, power, and water. Wells and springs were major sources used by all. Roads unpaved little better than dirt tracks, with no street lighting. Larger villages possessed a mosque, school, possibly an administrative building and a police station.

Life in general was tied to the land, and wealth would include their donkeys, goats, sheep and other animals. Historically life had changed little. Their habitat existed as a record and in their minds. Village trees, orchards, and family pedigrees were remembered in tales and poems. I realized that one should take care in framing one's thinking on the basis of materialism that is purely a modern western concept that did not apply here. As the days passed by, we heard of more and more rumors of aggression, theft of property, and bodily injury. But at this time, we saw no evidence.

Whilst the implications of UN Resolution 181 unfolded, another disaster was taking place that was not common knowledge for some time. King Abdullah of Jordan had a secret understanding with the Zionists, and had agreed that his army would not interfere or support the Palestinian Arabs in return with the agreement that he would seize possession of the West Bank Thus any Palestinian expected support of this fellow Arab country with a well trained army had been neutralized through treachery and greed.

Roger received a telegram early December. Two defenseless villages had been attacked by the Haganah. Earlier we had received reports that the Haganah was engaged in systematic intimidation entering villages and claiming to be searching for *"Infiltrators"*, and warning the local people not to cooperate with the so called Arab Liberation Army. The Jewish troops often fired at random, and any resistance by villagers due to Haganah aggression were killed.

Now the villages of Dayr Ayyub in the Al-Rama district and Beit Affa in the Gaza ditrict had been attacked. Dayr Ayyub (population 500) mainly Muslim were celebrating the opening of their new school for their many local pupils. But all that changed late at night. Twenty Jewish troops entered the defenseless village, and fired randomly at many houses. Down south in the Gaza district, a similar attack took place in Bayt Affa, but in this instance the criminal invaders were repulsed.

We drove to Dayr Ayyub 20 miles south east of Jaffa. The village was in a complete shock. The damage caused by the random shooting was evident on many buildings. The villagers claimed that Hebrew voices and shouts were heard throughout that night - there was no mystery who was responsible for the attack.

The damage, fragmented holes in stone and mud walls, told little of the dreadful attack. It did not reflect the horror of being attacked at night, hearing hostile threatening voices, the crack of rifle fire, all part of that nightmare attack, always to be remembered.

We identified our presence, and noted small huddled groups of women weeping suffering from shock, children solemn with fear, and men both sullen and angry who all offered fragments of what they knew. Every one had retired to sleep, and were woken by hideous shouts, threats, and the firing of guns. Little else was known other than the conviction that the voices heard were Hebrew, and that the attackers arrived and departed by trucks.

There was little that we could do. Hopefully the British Army and Police would investigate, and catch the perpetuators. Roger decided that we would   drive to Bayt Affa. It would be a long day.

" Why do they think that the attackers were units of the Haganah?   It was dark, everyone was bewildered, and naturally shocked. But why the Haganah?"

Roger slowed down a little, and finally responded.

" Why the Haganah? I will tell you why. First remember that the Arab people have lived side by side with the Jews all their lives. If they say they heard Hebrew voices and shouts, you can be rest assured that is precisely what they heard.

Now this is confidential We have learnt that Ben Gurion with other Zionist leaders held a meeting at the Red House in Tel Aviv and resolved that the Partition of Palestine was not enough. They want the whole country, and they have decided to drive out all the Arabs.   These attacks are the beginning.

The Haganah was termed a Hebrew defense force when first established in 1920. Orde Wingate one of our British officers trained these men, and he demonstrated how populations can be expelled and moved through military action involving the total destruction of villages and infra structure, and general brutality. Wingate was of a religious family which says little of such people. One of his sergeants, demonstrating the bestial efficiency of killing with bayonets to Haganah recruits, is quoted to have sarcastically remarked " You men need to be educated"

I'm told that the Haganah has recruited large numbers of Jewish thugs from the recent immigrants from Germany, Romania, and Poland."

We eventually drove into the village of Bayt Affa located in the Gaza District. The population 750-800 again were mainly Muslim. Fortunately they had proved very much more aggressive in retaliation to the attackers whom they identified as Hebrew Zionists. Despite their success in fending off this unexpected and unprovoked attack, the clusters of people seen and interviewed were clearly frightened, upset, and very much concerned.

Late in the day, we returned to Jaffa. Roger made a significant observation

"Did you notice that in neither village did the British Authorities intervene."

" Well" I retorted.

"That is understandable. The attack was completely unexpected at night"

" That is very true but there was no evidence of the authorities and their presence today. I sincerely hope this lack of concern does not become a trend"

I also had that hope, but had my doubts.

Late in December I handed my report of events for the month of December. Roger examined my report and whistled.

" You know Paul. Without such a Report, one can be totally aware of the gravity of the situation"

He slowly went through the list of events.

" By Giminy - look at that. Sixteen villages attacked, and an attack on Haifa. About 100,000 people have been subjected to attacks, about 1500 expelled, and about 100 killed.

No one can claim that this kind of nonsense has not been planned. Districts all over Palestine have been involved. This is dreadful."

I returned to my desk, typed up the Report, and arranged for it to be sent to Ibrahim.

Report - December 1947

Accra District	- No Reports
Baysan District	- No Reports
Beersheba District	- Village attacked- (Number?) -Al-Imara
Gaza District	- No Reports

Haifa District
- Village attacked- (11,000) -Balad Al-Shaykh **(60)**, -Khubbyayza, -Al-Tira **(13)**, Wadi'Ara
- Town attacked - (60,000)
- Town suburb expelled -(Number?)- Wadi Rushmiyya

Hebron District — -No Reports

Jaffa District
- Village attacked- (13,700) Al'Abbasiyya **(14)**, Al-Khayriyya, -Salama, Yazur
- Village expelled -(1,350) -Al-Mas'udiyya, Al-Muwaylih

Jerusalem District	- No Reports
Jinin District	- No Reports
Nazareth District	- No Reports
Al-Ramla	- Village attacked- (1,400) Dayr Ayyub, Qazaza
Safad District	- Village attacked- (600) Al-Khisas **(12)**
Tiberias District	- No Reports

Tulkarm District
-Village attacked -(1,450) Wadi Al-Hawarith
- Village expelled- (Number?) -Tabsur

Villages attacked	16
Town attacked	1
Inhabitants attacked	96,000
Inhabitants expelled	7,000

Haifa's Destruction Begins

Immediately after the announcement of United Nations Resolution 181, the 75,000 Palestinian Arabs in Haifa were subjected to horrific attacks by the Irgun gang and the Haganah. From the heights inhabited by the Jewish community overlooking the city, shelling and sniping commenced.

The attacks intensified with troops rolling barrels of fuel and explosives down the slopes into the exposed defenseless neighborhoods. And with unbelievable barbarity, the troops ignited streets with oil and fuel, and when the terrified inhabitants ran into the streets, they were subjected to machine gun fire.

It is difficult to imagine the terrible nature of these attackers. Not only was their intention to kill and injure, it also was to seriously intimidate the Arab people. Imagine the frightening confusion. Attackers disguised themselves as Palestinians. Attackers would bring to Arab repair shops cars for repair, the cars booby trapped with high explosives.

Understandably such criminal provocation upset the relationship of Arab and Jewish workers within the city. Thus the Irgun, well known for there past record of throwing bombs at Arab crowds, threw a bomb into a large group of Palestinian Arabs outside the Iraqi Petroleum Company. This took place as the Irgun and the Haganah were participating in their terrorizing of the Arab people in Haifa. In this instance the Palestinian workers revolted and killed 39 Jewish workers.

But the unprovoked attacks did not apply merely to the city of Haifa. The villages of nearby Balad Al-Shaykh, Khubbayza, Al-Tira, and Wadi'ara were attacked - a total population of 11,000 - sixty Arabs were killed at Balad Al-Shaykh, and thirteen at Al-Tira. The attack of Balad Al-Shaykh was supervised by a local commander Haim Avinoam. Within three hours over sixty Palestinian Arabs were dead.

About the same time, the Haganah went into the Haifa city neighborhood of Wadi Rushmiyya, expelled all the inhabitants, and blew up their houses. It is significant that the British Authorities responsible for law and order were present and did nothing!

Roger and I decided to visit Haifa early January 1948. We found the local Arab population in shock, bewildered, and leaderless. Possibly 15,000 to 20,000 of the Arab elite had departed with the intention of returning when conditions had improved. These individuals, who moved to their properties in neighboring countries of Lebanon, Egypt, and the like, never returned. 55,000 to 60,000 Arabs were left to defend themselves without any form of leadership.

We interviewed a property owner who had witnessed the terrible attacks within Haifa. The poor man *Abd Al-Kaladi* terrified, haggard, unshaven grey, with sunken eyes that had witnessed inconceivable horror, spoke with tears of his experience a few days earlier late December.

" I woke up - there was rifle fire, and a loud speaker was cursing us, and telling us Arab scum to get out of the country. From the window, I saw a heavy truck slowly moving down the road, with men on the back firing indiscriminately.

I immediately instructed my wife to keep the doors closed, hide under the bed. And I told her I would check the safety of my parents down the street, and would soon be back.

I ran to the back door, rushed to my parent' s house about ten buildings distant, hammered at the door, and eventually it was opened. My parents were safe. I told them to hide under their bed, and keep the front and back doors locked. I did not have time to explain, and assured them I would be back soon.

The truck in the street continued down the road, and halted outside a residence. Men shouted, pointed, and three men got off. Two with heavy boots kicked down the small entrance door, and sprayed the inside with bullets. Then another man threw in a bomb.

As I left my parents house, I heard a terrific explosion. There was a great deal of dust, smoke, and the smell of explosives. I rushed back to my home, and discovered that it was no longer standing. My wife and three children lay buried under piles of rubble. My neighbors tried to assist me but the weight of the stone and rubble was too great.

More explosions and firing of guns occurred further down the street. Later I returned to my parent's house to use their phone for help. It also had been destroyed and my parents no more."

The distraught man cried and demanded

" Why me - what have I done to suffer this absolute hell?"

Many others had similar tales to relate - all heart broken cried

" Why us. Why us?"

Walking around the attacked neighborhoods was a very depressing experience. One did not require a vivid imagination to identify the horror of being woken in the pitch dark late at night to eventually realise that monstrous criminals were creating rivers of fire in the streets, rolling explosive drums of oil and fuel down from the hills, spraying houses with machine gun fire, attacking individual houses with bombs, and all the time screaming obscenities over some unearthly loudspeaker.

Roger and I stared at each other. Roger shook his head wearily

" I just cannot believe anyone would commit such cruel and inhuman acts."

I was bluntly *"pissed off"* The crimes committed unbelievable. What was beyond my comprehension was that the British Authorities had done nothing to stop these crimes.

" You know Roger. Everyone in this city must have been aware of these events. One cannot claim ignorance, and stress that they were unaware of these happenings."

Standish agreed. One wondered what was worse. Those committing the heinous crimes, their fellow people watching, or those responsible for law and order who knowingly permitted the crimes to occur without making any effort to stop them.

We departed from Haifa depressed and disheartened. The city's future appeared bleak with further attacks impending.

A couple of weeks later, the Palmach attacked the isolated neighborhood of Hawassa to the east of Haifa. It was the home of the poorest Arabs. Homes were blown up including a school, and 5000 expelled. And so unfortunate Haifa and its Arab inhabitants was gradually destroyed.

And during the month of January, the Haifa district villages of Khubbayza, Al-Tira, Umm Al-Zinat were attacked.

Looters and   Demolition Squads

I had just completed my Report for January. Reviewing the reported events, it was evident that acts of aggression had increased enormously throughout Palestine. 34 Villages had been attacked, the towns of Haifa and Safad attacked, and a total population of 133,000 had been subject to aggression.

Over 8,000 had been expelled from their villages, and at least 65 killed. Within one month the level of aggression had doubled! But did that tell the whole story? What was the cause of this aggression, looting, and destruction? Who was involved? Was it spontaneous or planned? And if planned, did this planning commence way back in time?

The nature and cause of the aggression very much differed according to David Ben Gurion! I was hearing that Ben Gurion and senior Zionist leaders were claiming that their people were facing a Second Holocaust!. And presumably the Palestinian Arab population and the neighboring Arab countries were considered the assailants. But where was the evidence?

I scratched my head. There had been a few Arab attacks of Jewish convoys on some highways, but those attacks appeared to be retaliation to unprovoked Jewish aggressive attacks on villages. When one examined the record, the appalling massacres, the diabolical raids, the demolition of complete villages, one can understand that Arabs would be upset. In fact what was amazing was how pacified the Arab population had been to date. One certainly could not identify the possibility of a Holocaust on the basis of a few minor   attacks in retaliation to Zionist aggression.

Then there was the constant claim of hostile threatening forces of neighboring Arab countries entering Palestine on behalf of their Palestinian cousins. But where were they? Certainly immediately after the United Nation Referendum 181 announcing the inequitable Partition there was a lot of shouting and threats. But it all appeared to be typical *Hot Air*. Where were these forces? There was no evidence of forces entering Palestine. And certainly no evidence to support a claim of a Second Holocaust.

And yet one would imagine that there had to be some truth in Ben Gurion's claims which were broadcast throughout the Zionist world. World authorities appeared to be willing to believe these claims, and to sympathise with the Jewish people who had suffered so terribly in Europe a few years earlier. He certainly had plenty of support abroad.

What troubled me was that what had taken place over the past three months required an enormous amount of planning for its implementation. One cannot simply decide at a toss of the coin to have a highly organized military institution, with the necessary equipment, arms and training to attack a complete country. Already there was evidence of considerable numbers of troops, equipment, and arms. Over one hundred and thirty thousand Palestinian Arabs and the thirty four villages had been subjected to aggression in January. I felt fairly certain that this   provocation was the product of planning and organization which had commenced many years past.

I voiced my puzzlement and concerns to Roger Standish, hoping to get a brief explanation. I imagine I irritated Roger, because he responded with some anger and exasperation.

" Look Paul. Start thinking, and start some serious investigating. Get with it chum?"

He was despondent, and no doubt the deteriorating situation throughout Palestine was upsetting.

" Look Paul. Call on As'Ad Kamal. Here is his address. He will appraise you of what has been going on behind the scenes"

He busily scribbled name and address, wrote a short letter of introduction to As'Ad and handed the note and letter to me.

"Visit him this evening after dusk. Make sure you are not seen by anyone"

Whilst I examined the name and address, he stressed again.

" Be very careful - get caught, and As'Ad and all of us will be in deep trouble"

Jaffa was one of the Palantines, prosperous, and possessed a large population of over 100,000. Jaffa District was the only district in which the Jewish population well exceeded the Arab. The population of the district was about 70% Jewish and 30% Arab. Tel Aviv, adjoining Jaffa, and the northern communities were predominantly Jewish, and their materialistic commercial interests differed very much from the Arab quarter.

Regardless the United Nation Partition Plan had designated the city of Jaffa to be Palestinian Arab controlled although it lay within the proposed Jewish State.

The city of Jaffa was essentially Arab in character, planned, designed, and created by Arabs, Ottomans, and complemented by British institutional buildings during the Mandate that commenced in 1919, and rumored to end in 1948. Although the British Administration seemed severe and perhaps hostile, education was encouraged. Commercially Jaffa was a success - Jaffa oranges were commonly seen on European tables.

As'Ad Kamal carefully read Roger's note, and graciously welcomed me within his apartment llocated close to Tel-Aviv. Seated at an armchair, he gazed at me with care.

" *So you are a friend of Roger Standish?* "

I nodded, and explained my relationship in England.

" *Yes. Mr Standish is a good friend, and is well respected. Currently my country has troubles, and Mr Standish's concern is of considerable value. And I understand that you are undertaking similar work?* "

He looked at me curiously. The man was no fool, and no doubt suspected that I had limited experience. Was I to be trusted he probably wondered, but such thought would have been countered by Roger's introduction.

"*Well. Well. Now Mr Blackberry. How can I assist you?* "

I explained my lack of knowledge regarding the cause of the unhappy aggression taking place. I wondered if As'Ad could briefly explain the strange claims, so they appeared, of Ben Gurion and his Zionist leaders, and the obvious hostility of his supporters.

As'Ad stared at me thoughtfully, and then asked what I thought was a strange question.

" *What aggression Mr Blackberry? Rumors . Just rumors. Perhaps you should wonder who is the cause of those rumors* "

There was a touch of sarcasm in his voice which irritated me. What was his objective in that question. I immediately responded strongly , no longer relaxed. What the heck was his purpose.

" *Mr Kamal. Your question makes no sense. I have already witnessed some terrible crimes against innocent defenseless people. This is not the time to play with words. Come with me and see the atrocities of Haifa and Balad Al-Sheykh, and many other unhappy places. Are you telling me that these unfortunate people are spreading dishonest rumors?* "

I imagined my eyes hardened, and I stared firmly at As'Ad. My response clearly satisfied my host, and he sighed.

" *You have some questions Mr Blackberry?* "

" *Your explanation may satisfy or modify my suspicions and conclusions.* "

" *What are your suspicions and conclusions?* "

"A Conspiracy that probably commenced many years ago"

As'Ad scratched his forehead, and decided to get to the root of my concern.

" Yes. You are correct. A terrible conspiracy that started many years ago. Cross over from here to Tel Aviv, and you will see a building located in Yarkon Street close to the Mediterranean known as the "Red House" Last year that building became the headquarters of the Haganah which is the Zionist underground military.

It is Ben Gurion's office where he has planned the political future of the Zionist party with other Zionist leaders, and planned and arranged a military machine whereby such political plans could be achieved irregardless of equity and public opinion.

His political plans were particular ambitious, and he was fortunate to have the support of extreme Zionist organizations in America and Britain. The Zionists objective was an independent Jewish State within the borders of present day Palestine. How it would be achieved would be political with the aid of the British, and at the expense of the Palestinian Arabs who owned 95% of Palestine. This objective commenced seriously in 1917 when British Foreign Secretary Balfour gave the Zionists his promise to establish a national home for the Jews in Palestine without any consideration of the inequity of the proposal.

Another serious matter was the desire of the Zionists to have an exclusive Jewish State that meant the expulsion of the Arab population. This desire has existed in theory for fifty years, but has become increasingly a reality.

Before the possibility of Partition occurred, there was considerable planning. For example during the past 15 years Jews have made careful surveys of every village and town, and possess information invaluable for the elimination of Arab leaders, the seizure of real estate and personal property, the location of all water sources, minerals, agriculture, and aerial surveys that provided the vulnerability of such places when attacked by hostile forces. It is my understanding that these surveys now include the names of "wanted" persons in each village.

Whilst these detailed surveys were undertaken, Ben Gurion was building up an efficient military. The British officer Orde Charles Wingate gave the Zionist leaders the idea that to become a State would depend on possessing power whereby their numerous settlements could be protected, and Arab populations relocated. In 1936 he actively encouraged the Jewish settlers, and trained them as troops to be more effective in attack and retaliation. The Jewish settlers proved good students. In 1941 the Zionist's military might was improved through the training of special commando units, the Palmach, who initially directed their efforts against the Germans. Then in 1944, their efforts were redirected to Palestine assisting in the formation of Jewish settlements.

Then one must remember two other extreme groups - the Irgun gang who parted from the Haganah in 1931, and in 1940 was led by Menachem Begin; and the Stern gang which split from the Irgun in 1940. And finally we must not forget that the Haganah had an intelligence unit founded in 1933 which was responsible for the collection of information, and set up the evil network of spies, informers, and collaborators that exist everywhere in Palestine.

Now we need to consider the creation of Zionist policy. Even in the 1930s Ben Gurion realized that the success of the Jewish State would be subject to the population within the State being preferably 100% Jews. The question gradually became critical - the need to expel the Arab population. For the past year many of the following individuals met with Ben Gurion at the Red House with the purpose of determining the Zionist future policy.

Yigal Allon	*Head of Palmach commanded forces East and South*
Zvl Ayalon	*Deputy to Galili - commanded forces Central Front*
Shimon Avidan	*Led forces South*
Menachem Begin	*Leader of Irgun/Stern/Haganah, created laws for control Arabs*
Yitzhak Ben-Zvi	*Zionist leader and political historian.*
Moshe Carmel	*Commander Northern Front. Responsible in Galilee.*
Moshe Dayan	*Military Commander*
Ezra Danin	*Syrian Jew - Senior Intelligence*
Dan Even	*Commander forces coastal plain*
Abba Eban	*Ambassador at United Nations. "disclaimed any responsibility."*
Yehoshua Globerman	*Commander Haganah (assassinated 1947)*
Israel Galili	*Head of high Command*
David Ben-Gurion	*Zionist leader and master planner of Plan Dalat*
Isar Harel	*Head Intelligence Mossad and Shabak*
David Horovitz	*Committee for Arab Affairs.*
Moshe Kalman	*Deputy Commander of the Palmach - operations in North*
Sasha Goldberg	*Purchased and Manufactured Flame Throwers*
Ephraim Katzir	*Headed biological warfare - gasses caused blindness*
Tuvia Lishanski	*Information collector Arab villages.*
Gad Machnes	*Orientalist-DirectorGeneral Israel Ministry for Minorities.*
Golda Meir	*Senior Zionist Leader.*
Yossefi Nachmani	*Close aid to Yossef Weitz.*
Yehoshua Palmon	*Second to Danin - trained with British Commando.*
Yitzhak Pundak	*Assisted Shimon Avidan - forces in the South.*

Yohanan Ratner	*Strategic adviser to Ben-Gurion.*
Yitzhak Rabin	*Head of Harel Brigade. Second in command to Yigal Allon*
Eliyahu Sasson	*Syrian Jew - consultant adviser*
Reuven Shiloah	*Aid to Sasson - Orientalist*
Moshe Sharett	*ForeignMinister,head political department Jewish Agency*
Pacti Sela	*Intelligence*
Ariel Sharon	*Commando officer - Bersheba district*
Yaacov Shimoni	*German Jew Orientalist - Information gatherer*
Bechor Shitrit	*Minister of Minorities*
Yitzhak Sadeh	*Head of Armoured Units.*
Shlomo Shamir	*Senior Officer representing Ben-Gurion.*
Dr Yaacov Tahon	*German Jew who planned Jewish Colonization*
Yossef Weitz	*Head Settlement Department Jewish National Fund*
Yigael Yadin	*Head operations, acting chief Haganah and Israel Army*
Tuvia Zishanski	*Information gatherer - planned Arab evictions*

One has to give them credit if the word credit applies to their horrendous deeds. Already the Zionists have received large stocks of arms, guns, mortars, and equipment from abroad, and their military structure, so I understand, is about 50,000 troops ready for action. There is talk of an aerial squadron of fighters and naval ships.

And finally Ben Gurion has intimated that not only is he prepared to agree to any form of Partition with the United Nations, he has no intention to be held to such an agreement, and the Zionists will act aggressively against the Arab people."

As'Ad paused.

Sunk in thought, I chewed my pencil.

" What you say is incredible Mr Kamal. Where and how have you managed to get this information?"

As'Ad gazed at me, no doubt incredulous of my naïve question.

" Mr Blackberry. According to friend Roger Standish you are quite an astute individual although I realise that you are not well versed with my country. Now tell me. What advantage is there for you to understand how I collect my information? Why should I risk my neck advising you of my secrets. It is better that you do not know for my sake.

What I suggest is that you equate the information that I have given with your knowledge to date of all the terrible happenings that have occurred. Also use logic - the Zionists have devoted years of planning for what is developing this very moment. No organization could successfully plan and develop their current strategy without many years of planning, obtaining the needed financing, and implementing their policy."

Of course As'Ad Kamal was correct and wise - it was not in his interest to reveal how he obtained his information. I thanked him for his advise, apologised for my thoughtless question, hoped that I would make his acquaintance again, and departed.

I walked back - was it my imagination. There seemed to be many ominous shadows and alarming sounds all around me. Furtive movements seemed to take place around street lights that only suggested hidden danger and more danger.

Back in the security of Roger Standish's apartment, I shook my head with disbelief. That Mr Kamal had an axe to grind. It made so little sense that the Jewish people, survivors of the Holocaust a mere three to four years past, would even contemplate the ruthless expulsion of an entire defenseless Arab population, and the theft of all their real and personal property.

But what other explanation could explain the many many aggressive attacks, massacres, and expulsions. The following morning still depressed, I looked around Roger;'s room. Already I felt attached to the city and its Arab people - a city and a people that might change radically if As'Ad Kamal's advise and forecast was correct.

Report - January1948

Accra District

- *Village attacked- (1,100)Kuwaykat*

Baysan District

- *No Reports*

Beersheba District

- *No Reports*

Gaza District

- *Village attacked- (13,500) Arab Suqrir **(8),** Barbara, Al-Majd*
- *Bayt 'Affa, Burayr, Hamama, - Kawkaba, Yibna,*

Haifa District

- *Village attacked- (7,700) -Khubbayza, Al-Tira, Umm Al-Zinat*
- *Town attacked - (60,000)- Haifa*
- *Suburb expelled- (5,000) Hawassa*

Hebron District

- *Village attacked- (4,000) Bayt Nattif, Zakariyya, Dayr Aban*

Jaffa District

- *Village attacked- (16,000)Bayt Dajan, Salama **(10),** Yazur **(9)***

Jerusalem District

- *Village attacked-(3,100) Al-Burayjr, Dayr Aban*
- *Village expelled-(2,800)   Lifta **(7),** Romena, Shakkh Badr*

Jinin District

- *No Reports*

Nazareth District

- *No Reports*

Al-Ramla District

- *Village attacked- (2,150) Sarafand, Al-Vamar, Al-Kubra*

Safad District

- *Village attacked- (1,150)Ayn Al-Zayjun **(1),** Mansurat Al-Khayt*
- *Town attacked -(12,000)   Safad*
- *Village expelled-(300) - Al-Ulmaniyya*

Tiberias District

- *Village attacked-(4,300)-Ghunayr, AbuShusha**(2),** Lubya**(1)***

Tulkarm District

- *No Reports*

Villages attacked	*33*
Towns attacked	*2*
Inhabitants attacked	*133,000*
Inhabitants expelled	*8,100*

The Storm Breaks

Roger stared at the summarised Report for the month of January.

" Bloody Hell. Villages are being attacked all over. I am willing to bet the number killed is closer to double that reported. There are mortar and bomb attacks on land, sea, and the air."

Seated at my desk, he examined the large pile of serious reports that had been received.. Shaking his head with concern, he made a decision.

" We will have to get on the road immediately, verify the reports, and make our own records. I suggest that we visit the districts of Haifa, Accra, Safad, and Tiberias. We will return back here and complete our findings. Then we will visit the districts of Hebron and Gaza."

We left early - the sun barely risen - and drove through Tel Aviv and its immediate neighborhoods along the coast, and entered the district of Tulkarm. Here both the villages of Tabsur on the southern border and Wadi Al-Hawarith on the northern border had been attacked by Jewish forces last December. Both places were ominously quiet. Both villages had Jewish settlements close by.

A most alarming and disheartening feature on the roads were the thousands of refugees expelled and fleeing from attacks presumably in the north. Some were in a desperate condition lacking possessions, food, and transport. There was a sense of panic and extreme fear, and talk of bombing, the desolation of their villages, and the murder of village men.

As we progressed northwards, the roads became increasingly clogged with refugees. In the district of Haifa , we drove along the coastal road, and passed by the villages of Khirbat Al-Burj and Qisarya already occupied by Jewish forces. Also the villages of Jaba, Al-Tira, and Khubbaysa that had been subjected to attacks.

But it was not only the coastal areas that had suffered aggression. Inland the villages of Al-Butaymat, Daliyat Al-Ranha had been occupied, and Lid Khirbat, Ha'Arat Al-Sarris, and Wadi'Ara had been subjected to serious attacks.

We were now passing village after village that had been bombed and demolished, and the inhabitants driven out and trudging the dusty district roads to unknown destinations. Smoke rose from structures purposely set on fire.

Roger groaned.

"This is far worse than anything I imagined. They are attacking the whole nation of Palestinian Arabs. And it would seem that the British troops are doing absolutely nothing to prevent these attacks."

We stopped and spoke to a few refugees. All had similar experiences - gangs of Jews machine gunning, mortar bombing, looting, blowing up buildings, and forcing the villagers out of their houses. They claimed that many individuals were blown up within their own homes.

And often it was claimed that the people responsible for the attacks were often assisted by local kibbutz settlers who took advantage of these attacks to seize real and personal property irregardless of the law.

The population in the Haifa district was approximately equal Arab and Jew. Already massacres had taken place, and the fear of further massacres was apparent. Over 60 were killed by a local Jewish force at Balad Al-Shaykh, and 13 at Al-Tira. The Haifa neighborhoods of Hawassa (5000) and Wadi Rushmiyya had been cleared, the houses blown up, and the people expelled. The British simply watched.

Now every Arab was distraught with fear very much aware of the terrible atrocities and the heartless diabolical cruelty of the Jewish attacks. There was no Arab leadership. There was no British intervention. The Arab people simply waited for their fate. The ethnic cleansing of Palestine had commenced. Jews were observed walking insolently the streets - it was not difficult to guess their evil thoughts.

In Haifa the attacks continued. We viewed evidence of the terrible damage caused by drums of fuel and explosives rolled down from the adjoining heights. And we listened to so many who had suffered the horror of night time attacks and the frightening loud speaker demands. And perhaps more frightening, there was an awareness that the attacks were intensifying, and a feeling of helplessness.

The following morning we departed for the district of Accra. The ancient city of Acre, the principal town, is located on the coast, and was first recorded at the time of the Crusaders. What a great tourist center it could be free of hatred. The ancient stone walls abutting the Mediterranean, the curved swept shores to the south, and the fascinating variety of historical buildings and mosques.

Alas, the year was 1948, and the British clearly indicated their disinterest in the responsibility of ensuring safety and security for the indigenous Arab population. Actually these people in the district of Accra demonstrated some spirit, and the villages of Al-Kabri, Kuwaykat, and Al-Manshiyya resisted attacks from Zionist groups who used bombs and machine guns.

I remarked, probably for the umpteenth time, as we drove by

" This has all been planned. These attacks are taking place all over the country. It is not just the Haganah, the Stern gang, the Irgun gang, the Palmach - there is evidence that the local

settlers are involved"

" I'm afraid you are right. Somehow they know the British will do nothing to stop their attacks and killings. "

It was typical winter weather, the car heater operating, and the occupants deep in thought. Roger revealed his concerns.

" These thousands of refugees - do they even know where they are going? Many have absolutely nothing. Their destination and haven perhaps 100 to 200 miles. Who will provide habitation , warmth, and food there and on the way? Already the Jews are claiming that these hundreds of thousands are departing through their own free will.. No doubt that lie will persist for many years if these people are not permitted to return. "

I did not respond - my thoughts were far too depressing.

Roger directed the car from Acre to Safad, and eventually branched off for the village of Kuwaykat. It had a population of about 1,100, and had been attacked in January. It was a charming attractive rural village that depended on agriculture, and it was difficult to imagine that it had been subjected to destruction and murder. A village built of stone, it was set at the edge of the hills, and comprised of dwellings, a school built by the Ottomans, a mosque, all connected with narrow twisting alleys. Water was plentiful in wells, and the very fertile district provided fine olive orchards, water melon crops, livestock breeding, and mill products. Later this year it would no longer exist.

We continued on eastwards making our way along the main valley between Acra and Safad with high hills 1000 to 2000 feet on both sides.

Safad with a population of about 12,000 (9,500 Arabs and 2,400 Jews) was a town of modest buildings, white in appearance, built of stone located on a treed slope dominated over by mosques and institutional buildings. We   obtained accommodation, and remained in Safad for five days.

The district of Safad had already suffered hostilities commencing in December 1947 with an attack against the village of Al-Khisas (1450) in which 12 were killed. In January four villages had been attacked, the town of Safad attacked, and the people of Al-Ulmaniyya expelled.. Now in February seven villages had been attacked, and about 20 killed at Harrawi and Sa'Sa.

Everyone was very much concerned about the attacks, and there was hope that the Arab League members of Syria or Lebanon would intervene, and provide security. However that hope appeared of no value. The Arab League truly were screaming *"Blue Murder"* but unfortunately   provided little evidence of support. All the shouting was just   *"Shouting"*

The attack on Sa'Sa, a village of about 1,100, and the massacre of 10 to 20 individuals in February truly frightened the population. The Palmach, a special Jewish commando unit founded in 1941 raided the village. The attack took place at night, and at least ten houses were blown up with their owners inside.. Widespread fear and panic was caused throughout the district.

We visited the village, walked around noting the damage, and were depressed at the sight. Such a tragedy - a tranquil rural valley growing olives, figs, fruits, barley, wheat, and accompanied with vineyards, bee hives, goats, and sheep - now a place of horror.

Then we visited the village of Taytaba located close by which also suffered attacks possibly by the same group of attackers that attacked Sa'Sa.

Also we learnt of an Arab bus en route from Al-Huga to Safad ambushed at Harrawi by a Zionist military unit. A mine was exploded under the bus, and the passengers subjected to firing and fire bombing.. Four passengers were killed.

Harrari was located fairly close to Safad set on a peak. The people of this village were descendents of the Bedouin tribe of *" Arab Al-Hamdim"* Some pursued animal stock and grazing, whilst others grew cereals. A typical rural village.

We drove across, and viewed the shattered burnt out hulk of the bus. A witness described the horror of viewing attackers who thoroughly enjoyed the spectacle of attacking the defenseless passengers.

I had enough. I told John I could not stomach any more of this bestial cruelty, and requested that we return to Jaffa.

" Sorry Paul. It is dreadful. I know its dreadful. But we have to witness what is happening, Otherwise our work is meaningless. We will now return to Jaffa after visiting the districts of Tiberias, and then hopefully Hebron and Gaza"

Tiberias with a population of about 5,000 to 6,000,located   about 15 miles south of Safad, is set on the edge of Lake Tiberias. The district, according to the United Nation Partition Resolution 181, was part of the proposed Jewish State.

On our arrival, we learnt that two Arab taxi drivers had been murdered by Irgun troops. The local Arab population was nervous and apprehensive, and had no faith in the British providing protection, law, and order, and no confidence in the assurance of U.N. Resolution 181 of their welfare.

The attack of the Jewish military against the village of Ghawayr Abu Shusha (1500) early January resulting in the death of two including the son of the village *Mukhtar*. It was very disturbing. And attacks in February against village Lubya (2500), the death of a villager, Al-Shajara, and also the town of Tiberias created further fear. Viewing all these destroyed villages which until recent were vibrant habitations continued to upset me.

" Let's go Roger. I cannot take any more"

Roger Standish was not oblivious to the horrors, and agreed that it was time to move on. As we headed south to Jerusalem, I demanded with some despair.

"When will it all end Roger?"

Standish shook his head glumly - he had no answer to these terrible crimes. The distance Tiberias to Jerusalem was about 90 miles following the road adjoining River Jordan. In the district of Baysan, we passed by the villages of Farwana, Al-Fatur, and Al-Zarra with small populations 500 to 1000 which had been subjected to attacks by Zionist forces. The more we saw, the more depressing it became. It was so upsetting noting peaceful rural settings with plentiful water and orchards that were being destroyed by criminals.

We had just arrived at the border of the districts of Baysan and Nablus. What made me aware of the car behind us I cannot explain. Perhaps my experience with Ahmad being tailed from the Lebanon border had made me apprehensive. Anyhow initially I noted that the car was a Mercedes - a fine vehicle that any driver would love to possess. The color silver grey.

I gave the car no further thought, and examined the Nablus district countryside. We must have traveled another 15-20 miles, when I became aware again of the Mercedes still behind us with two men in front. I did not wish to sound like a nervous old woman but there was no option
Quietly I murmured to Roger.

" I think we are being followed - the Mercedes behind us has been there for the past 30 miles."

Roger continued to look straight ahead, and tensely responded.

" Correction Paul - the last 50 miles. That car turned up immediately we left Tiberias. Now don't look back and relax. We will rid ourselves of our friends in Jerusalem"

Roger slowed down as we approached the outer north city walls of the Old City. We drove past Herod's Gate, Damascus Gate, and then New Gate, and continued on slowed by a street. packed with vehicles. In the corner of my eye, I noted that we were definitely being followed.

We approached an intersection controlled by a British policeman who signaled us to stop for cross traffic. Roger dutifully slowed down, then suddenly gunned the engine, turned right and raced away down the intersecting street. The startled policeman, very much aware of a serious traffic infraction, waved his arms in futility at our car. However there was no question that any other vehicle would be permitted to repeat that illegal turn. The Mercedes with two thugs swearing and cursing remained halted at that intersection. Our tail was lost.

Rapidly Roger, very anxious, drove through the close neighborhoods of Jerusalem, and eventually entered a courtyard in a quiet alley in Suba. The courtyard's gate was immediately closed. Roger entered the house, and spoke urgently to the house owner. The situation   clearly understood, Roger waved me across, and introduced me to Hikmaj Abd Al-Hadi.

Hikmaj, a solid muscular man difficult to upset, gave me a warm smile.

" Welcome Mr Blackberry to my house. You are a very welcome guest. You will be shown your room - later we will have a meal, and discuss current events."

I collapsed on my bed, and within moments was fast asleep The strain viewing the terrible sights of demolished villages, fleeing refugees, the dreadful tales of killing, torture, massacres, the bestial hostility of the attackers, and finally being tailed for the second time. I sensed I no longer had control of my life. My dreams reflected a very concerned Correspondent.

I woke early evening. Roger Standish was seated at a desk busy writing, and turned now aware that I was again with the living.

" Dinner in half an hour Paul. Now some important matters to remember. Hikmaj is an associate of Ahmad. Their activities involve enormous risks to themselves and everyone connected to them in any form or fashion. This is a "SAFE" House. We will remain here low for a few days. Hopefully our trackers will lose interest. However knowing the nature of the Mossad, it is very doubtful.

Now while we are here. I propose you complete your February summarised Report. Ibrahim is anxious to receive your latest information."

Roger returned to his writing, and then decided he should explain our next movement.

" By the way when we leave for Hebron and Gaza, we will travel in a different car. I propose that we wear Arab clothing. British dressed in conventional English clothing tend to stand out like a sore thumb. We need to travel without attracting attention. Life is becoming rather difficult."

Report - February1948

Accra District	*- Village attacked-(3,600) ,Kuwaykat, Al-Manshiyya*
Baysan District	*- Village attacked(500) a, Al-Fajur, Al-Zarra*
Beersheba District	*- No Reports*
Gaza District	*- Village attacked- (6,100) Bayt Jima, Burayr, Dimra* *- Al-Faluja ,Hamama, Ibdis*
Haifa District	*- Village attacked- (9,500) -Jaba, Lid Khirbet, Al-Tira, Hai'Ara* *-Wa'Arat Al-Sarris* *- Village expelled- (2,500) -Al-Burj Khirbat, A;-Butaymat* *- Qisarya,Daliyat Al-Rawra* *- Town attacked - Haifa (60,000)*
Hebron District	*- No Reports*
Jaffa District	*- Village attacked- (31,000) -Al'Abbasiyya **(2)**, Bayt Dajan **(3)*** *- Biyar'Adas, Migdal, Fajja, Salama,* *- Al-Khayriyya, Yazuk **(2)**, Abu Kabir* *- Village expelled- **(200)** - Al-Mirr*
Jerusalem District	*- No Reports*
Jinin District	*- No Reports*
Nazareth District	*- No Reports*
Al-Ramla District	*- Village attacked- (2,200) - Dayr Ayyub, Al-Maghar*
Safad District	*- Village attacked- (2,850) - Harrawi **(4)**, Jubb Yusuf,* *- Mansurat Al-Khayt, Sa'Sa **(20)**, Taytaba,Al-Mansura*
Tiberias District	*- Village attacked- (3,450) Lubya, Al-Shajara* *- Town attacked - Tiberius (12,000)*
Tulkarm District	*- Village attacked- (2,000) - Bayt-Lid Khirbat, Bayyaray Hannun* *- Umm Khalid*

Report - February 1948

Villages attacked	*44*
Towns attacked	*2*
Inhabitants attacked	*133,200*
Inhabitants expelled	*2,700*

Two Arabs Survey the South

By the week end I had completed my reports, and summarized events in Palestine for the month of February. No doubt it was deficient of many events, but was more than adequate to indicate a grave tragic trend.

Ibrahim visited our Safe House Sunday morning. He appeared worn and tired, yet regardless he demonstrated delight in seeing his young correspondents, and expressed approval of our work.

" I wish to tell you Paul that your January Reports, and your summarized Report for the month were extremely good. I am very proud of your accomplishments - your work could not be better. Now you tell me that you have completed your reports for the month of February "

He nodded with concern pinching his chin as he read the reports. He sighed.

" Terrible - Terrible. Everywhere terrorist attacks by the Palmach, Irgun, Stern, Haganah, and clearly by members of the kibbutz settlements. This is no isolated happening. This is the result of many years of diabolical planning by the Zionists. There is no way these frightful people could have accumulated the weapons, bombs, mortars, armored cars, tanks, guns, without long term planning and financing of the Zionists in America and Britain."

The elderly man squeezed his eyes in thought. What could be done to resolve this terrible tragedy. There was so little leadership and co ordination between the Arab Palestinians. The British obviously had sided with the Zionists, and the only Arab country Jordan with an efficient military force trained by the British had been muted by a treacherous agreement between the Zionists and the Hashemite King Abdullah of Jordan whereby he would have the West Bank in exchange for not confronting the Zionist troops throughout Palestine, and not supporting any Arab League forces that might become involved in the Zionist conflict.

" My poor poor people. There only fault an unwillingness to be aggressive and to work together to fight off the Zionists. Now they are suffering the ultimate penalty - expulsion and death."

He sat motionless for what seemed hours - perhaps communing with unknown others - perhaps resolving the impossible in his mind - a crisis beyond his imagination. Finally he rose, tired but resolved.

" Roger, Paul. We have a mission. The Truth must be recorded, and the Truth must be made known to the rest of the world. That is our mission. These diabolical thugs and their crazy religious beliefs must be defeated otherwise they will eventually destroy the world. What they cannot destroy is the Truth and our records of the present and past. When the world has the sense to rid itself once and

for all this dreadful scourge, my people will return again in peace with their past and memories. "

Ibrahim turned to Roger.

" Roger. You have accomplished wonders. Paul's work is excellent. I am very proud of you two. We will have a meeting tomorrow morning. There is much to be discussed of extreme importance. "

After an early breakfast, we sat at the table, and listened to Ibrahim. He explained that the acceleration of frightful   events, the aggressive attacks and expulsions, necessitated some important changes.

" You have to understand Roger and Paul, that your research and reports confront and contradict the terrible lies of the Zionist propaganda claiming that they are being subjected to a Second Holocaust. The Zionists are flooding the media in America   and Britain with their lies as a pretence to attack the Palestinian Arabs.

Our work, our very mission, is to blunt these terrible lies. Hopefully world opinion will eventually change based on the Truth rather than these Zionist lies, and world bodies will put an immediate stop to this persecution.

One matter is certain. As our information and reports become increasingly known, the Zionists will be alarmed and determined to find those responsible for circulating the   Truth. Our future will be increasingly dangerous. Ben Gurion and his fellow criminals are extremely intelligent, and have the considerable advantage of possessing a highly organized intelligence.

We know the country has informers, spies, collaborators, and the like everywhere. Treachery is commonplace. Every activity in the Palestinian world is being recorded. One does not have to be a rocket scientist to identify the increasing risks that we face. And the gravity of our organization being destroyed is real. "

The Information Service leader dwelt over what he had said, and realized the necessity to stress the dangers faced.

" Paul. I realise that it is very difficult to believe much what is happening. To imagine that the very people who suffered so grievously in the hands of the German Gestapo are now committing far worse crimes against my people a mere three to four years later. Bluntly I suspect many of these Zionist criminals worked with the Gestapo. "

Anyhow Colonel Issar Harel heads this ghastly intelligence organization. I understand that it has collected over the years an enormous amount of data of every Arab, every potential community leader opposed to the Zionists. With that information the fate of thousands is sealed with their death. Harel and his criminal workers represent a terrible danger to all Palestinian Arabs who will be subject to interrogation, blacklisting, imprisonment, torture and death. This is the purpose of the Jewish secret service."

Roger Standish interjected.

" Harel's organization not only represents a threat to the Palestinian Arabs. It is a direct threat to our activities. We will have to plan a system whereby it is difficult to link any of us to each other. If any of us should fall into their hands, we need to be ignorant of vital information that can destroy us."

" Yes Roger - you are right" agreed Ibrahim

" The success of our information service is in jeopardy if any of us is linked to others in our group. Now I have prepared a system which I hope will protect our individual safety."

Ibrahim gave to each of us a copy of his proposed system.

" Please study the suggested system with care, and let me know any potential faults. We will meet later this evening, and discuss the system in detail, and iron out any possible weaknesses."

The meeting that morning ended in a subdued manner. We retired to study Ibrahim's ideas that might secure our very safety in the future. The paper contained the methodology whereby we would communicate with each other, passwords to identify ourselves, post boxes addresses recorded to fictitious owners, the opening of obscure bank accounts, and how we would be compensated in cash.

I could not fault Ibrahim's proposal. My only fear was my cowardice if exposed to torture. I could not envisage my ability to suffer the agony of torture under any circumstance. That evening, we convened. All agreed that the proposal was well thought out. Ahmad was present, and he made one significant observation addressing Roger and I.

" You two are far too conspicuous - English faces, English clothes, English mannerisms. When you travel, I suggest that you wear Arab clothing. Another serious matter. That Morris Minor of Roger's is no doubt recorded all over Palestine by now. I will make available a beat up Volkswagen which will be ideal for your needs with it's air cooled engine. And more important it will not draw very much attention"

" Good thinking Ahmad" responded Roger

" We have already realized the danger of identification, and will adopt your suggestion when we survey the Hebron, Beersheba, and Gaza districts"

After our meeting, Ibrahim advised me that I had a visitor. Noting my puzzlement, he smiled mischievously, and said no more. My mysterious visitor entered. It was dear Ghada. I immediately rose and welcomed her. What a wonderful surprise - and she appeared so well.

Ghada gazed at me with some concern.

" Paul. You are thinner. You must look after yourself"

Was I thinner? That is the problem when one sees the same face every day in the mirror. Nothing appears to change. I grinned.

"Blame your father - I am being made to work such long hours!"

Ghada turned to her father, and demanded with some concern

"Is that true father?"

Ibrahim smiled rather sheepishly.

" Possibly my dear but I promise not to be so demanding in the future"

Ibrahim's assurance appeased Ghada's concern. We shared our latest news. It was so wonderful seeing her again, and time passed by far too fast. We all retired early for the night. The following day would keep us well occupied.

Early the next morning, it was time for us to leave Hikmaj's Safe House. Already we wore our new Arab clothing and black and white head dress *(Kaffiyeh)*, and gradually became accustomed to the freedom and comfort of robes so appropriate for the Middle East.   However our appearance did not meet Hikmaj's approval. He placed two chairs in the middle of the room, and directed both of us be seated.

He then returned with a bowl of stain, and liberally applied it to our face and exposed parts. Finally he was finished, and then sighed deeply.

" What is it now" Roger demanded.

Hikmaj shook his head in desperation, and muttered.

"God could not have created two such ugly Arabs!"

Ahmad took over, and demonstrated our new car, the Volkswagen, and assured us that it was in excellent condition although its appearance was battered and unloved.

With regret two of God's ugliest departed, quiet and discrete, and headed for Hebron about 20 miles distant.

The district of Hebron provides evidence of the ever increasing aridness of the south. Most of the Hebron district villages are   in the north west part of the district.

The villages of Bayt Nattif (2400), Zakariyya (1300), and Dayr Aban   suffered attacks in January by a Haganah unit of about 100 men, but apparently the villagers were able to resist the attacks.

Bayt Nattif, close to Zakariyya and Dayr Aban   was set on a flat ridge between two valleys adjoined the Bethlehem -Aijur-Bayt Jibrin road, a strategic highway. The residents Muslim had an elementary school, and relied on three wells for water. Agriculture mainly cereal, orchards, grapes, and olives.

At this time, there was no evidence of hostile aggression which took place later in the year. We continued our way to the district of Beersheba.

Beersheba, about 35 miles south west of Hebron, is prominent with   very wide streets. To the south the desolate Negev and its long border with Egypt. - the home of the Bedouin. T.E.Lawrence accurately describes the Bedouin in *"Arabia Deserta":*

" The Bedouin has been born and brought up in the desert, and has embraced this bareness too harsh for volunteers with all his soul, for the reason ----------- that there he finds himself indubitably free. He loses all natural ties, all comforting superfluities or complications, to achieve that personal liberty which haunts starvation and death --------- He finds luxury in abnegation, renunciation, self restraint. He lives his own life in a hard selfishness."

There are about 90,000 Bedouins in the Naqab (Negev). The people have inhabited this arid area since the Byzantine period, and have conducted a semi nomadic life at least as far back as the 1500s. There are 96 Tribes, each of whom has grazing rights and access to water sources.

.
The Bedouin reject all authority, and any rules of conduct are their own. Whilst grazing land and water is considered common property, the constant skirmishes often involve the theft of camels, sheep, and goats, occasionally murder and the taking of women which suggests a certain inconsistency in recognizing property ownership and individual rights.

We visited the village of Al-Imara located close to the Gaza strip, which was subjected to an attack by a Zionist patrol in December 1947, and   driven off by the local inhabitants. Rainfall in this arid area was very small, and the local people relied on a major seasonal watercourse Wadi al-Shalala and a spring Ayn al-Shalala for seasonal agriculture. What was very significant the number of Jewish settlements in the area, and the kibbutz of Urim which relocated at an area close to the British police station.

Like the district of Hebron, little aggression had taken place. That would take place later in the year. We decided to drive on to Gaza.

The district of Gaza is located on the coastal plain adjoining the Mediterranean with a coast line of about 55 miles. During January seven villages with a total population of about 13,500 were attacked.   February six villages were attacked with a total population of 16,100.

Despite the district of Gaza being designated part of the United Nation's proposed Palestinian State, it was quite obvious that the Jewish settlements nearby desired the rich agricultural land within Gaza.

Any brief examination of the U.N. 181 Partition Plan, would suggest that the individuals in UN must have been working for the Zionists. Not only was all the prime land, transport, ports, communication, and waters sources awarded to the Jewish State, the plan was devised to fragment and seriously weaken the Palestine State into three isolated areas which would all be subject to Jewish control .

Gaza was a classic example - a strip of land a mere five miles wide and fifty miles long adjoining the Mediterranean, and another strip five to fifteen miles wide and forty miles long adjoining the Negev Desert and Egypt. Immediately next to the strip a number of Kibbutz settlements with occupants desiring to possess the land.   And the obvious economic link with the West Bank subject to hostile Jewish interference and blockades.

From Gaza City as we drove north to the village of Barbara, I complained.

" What a scam. Do you realise Roger that somehow a large community of Palestinian Arabs are expected somehow to survive on a strip of land only five miles deep with hostile Jewish settlements next door. There is no connection with the West Bank which means that the Jews have a strangle hold on the economy of the Gaza District. All movement of people and goods will be subject to the questionable cooperation of the Jews.   Any blockade and controls makes Gaza   a prison"

With some sarcasm, Roger responded.

" My dear chap. You are viewing the obvious corruption of United Nations complying to Zionist interests. Ghandi forecast the failure of the Jewish State through corruption and aggression. And no doubt he would have forecast the failure of United Nations through   corruption"

The village of Barbara located about 15 miles north east of Gaza is perhaps a typical example of villages within the district. Set on the east side of the sand dunes that parallel the coast, it is located west of the coastal highway and the railway line, with access to urban centers south and north. Historically there are records back to the 1300s when it was the hometown of the renowned Muslim scholar Ahmad ibn Dawud.

During the 19th Century, the village was rectangular in shape and had two ponds and gardens to its sides.. Population was Muslim. Dwellings were adobe brick with a centrally located mosque. In recent years an elementary school was founded. Agriculture was known for its grapes, some of the best in the country, also orchards of almonds, figs, olives, oranges, guavas, and crops of water melons, cantaloupes, and grain. Wells and irrigation provided much of the water.

But all this peace ended early this year. In January there were a number of skirmishes, and a Jewish bus passing through the village opened fire on the villagers. Further attacks that month included gunfire, and several windows were broken of the local school.

Arab Suqrir, a village 25 miles north east of Gaza, suffered a Haganah attack early January. A party of Jews attacked Wadi Sukrayr with gunfire January 9th, the police arrived, and counter attacked. Finally 8 Arabs and 12 Jews were killed. Then about two weeks later the Haganah bombed fifteen to twenty houses in the same area in retaliation.

Hamama, about 5 miles north of Barbara, with a population of about 5.500 Muslims suffered attacks in January and February. Topographically its features were similar to Barbara. It's history first recorded being the site of a battle between the Crusaders and Muslims.

The village had two schools and a local council administered its affairs. Attacks commenced in January with village laborers attacked in the fields by Jewish settlers. Fifteen men were wounded. Two days later the Jewish settlement again opened fire on villagers from Hamama, killing one and wounding another. Then in February a group of villagers were attacked at a bus stop on the main road between Hamama and Isdud, and two were wounded.

Roger and I made a few discreet enquiries with a number of witnesses of the attacks. One laborer, still bewildered and hurt, explained that he was working with others on fields between Hamama and Isdud January 22nd, and were attacked by Jewish settlers from nearby settlement Nitzanim. They had done nothing to provoke the settlers, and yet 15 fellow workers had been wounded - 2 seriously!

Another man still suffering from shock and wounds described that he and others were waiting for a bus February 17th, and were attacked, fired upon, and he and another man wounded. Those attackers returned to the Jewish settlement of Nitzanim.

We then drove to Burayr not far distant from Hamama with a population of about 3,000.

Muslims. The village center quite prominent with a market, clinic, grain mill, and two schools. Water was plentiful from three wells, and recently a number of artesian wells had been drilled. Agriculture included grain, fruits, citrus, figs, grapes, and vegetables.

Again there was no difficulty finding witnesses to a number of attacks. The first attack occurred January 27th by five Zionist armored cars which was repulsed. Then February 14th, a similar attack took place, and that in turn was repulsed. Despite these two serious attacks, the British intervened the following day, forcibly removed some village barricades, and wounded two villagers. There was a general sense of bitterness about the British, helplessness, and fear.

Further attacks took place throughout the district in January, February, and now in March. We were advised that the village of al-Faluja had suffered a serious attack 14th March a few days prior to our arrival.

We drove to Al-Faluja, a few miles east of Barbara. It was a fair size village of about 5,100 all Muslim. Surrounded on three sides by a wadi, it had two wells and a pool to the east. There were two schools, a local council, and a large mosque with three domed halls. Agriculture of this rural village was mainly rain fed producing grain, vegetables and fruit.

Here there was no difficulty finding witnesses. A Jewish supply convoy escorted by Haganah armored cars had engaged in a battle with the villagers in which 37 Arabs and 7 Jews were killed, and many were wounded. Later that day a Haganah demolition squad arrived, blew up ten houses, the post office, and the three storey municipal building. The tales were all similar - the attacks unprovoked.

We returned to our safe house in Gaza. That evening Roger received a message. We had to return to Jaffa immediately. I remarked to Roger on the way back.

" *Despite the district of Gaza being proposed by U.N. part of the Arab State, the Jews are clearly indifferent, and act as if the whole of Palestine is their domain*"

" *It certainly seems that way. The British troops are not doing a darn thing to stop all this nonsense*"

In Jaffa I was busy for the rest of the month collecting and preparing my reports whilst Roger attended to some immediate matters.

Report - March 1948

Accra District	*- No Reports*
Baysan District	*- No Reports*
Beersheba District	*- No Reports*
Gaza District	*- Village attacked- (8,100) - Bayt Daras (9), Al-Faluja (37)*
Haifa District	*- Village attacked- (13,000) -Ayn Ghazal (1),Al-Ghubayya* *- Al-Fawqa, Mar-ibn'Amir, Al-Tahta, Jaba, Al-Tira* *- Village expelled- (1,600) - Qannir, Qira* *- Town attacked - Haifa (60,000)*
Hebron District	*- No Reports*
Jaffa District	*- Village attacked (12,000) - Abu Kishk, Biyar'Adas, Migdal* *- Salama, Al-Shaykh Muwannis* *- Village Expelled (1,000) - Al-Mas'udiyya*
Jerusalem District	*- Village attacked (8,200) - Artuf, Bayt Mahsir, Ishna,* *-Dayr Aban, Al-Malina, Al-Qastal*
Jinin District	*- Village attacked (2,200) - Nuris, Zir'in*
Nazareth District	*- No Reports*
Al-Ramla District	*- Village attacked (3,500) - Dayr Ayyub, Al-Maghar, Qatra*
Safad District	*- Village attacked (1,200) - Jubb Yusuf, Al-Mansura, Taytaba* *- Village expelled (750) - Kirad Al-Ghannama, Al-Musayniyya*
Tiberias District	*- Village attacked (2,600) - Lubya (6)* *- Village expelled (2,000) - Al-Manara, Al-Manshiyya,* *- Al'Ubaydiyya, Wadi Al-Hamam*

Report - March 1948

Tulkarm District	- *Village attacked (3,150) - Fardisya, Ghabat Kafr Sur, Qaqun*
	- *Al Talama*
	- *Village expelled (4,000) - Bayyarat Hannun, Rami Zayta,*
	- *Umm Khalid, Wadi Al-Hawarith, Wadi Qabbani,*
	- *Arab Al-Nufay'at*

Villages attacked	*49*
Towns attacked	*1*
Inhabitants attacked	*123,000*
Inhabitants expelled	*9,350*

Caught by Jewish Security

When we returned to Jaffa late that evening, we faced more serious news; the situation increasingly grim. Six villages in the Jaffa district had been attacked whilst we had been away. Over 12,000 had been subjected to fearsome attacks, bombing, and machine gun fire.

Despite the village of Al-Mas'Udiyya's arranged truce with the Haganah late 1947, the entire population had been forced out and expelled. The village of about 1,000 was located close to the outskirts of Tel-Aviv.

Our city of Jaffa, with its population of about 100,000, was now a city of extreme fear. Everyone complained that the British, supposedly responsible for law and order, had done very little to stem the violence, and gave one the impression that they had washed their hands of their responsibilities.

I shook my head in disbelief - my Palestine, as I knew it, was being destroyed, and there was no evidence that the destruction would be stopped. I slept poorly that night, and woke the following morning quite shattered.

Roger and I sat in the Study appraising events for the past month. I had a rough draft of my summarized Report for March, and read out some statistics.

" 34 Villages attacked in all districts with the exception of Accra, Baysan, Beersheba, Hebron, and Nazareth. Also the town of Haifa. About 123,000 subjected to bombing, machine gun fire attacks, and the like.

15 Villages attacked and expelled. A population of 9,400 expelled.

50 to 100 Killed."

I summed up the situation.

"The neighboring Arab countries (The Arab League), despite a lot of hot air have given no evidence to be involved and assist the Palestinian Arabs. The Jordan Army and the British troops are simply watching. In fact the British are making life even more difficult for the Palestinian Arabs."

Roger did not bother to examine the report in detail.

" These attacks are all over the country, and must have been planned years ago. Just imagine the purchase and stocking of the huge arsenal of arms, bombs, and guns. The acquisition of armored cars and tanks, fighter planes and the like.

And just think - all this aggression demanded planning, direction, and co-ordination, and definitely required large sums of money and backing. This is no spontaneous hostile rising. This aggression has been in the works for many years."

He slid the draft report .back to me.

" Paul. We have a large task somehow or other covering the whole country. Ibrahim tells me that his clients demand first hand reports - not merely the quotation of statistics and second hand advise.

Now it seems pretty obvious to me that the Zionists are intent on aggressive attacks on all villages and towns with Muslim populations. And the way they are behaving, intimidation is the name of the game, and the purpose to encourage the people to leave.

U.N.Resolution 181 sets out the terms of the Partition, but there is no evidence that the Jews intend to comply to the terms. Their aggression suggests that the Winner takes all! My guess is that the two major port cities Haifa and Jaffa will be subject to more bold attacks with the object to expel the Arab populations.

As Ibrahim demands first hand reports, you shall go to Haifa, and I will remain here to record local troubles. Is that in order?"

I nodded *" Agreed"*

" Right. You take the Volkswagen, wear your Arab clothing, and be very careful. This country is becoming increasingly dangerous for us, and no doubt the Haganah, Palmach, Irgun, Stern, and others will try and seek us out. Report to our Safe House in Haifa.

Haifa is full of informers and spies, so take care with whom you enquire, and try and remain in the background. By all means get pictures and reports of villages attacked, but Haifa is the place of concern. I'm told that the British troops, despite the appalling attacks, have done nothing, and in fact seem to be hindering the Arab people.

And remember an Arab with an ugly British face writing notes and taking photographs can only invite suspicion and hostility. "

Roger, tired and stressed,   smiled wearily.

" Congratulations on your promotion. You will do well, I know. Give me a ring via the Safe House if you need any assistance. OK?"

I returned to my office, and immediately finalized my summarized March Report. On a map of Palestine, I recorded all the villages subjected to attacks over the past four months. It was a grim reminder that hostilities were taking place everywhere, and that they would probably increase. I decided to study recent happenings in Haifa.

Haifa, a major Mediterranean port, had a population of about 75,000 Palestinians, with a considerable number of Jews living in close by neighborhoods. There had been many attacks on the Arab population in recent months, and it was rumored that a Zionist DanI Agmon headed a Haganah unit called *"Hashahar"* which specialized in causing intimidation.

Arab housing had been subjected to rolling drums of explosives, streets of fire, loudspeakers screaming threats at night, and individual attacks of houses with bombs and machine gun fire. The Palestinian elite, perhaps 15,000 to 20,000, had fled to Lebanon or Egypt, leaving the remaining 55,000 to 60,000 leaderless.

A despicable attack by the Irgun throwing a bomb at a group of Palestinians waiting to enter the local Refinery December 1947 was the last straw, and for once the Arabs retaliated and attacked their fellow Jewish workers. The Haganah High Command decided to retaliate by ransacking a whole village and massacre its inhabitants. The village chosen was Balad al-Shaykh, a few miles east of Haifa. A local commander Haim Avinoam with his force encircled the village, and within three hours over sixty Arab Palestinians had been killed.

Not satisfied, the Haganah then entered the Haifa neighborhood of Wadi Rushmiyya, expelled its inhabitants, and blew up their houses. A few weeks later the Palmach demolished the neighborhood of Hawassa, and expelled its 5,000 inhabitants.

It was appalling that the British had simply watched. Thus the people's hope of security provided by the British was merely a dream. It was also a reminder that conditions might prove quite difficult for me. I prepared for my solo visit taking as little as possible - a camera, pads of writing paper, and two spare one gallon cans of petrol.

Roger shook my hand.

" Take care Paul. See you back soon"

As I slowly drove through the predominantly Jewish communities of Tel Aviv, I realized that I was very much on my own. The Jewish neighborhoods quiet and depressing, the people hard, hostile, and indifferent..

Traveling on the coast road through the district of Tulkarm, I briefly checked the villages of Bayyarat Hannun, Arab al-Nufay'at, Wadi Qabbani, Umm Khalid, Wadi al-Hawarith, and Rami Zayta. All inhabitants had been expelled - the villages bombed and destroyed. In some instances only rubble and a few broken walls remained.

No doubt some of the unfortunate people seen trudging along the main roads were refugees from these very villages, hot, dusty, hungry, with no evidence of assistance. The district of Haifa adjoined Tulkarm. There further villages could be seen that had been recently attacked. Houses bombed, roofs destroyed, and a general feeling of gloom and lack of activity. I stopped no more. I had seen more than enough.

My car safely concealed in the Safe House courtyard, I was now provided with the latest news by Ghalib Al-Masri who was distracted, fearful, and indignant.

" What are you doing here - are you mad?. Everyone is leaving. You British are so strange. You are concerned about us whilst your army commander Hugh Stockwell does not give a damn.

Do you not realise that over thirty villages within the district of Haifa. have been attacked, and in the majority of villages the people have been expelled. About 35,000 to 40,000 have been subjected to attacks, and about 24,000 expelled. What is of considerable concern is that it was not only the Haganah, Irgun, Stern, and Palmach responsible for the wholesale murder and destruction - the local kibbutz often were guilty. Members of the Zionist socialist party of Hashomer Ha-Tza'ir, participated and worsened the fate of many unfortunate Arabs.. "

In Haifa there was total despair. The British obviously would not intervene. There was no leadership - just fear and panic reigned. The date 18th April. - I warily walked around the city. Loudspeakers could be heard blaring out threatening messages, and urging all to flee. The threats and attacks intensified.

By the 21st April the Jewish Carmeli Brigade was entering into Haifa suburbs, killing anyone it confronted, house entrance doors forced open with explosives, followed by looting and bombing. By now the Arab population had lost all hope.

Early the 22nd April, the population fled to the harbor with the intention to escape by boat. There was panic, fear, and chaos., and that sense of fear, panic, and chaos spread to me. Hidden in a graveyard overlooking the harbor, I viewed the unhappy chaos, scared that I might become part of it. People were being urged to congregate at the Old Market Place close to the Harbor.

But there was no leadership or organization - just panic and fear. And the attackers without any mercy heartlessly bombarded the helpless Arab people in the Square with 3" mortar shells and sniper fire. The panic increased, and suddenly the gate to the harbor was forced open. Immediately the terrified crowd fled into the harbor, the weak, young, and helpless left behind crushed to death.

The poor people were screaming, shouting, weeping, crying, demanding for assistance. Many were forced to wade out to overloaded boats, some carrying their elderly parents and children. Boats completely overloaded, overturned, sank, and many drowned. The bombardment continued mindlessly without any evidence of pity or concern.

It was a memory I can never forget - one of total horror - one in which to my own shame I simply stood petrified with fear watching. Poor women were desolate, screaming, wailing, moaning, and sad frightened little children wide eyed in fear and bewilderment with or without parents. Men panic stricken literally treading over motionless bodies hurt, crushed, and dead.

Frozen with fear, I somehow forced myself to take one photograph of the frightened people wading out to boats that could not possibly accommodate them. I could take no more - it was far too horrible.

My hands and fingers stiff like pieces of lead were forced to make some notes. I had difficulty writing - my mind stunned with the scenes of death and agony of frightened hordes. It was a scene I wished never to experience again.

It was then I was aware that I was being observed by two men. Two very solid hard looking men with steely eyes and tight mouths. One, clearly the leader asked.

" Good morning Sir - what are you doing?"

The question suggested that my activity did not meet their approval. I returned my writing pad into my file, and looked up.

" Just making some notes"

My explanation did not appear to satisfy them. The man who had asked me the question spoke again in a demanding fashion

" I am Inspector Mendlesohn, and this is Sergeant Gerber. Please identify yourself"

I felt I was at a disadvantage not knowing these strangers or the purpose of their question. Rather weakly I responded

" Paul Blackberry visitor seeing your country"

The inspector turned, and addressed the Sergeant.

" Sergeant - he is seeing our country"

He turned back, and addressed me more officiously

" Mr Blackberry - forgive my curiosity - you are British and yet dressed in the clothing of Arab scum. And here you are recording the irresponsible behavior of a crowd of criminals. Have you authority from the State of Israel to be here?"

" Of course not"

The inspector addressed the Sergeant again.

" Sergeant. Here is an individual disguised as a local Arab recording unlawful events without State permission. This is a very serious matter. Take this individual to Judge Abramson"

I was completely taken aback, and weakly protested

" You have no right"

The inspector interjected

" Excuse me Sir - it is you that has no right"

And I discovered, regardless of my rights, that a light weight of 135 pounds is helpless in the hands of two heavy particularly strong men, and rapidly I was conveyed to a nearby building titled Jewish Security, placed in a secure room for an hour or more, and finally brought standing before Judge Abramson. With cold eyes, he studied me whilst Inspector Mendlesohn submitted his complaint. The complaint understood, the judge advised me of the court's leniency.

" Mr Blackberry - you are very fortunate to be in a law abiding country. As you are a visitor, I accept your ignorance of the law, and will take no further action regarding this very serious infraction. Please never visit the State of Israel without our authority. You are to leave this district immediately"

Icily he instructed me that I could go. The Inspector returned my file and camera. Bewildered and disturbed, I left the premises, and sincerely hoped I would never meet those unsavory characters again. Eventually I returned to the Safe House after double checking a number of times, and certain that I was not being followed.

I reported my experience to a very concerned Ghalib Al-Masri retrieved my car, and took off for Jaffa. But my troubles had not ended. As I leaving the outskirts of Haifa, I was stopped by a British Police check point. A Sergeant strolled across, and stared at me curiously.

" I would not wear them Arab togs - you will get shot at"

I stared at the soldier, and asked.

" What's going on Sergeant. I have just been hauled in by Jewish Security to a Judge"

I told him of my recent experience. He listened expressionless and without comment

" So you tell me that you got caught by Jewish Security personnel. Come off it mate - there ain't no such thing. Might I suggest you get back to Limey Land before you get into some real

trouble. There are plenty of better things to do rather than record the activities of some Arab criminals"

I stared at this man in disbelief. Furiously, without thought, I lashed out

" Instead of wasting tax payers money harassing innocent people and refugees, go into the city and protect the tens of thousands of defenseless people fleeing from mortar shelling and machine gun fire"

Mouth turned down, the man snarled.

" Listen mate - keep your damn mouth shut. We know what we are doing. Keep your fingers clean or you will get thrown out of the country. Now get going. And don't you ever get caught again in them Arab togs."

As I departed, I observed that he read and wrote down my car registration. I was becoming far too famous or notorious without even trying.

I was being followed by a small foreign car. Whether or not the two occupants were my old friend the Inspector and his Sergeant I did not know, but I had an unhappy feeling that it was them. I wasted a few moments wondering how they had got onto my track - perhaps as simply as waiting to be advised of my presence at the British Police check point, Regardless I had to lose them.

I rapidly turned off the coastal road, and drove to Tulkarm. Within the town, I purposely drove down some narrow streets and alleys, and parked the car beneath a dark Cedar adjoining a hotel parking area. Within ten minutes I reported at the Tulkarm Safe House. Jaffa was contacted and advised that I would be driven to Jaffa. The Volkswagen would be collected later when it was certain that the vehicle was not being observed.

Roger listened to my account of the Haifa visit.

" You do not need any authority - that is utter rubbish. "

Roger smiled sympathetically.

" Never mind Paul. You were in a very difficult situation. I am afraid they conned you. I have a feeling you will discover that your camera film is missing. You had better lie low for a few days. You can write up your report on Haifa."

Some other precautions would have to be made.

" *The Safe House in Haifa has been relocated. Tulkarm will change the registration plates of the Volkswagen.   Regarding the Jewish Security, I sense that they do exist regardless what the British check point say. So we need to keep our eyes open for that inspector and his sergeant.* "

Plan Dalet

Perhaps it was just as well I was rewriting the recent events in Haifa. The note taking at the scene could not possibly cover the terrible scenes and happenings that took place prior to the final panic. As I jotted down some of the many recollected events pertinent to the disaster, I wondered how such a large population could have permitted itself to disintegrate so rapidly.

Fear and self preservation? Lack of confidence in the security of the prevailing law and order authorities. The omission of recognized leadership and authority. All were factors, but were they the primary cause.

Examination of events in the district of Haifa over the past six months suggested a conspiracy, an evil and well coordinated plan, to expel the Arab population through intimidation. It could not possibly have been caused by a few un-coordinated attacks by irresponsible hostile individuals.

Of course the ill thought United Nations Referendum 181 announced late November 1947 no doubt was the catalyst. The district of Haifa was designated part of the new Jewish State, and probably some extreme Zionist groups would have desired the expulsion of their Arab neighbors. But the possibility of such small groups conspiring together and the magnitude of the crimes did not seem a feasible explanation.

As early as December 1947 villages were attacked with 60 killed at Balad Al-Shaykh and 13 killed at Al-Tira. Both massacres took place at villages very close to the city of Haifa, and both committed by the Hagana and the Irgun. Haifa itself with a population of about 60,000 Arabs suffered constant attacks that involved high explosives, machine gun attacks, and the bombing of houses. The neighborhood of Wadi Rushmiyya was demolished and the people expelled.

January the attacks continued at Haifa. Also a number of villages were attacked with a total population of 7,500. The Haifa neighborhood of Hawassa was demolished and 5, 000 expelled

February the aggression applied to ten villages attacked (population 12,000), and 2,500 expelled. The Haifa population of 60,000 continued to suffer attacks. March nine villages attacked (population 13,000) and 1,600 expelled, and the population of Haifa still subjected to attacks.

Now in April the town of Haifa succumbed to the attack of the Carmel Brigade, and the population expelled. Seven villages (12,500) attacked, about thirty villages attacked and the inhabitants expelled (26,500)

Later I discussed my findings with Roger Standish hoping to glean an explanation. Roger shook his head.

" I could take a guess but do not possess any facts to support it. Why don't you have another chat with As'Ad Kamal. "

As it grew dark, I carefully walked to As'Ad's apartment. Again he eyed me carefully, as I explained the reason for my visit. I described my recent visit to Haifa, the horrifying scenes, and finally my upsetting episode with the Jewish Security. He was concerned to learn that I had been apprehended wearing Arab clothing.

" You are very fortunate that they permitted you to leave. My guess is that they hoped to track your movements, and make a connection with others."

" You think so?"

" Of course. These people have thousands of years of experience dealing with their fellow people in the risky occupation of financing and money lending. They are very astute in matters that are foreign to us."

" In what ways?"

" Consider, for example, the crazy religious claims of the extreme Zionists. Their claims differ no more than the claims of thousands of other religions. And yet in their case, the demand of an exclusive State within which only their fellow people may dwell. Initially it was an idea which never had much support. And yet in recent times the idea has been increasingly supported for a multitude of reasons   which have little to do with any kind of religious desire."

Puzzled, I asked. *" What other kind of reasons."*

" The opportunity to gain individual power utilizing the finance and support of the extreme Zionists living in the USA and UK.   The individuals involved in the current campaigns against the defenseless Arab are not interested per se in religious exclusivity other than as an excuse to accumulate oppressive power against others, and to steal real and personal property of the Arabs. Of course with such dishonest thinking, it attracts the bottom of the Jewish scum - no doubt many the evil dregs of European society. "

" You truly think that is a possibility?"

" It is not a possibility Paul. It is a fact"

As'Ad Kamal did not take kindly to my doubts, and irritably decided to further my education.

" Make some notes young man because it is time you understood precisely what is happening in this unfortunate country.

Commencing with Theodore Hertz late 1800s, and more individuals at the beginning of this Century, Zionism to them meant a mix of ideology and colonialism. Gradually the idea was adopted to acquire property in Palestine and pursue Zionism in a more positive manner.

At that time, the dream of a Jewish State existed, but no hope of achievement through political means. As you no doubt know Balfour (British Foreign Minister) provided some momentum 1917 by declaring the promise that a home for the Jewish people would be established in Palestine. But of course the declaration was not practical. The Arab people had not been consulted and would automatically reject the idea for many reasons including the obvious one that they owned 95% of the land.

Ben Gurion led the Zionist movement, commencing in the mid 1920s, and proved a very determined and hard working leader. He rapidly realized that the future of any Jewish State could not survive if it lacked security and defense. And rapidly he and his collaborators realized that no security or defense that met their ideals could exist with the current Arab population.

There were many who could be considered collaborators. However the following men may be considered the prime decision makers of the future policy of the Zionist forces commencing in 1948:

David Ben Gurion	*Leader of Zionist Movement.*
Moshe Sharett	*Foreign Minister*
Menechim Begin	*Leader Irgun Gang*
Yigael Yadin	*Head of Operations*
Yigon Allon	*Senior Officer Palmach*
Yohanan Ratner	*Strategic Adviser to Ben Gurion*
Yitshak Sadeh	*Chief of the Palmach*
Israel Galili	*Head of High Command*
Zvi Ayalon	*Deputy to Galili*
Isar Harel	*Head of Intelligence*
Yossef Weitz	*Jewish Agency - head of settlement*
Ezra Danin	*Jewish Intelligence*
Yehoashua Palmon	*Deputy to Danin*
Eliyahu Sasson	*Promoter of Divide and Rule Tactics*
Moshe Dayan	*Military Commander*
Yaacov Shimoni	*Head Information*
Dan Even	*Commander Coastal Front*
Shimon Avidan	*Commander Givati Brigade*
Moshe Carmel	*Commander North Front*
Yitzhak Rabin	*Commander Central Front*
Shlomo Shamir	*Spokesman for Ben Gurion*

And most of the above took a positive part in implementing the future policy known as Plan Dalet. It should be remembered that initially the policy was one of aggression and intimidation. However it was difficult to pursue this policy due to the pacifist reaction of the Arab people desiring peace, and unfavorable foreign indignation. There was so little retaliation.

The question arose at Ben Gurion's meetings " How could the aims of the group be achieved without an acceptable excuse for aggression."

The claim presented to the world was the immediate false danger of a Second Holocaust. The pretext of an universal uprising of the Arabs against the isolated groups of Jews and the hostile entry of the Arab League from neighboring Middle East countries. That claim proved more than adequate to raise the necessary sympathy of the outside world regardless of the truth, and the subsequent provision of adequate funds and military supplies for the Zionist aggressive campaign thereafter.

Ben Gurion's committee realized that most of the obstacles to their plans did not exist. The Palestinian Arabs presumed on the assumed security of the British troops which proved false. Palti Sela of Intelligence concluded "If these people are to be expelled, the excuse that it was due to retaliation would not be possible because of their lack of aggression"

The entry of the Arab League was merely "Hot Air". The United Nations and their wording of Resolution 181 were merely words which would not be enforced. There was no real physical opposition in existence to counter and excuse any aggressive tactics by the Zionists.

Rapidly early this year it was decided that the solution would be the forcible expulsion of the Arab people preferably to adjoining Arab countries, and the theft of all Arab real and personal property. Thus Plan Dalet became the master plan.

Ezra Danin. disappointed by the lack of aggression by the Arab people demanded a much more aggressive policy - to terrify them - to destroy their transportation - to sink their fishing boats - to stop raw materials delivered to their factories.

Early December intimidation in a greater massive scale commenced involving the attack, the demolition of buildings, the distribution of threatening leaflets, and a number of massacres. Ben Gurion's meeting in December discussed, and decided that future retaliatory operations should include the expulsion of the Arab people, and the resettlement by Jewish settlers. Haifa was the first urban center attacked under the new campaign of terror.

The new campaign commenced.   Balad Al-Shaykh close to Haifa was attacked and over 60 killed. Thereafter two neighborhoods of Haifa were demolished, and the inhabitants expelled. And the attacks within Haifa continued. The British, considered an obstacle,   did not intervene.

Yossef Weitz proposed January that all the Arab population should be expelled, their land seized, and acquired by Jewish settlements. There was general agreement to cause the optimal damage and kill as many as possible. The purpose of every attack to occupy, destroy, and expulsion.

Yigael Yadin, supported by his second in command Yigal Allon, proposed that in future an offensive should be undertaken rather than individual retaliatory attacks, Destroy complete areas and destroy the Arab economy.

In February David Shaltiel, Jerusalem military commander was instructed to destroy the neighborhood of Shaykh Jarrah and others, and to settle Jews in all evicted houses.

During February Ben Gurion continued his propaganda claiming the Jewish people were defending themselves from destruction by the Palestinians. That public relation ploy was highly successful, encouraged the Jewish forces to act, and obtained the maximum foreign sympathy.

Enormous supplies of armaments, weapons, bombs were purchased and delivered. The Jewish military was now involved in the manufacture of flame throwers and poisonous gas. Yigael Yadin again demanded massive invasions of Palestinian areas.

My Arab people were now being seized, falsely accused of being illegally present in the Jewish State not having newly issued identity cards, interrogated, tortured, and imprisoned. I understand that in Haifa, the center for interrogation is at 11 Daniel Street overlooking the harbor.

And so this terrible policy Plan Dalet is carried out. You no doubt have plentiful records as evidence of the ever increasing attacks and expulsion of my people."

As'Ad Kamal leaned back in his chair. He had spoken. What he had said confirmed my suspicions. All these attacks, their nature and intensity, had been planned and formulated over a long period of time.. What a grim sad subject.

During April, whilst the entire population of 55,000 - 60,000 in Haifa had been expelled in my presence, 143 villages throughout Palestine had been attacked, 4 towns attacked, 171,300 individuals suffered these attacks, and 150,000 expelled. Many massacres had taken place including those at Saris (7), Mu'Awiya (12), Sarafand Al'Amar (39), Biriyya (20), Nasir Al-Din (10), and the most horrific at Dayr Yasin (Jerusalem District) (245).

It is difficult to envisage the cruel inhumanity involved in the Dayr Yasin massacre - some of the village inhabitants were actually paraded along the main streets of Jerusalem (a proclaimed Jewish Victory Parade) amidst the cheering of Jewish crowds. These unfortunate men were then returned to their village and slain.

There was no way that all these unprovoked attacks were spontaneous acts of a few individuals These attacks were the product of years of planning and Plan Dalet.

" And by the way Paul, if you still have some doubts. Think very carefully, and forget everything I have said. Analyse Ben Gurion's claim that the Zionist Military has an aggressive armed force of 50,000 men - that is every fit Jew between the age of 8 and 50; the arms, armaments, mortars, explosives, armored units, a fighter squadron, destroyers, and the organization and money to plan and direct these forces. Many years of planning is necessary for such a status. Ask yourself how that could happen - and your answer is a long planned conspiracy.

No doubt the idea is repugnant, but consider the general reluctance of the British to intervene throughout Palestine and prevent these aggressive attacks. Consider the disgraceful conduct of general Hugh Stockwell British commander in the Haifa area who simply watched the Carmeli Brigade enter Haifa and commit so many atrocities. He was well aware of the Carmeli Brigade plans, and actually warned the Palestinian people of the expected attack, advised the inhabitants to flee, and provided no security and safeguards. And this outrageous dereliction of common decency took place whilst the Jewish loudspeakers could be heard urging the unfortunate Palestinians to leave.

I cannot explain who was responsible for advising the British Forces to not intervene, but the fact is just as disgraceful as the actions of Ben Gurion's thugs. Ernest Bevin British Foreign Secretary was furious with Stockwell, so it would appear that he was unaware of any conspiracy. No doubt Ernest Bevin was ignorant that Hugh Stockwell had an affair with a Jewish woman in 1945 who some claimed was an Israeli agent! And yet immediately your General Montgomery strongly defended Stockwell. Clearly this universal lack of intervention upholding the Mandate security law and order came from top authorities in Britain."

My mind was full of conflicting thoughts. The cause of recent events demanded an explanation, and yet the explanation might not be that welcome to my ears. I thanked As'Ad for providing me with his background understanding of the Zionist planning and implementation. He in turn shrugged his shoulders - the information must be made known. With surprising kind interest he asked.

" And young man. How are you enjoying Palestine and its people?"

" The people are of great interest. Although the majority apply their work to agriculture, there is no lack of intelligent professional individuals specializing in engineering, architecture, the law, and the sciences. Their desire for peace is highly commendable. It is so unfortunate that they easily fall prey to aggressive and dishonest people.

Regarding the country, the economic potential appears great provided adequate water resources can be found. The Palestinian is a good worker, and has succeeded in agriculture for thousands of years."

As'Ad led me to the door and shook my hand.

" It will be interesting to record the future - will the pacifist people survive and continue to   live in Palestine is a very important matter. It is a certainty that the Zionists, if they overwhelm the Palestinian Arab through aggression, will never succeed in peace. "

And so I departed full of thought. Possibly general Hugh Stockwell, tainted by his affair with a Jewish agent, was responsible for British policy in Palestine. Being defended by Montgomery meant very little - Montgomery's record   a irresponsible loose cannon, vindictive, and a mischief maker.

I was reminded by a recent talk by a Jewish student who claimed that the Jewish authorities at Haifa wanted the Arabs to remain, and desired peace. My files for the months of December 1947 to April 1948 recorded there had been 287 attacks against Arab villages, 10 attacks against towns, 673,000 Arabs had been subjected to attacks, and 172,000 expelled. And yet despite these deplorable records, this Jew and no doubt many more would claim that all the problems have been created by the Palestinian Arab, and that the Jews simply desired peace and friendship!

" Post everyone" announced Roger, as he entered the office. He examined the letters and advised.

" Letter from England for one lucky chap"

I immediately recognized Mother's writing. One of Mother's enduring qualities was a guaranteed response to any communication. My promised letters to Mother were religiously answered. Normally she used the standard blue airmail letter ideal for writers with limited imagination. Mother overcame the limited space by writing minutely. It is fortunate that few customers were like Mother otherwise the post office system would have gone bankrupt.

Her subject matter covered a wide range of subjects - the neighbors, the family, the latest obituary notices in the Telegraph, and always some valuable advise to her eldest son. And of course now her eldest was in Palestine, any news item relating to the Middle East would catch her attention.

Although Mother had weakened and acquiesced to my working in Palestine, she still suspected it was a bad decision, and that unhappy thought continued to fester. Seated comfortably in her armchair close to the Dining Room fireplace, her sharp eyes identified a most alarming headline.

" Palestine - Imminent Second Holocaust!"

Her heart stopped momentarily. Her immediate thought was the danger faced by her son. With care she carefully read the paper's editorial. The Jewish population in Palestine were facing the Second Holocaust, and in danger of being overwhelmed by hostile Arabs and the United Arab League. The paper stressed the gravity, and claimed that they must be supported - no way would it be permitted that they suffer again like in Europe a few years earlier.

Trembling Mother immediately phoned Father, and shared the alarming news with him. Father remained calm, and pacified Mother.

" *Charlotte. Nothing to worry about. Wait until I get back from the College, and we can discuss this editorial"*

Father never gave us the impression of alarm - his appearance one of composure and control - although I suspect his inside often racked with the fears of being a parent. Mother in the Kitchen heard the opening of the front door, and waited unhappily at the Kitchen stove.

Father gave her a kiss, and was immediately fed with a litany of fears, and the alarming editorial.

" *Well Charlotte - there is a lot of talk about possible hostilities, but the odd attack by some Arabs seems minimal."*

" *That is not the point Frank. It is what will happen!"*

" *I doubt it Charlotte. My understanding is that the Paris Peace Conference declared that the Jews shall have their own State within Palestine, as originally proposed by your Liberal leader and Prime Minister Lloyd George and Winston Churchill. We have the Mandate of Palestine providing administration, law and justice.*

And United Nations has just declared the Partition of Palestine so that the Jews will have a part of Palestine. The Arab people must have agreed to all this - there won't be a problem. And remember there is a large British Army contingent in Palestine"

Mother frowned. She so admired Lloyd George who at one time congratulated her for her Suffragette and Liberal activities. If Lloyd George gave his blessing to this Partition, it must be safe. Reluctantly she accepted this conclusion.

" *Well - I hope so. It is so very worrying"*

Father placed his arms around Mother, and hopefully provided the necessary assurance.

However it is difficult to calm a resolute woman and a concerned mother. Her steely blue eyes might be momentarily calmed, but that did not prevent her from warning her eldest son of his danger. Palestine definitely was not like her France and her Germany.

Her letter was quite explicit. Already she had cut out many articles addressing the imminent Second Holocaust. All signified a great danger to her eldest. Very significant questions were posed:

How Trustworthy were these Arabs?   Her concern was fed with so many stories and films of blood thirsty sheiks, enormous harems, heads often cut off, concealed faces and wild eyes, and a very disturbing lack of respect of law and order. Possibly their identity was confused by others who may have been Indians or whatever. Regardless all had brown skins, and all were very dangerous and unpredictable!

Is your Employer Mr Ibrahim Shiqaqi a Gentlemen?   Mother being British recognized the value of being a gentleman. Letters to Father were always addressed " Mr Frank Blackberry Esq"

She knew well that a gentleman's role in life was distinguished by honor, honesty, sound morals, and reliability . How could one be a gentleman if not brought up in England?

The possibility of a Second Holocaust is very real! The national papers say so. And the Jews should know having had first hand experience in Europe during the Second World War. These unfortunate people must be absolutely scared surrounded by hostile Arabs and hostile Arab Countries. I think you should return to England immediately.

You must not take any Risks! Your Father advises that the British Army has a large contingent in Palestine. Cannot you arrange them to provide protection?

Foreigners lack our education and civilization!

Mother's thinking no doubt was tainted by a life of experiences with unreliable Welsh " Never trust a Taffy",   rascals from Ireland " Never trust a Paddy", and no doubt many other scoundrels preying on innocent British.

I smiled, and showed Mother's letter to Roger.

" Here is evidence of the Zionist Propaganda machine"

Roger had some difficulty reading Mother's minute writing. However he rapidly realized the significance of Ben Gurion's propaganda   broadcast in British papers.

" Do you mind if I make a copy for Ibrahim?"

" Please go ahead. I can see that our work is cut out to defeat these lies."

Report - April 1948

Accra District	- No Reports
Baysan District	- Village expelled - (750) -Qumya, Al-Tira
Beersheba District	- No Reports
Gaza District	- Village attacked - (2,650) Barbara, Al-Majdal

Haifa District

- Village attacked - (12,500) -Abu Shusha, Ayn Ghazal, Ayn Hawd
-Al-Kasayir Khirbat, Al-Shuna Khirbat, - Al-Tira, Umm Al-Zinat

- Village expelled - (26,500) - Abu Zurayq **(6)**, Arab Al-Nufay'at
- Balad Al-Shaykh, Al-Damum Khirbat, - Arab Al-Fuqara,
- Al-Ghubayya, Al-Fawqa, Al-Tahta, Arab Zahraj, Atlit,
-Marj-ibn'Amir, Hansha, Al-Jalama, - Al-Rihaniyya
- Kabara, Al-Kafrayn, Lid-Khirbat, Yajur, ,Sa'Sa,
- Al-Mansi, Al-Naghnaghiyya, Qannir, Na'Arat al-Sarris
-Al-Dumayri, Barrat Qisarya, Byurayka

- Town expelled   - Haifa   (60,000)

Jaffa District

- Village attacked - (2,750) - Ranjiya, Al-Shaykh Muwannis

- Village expelled -   (30,000) -Bayt Dajan, Biyar'Adas, Migdal,
- Ijlil Al-Qibliyya, Ijlil Shamaliyya, Yazur,   -Salama, Saqiya,
- Kafr'Ana, Al-Khayriyya, Al-Safiriyya,Manshiyya, Al Qubab

- Town attacked   - Jaffa   (100,000)

Jerusalem District

- Village attacked - (2,900) -Al-Maliha, Nijaf, Suba
- Village expelled - (2,200) -Bayt Naqquba, Bayt Thul, Dayr Ayyub
- Dayr Yasin **(245)**, Qalunya, Al-Qastal, - Saris **(7)**

Jinin District

- Village attacked - (6,000) - Al-Lajjun, Umm Al-Fahm, Aqqaba,
- Ayn Abrahim, Khirbat Al-Buwayshat, - Mu'awiya **(12)**
- Murjafia, Mishayrifa, Mismis,

- Village expelled - (2,000)-   Ayn Al-Mansi, Zir'in
- Al-Naghwaghiyya

Report - April 1948

| Al-Ramla District | -*Village attacked - (8,400) -AbuShusha,DayrAyyne,Dayr Tarif* |

Al-Ramla District

> -*Village attacked - (8,400) -AbuShusha,DayrAyyne,Dayr Tarif*
> -*Al-Duwayriyya Khirbat, Al-Mansura,Qatra, Umm Kalkha*
> -*Al-Mukhayzin, Sarafand Al'Amar **(39)**, Sarafand Al-Kharab,*
>
> - *Village expelled - (4,800) -Al -Mukhayzin, Khulda, Saydun,*
> -*Wadi Hunayn*

Safad District

> - *Village attacked- (7,000) -AbilAl-Qamh,Biriyya **(20)**,*
> -*Dirdar-Hunin, Al-Ja'una, Al-Wayziyya,Khan Al-Dunayr,*
> - *Al-Khisis, Al-Manshiyya, Al-Mansura,*
> - *Al-Nabi Yusha, Qabba'a, Qaytiyya, Yarda,*
> - *Al Sanbariyya, Al-Shuna, Al-Urayfiyya*
> -
> - *Village expelled- (3,500) - Arab Al-Zubayd, Jubb Yusuf,*
> - *Karraza Khirbat, Kirad Al-Baqqara, Al-Ulmaniyya,*
> - *Kirad Al-Ghannama. Al-Malikiyya, Julayl, Madahil*
> -
> - *Town attacked - Safad (12,000)*

Tiberias District

> -*Village attacked -(2,500) -Awlah,Al-Dalhamiyya,Hadatha,*
> - *Yaquq,Ma'Dhar*
>
> -*Village expelled - (9,500) -Ghunayr Abu Shusha, Kafr Sabt,*
> - *Al-Nuqayb, Samakh, Al-Samra, Al-Wa'ra,*
> -*Al-Sawda Khirbat, Nasir Al-Din **(10)**,Al-Madjal*
>
> - *Town attacked - Tiberius (12,000)*

Tulkarm District

> - *Village attacked- (3,000) -Al-Jalama, Bayt Lid Khirbat*
> - *Fardisya, Ghabat Kafr SurQaqun,*
>
> - *Village expelled - (8,000) - Al-Manshiyya, Miska, Tabsur,*
> - *Qawuqji, Arab Al-Fuqara, Bayt Yerush'a,*
> - *Kefar Netter, Tel Yitzchaq,Zalafa*

Villages attacked	*143*
Towns attacked	*4*
Inhabitants attacked	*319,000*
Inhabitants expelled	*147,200*

Samiha

" Paul "

I looked up from my desk in the Jaffa office, and noted Roger's presence. His voice had that tone demanding immediate attention and concern.

" What is it? "

I imagine I sounded rather tense - work and life had been rather shattering, particularly my recent experience in Haifa.

" I would like you do me a great favor. A young lady will be here later today from the district of Haifa. I knew her family quite well. She has had a terrible experience recently, and needs understanding and comfort. I cannot assist - I think Freda would be upset if I took over that role. You know what women are like"

I nodded indicating my understanding of women - utterly ridiculous because I knew damn all. In fact I was rather scared of them. Regardless I was expected to assist and agreed with some reluctance.

" Alright - Don't think I am the ideal guy but will do my best"

Roger placed his hand on my shoulder.

" Thanks Paul - you are the ideal person. Please be very gentle with her. Avoid any discussion addressing the current Palestinian hostilities. Just allow her to talk if she so desires. Otherwise just keep her company and offer the comfort of your presence. "

Roger went to his office, and left me uncertain and concerned that I might not be ideal for this chosen role. Anyhow I was now committed. Late afternoon Roger entered with Samiha, and introduced the young woman to me.

" Paul. Meet Samiha. Samiha. Meet Paul. "

Roger then explained to me Samiha's role in the office.

" Samiha will assist you in the preparation of your reports "

Samiha smiled in an uncertain manner. She was a Palestinian Arab, perhaps 5'2" tall, of very slight build, and wearing the conventional Kheddiff. Perhaps not particularly striking on Western standards until one became aware of her eyes. Her eyes were so very beautiful and expressive. They expressed the loveliness of her soul - sadly not commonly observed in my world. I held out my hand, and shook her hand warmly.

" Samiha. I am so happy to meet you. We will be great friends. Would you like some coffee?"

She nodded. She was not talkative, and remained subdued. I thus took over the difficult role of an instructor unconcerned in having a silent student. Through my inexperience, some of the matters addressed became frozen in time as I desperately sought words and subject matter.

With some relief, Roger returned to announce that he would drive   Samiha to her new lodgings, and I was left to my own thoughts. It had been a rather difficult session - she was such a quiet subdued personality.   Hopefully she would be more talkative as she gained confidence.

It was late afternoon at the end of the week   Samiha was quietly sitting on the office sofa reading some information that had just arrived. She looked so lonely and forlorn. I had to do something to cheer her up. Summoning   courage I rose from my desk, walked across, and sat solidly at the other end of the sofa. I examined her sad face, and asked her in what I hoped was a sympathetic tone.

" Samiha. A penny for your thoughts."

She gazed down at her lap, tears welled in her eyes, her mouth tremored, and she began to sob. My heart was broken hearing her sad cries, and I moved across and placed my hand lightly on her arm.

" Please Samiha. Please do not cry "

She sobbed uncontrollably. Without any embarrassment I placed my arm around her shoulders, and gradually offered some comfort with my presence. We sat together quiet and close for many hours. Nothing was said. Her grief we shared   together with   the warmth and comfort of two lonely people.

Sometime the following week, Roger complimented me

" Wonderful Paul. Samiha appears far better settled. Your company is a good tonic for her."

" It is very pleasant having her in the office, but she is still very quiet and subdued."

" Yes "   Roger thoughtfully tapped his desk

" I had better tell you the facts. But please keep it to yourself. Samiha and her family lived in Sa'Sa not too far from Haifa. There was a massacre, and she witnessed the killing of her parents, brothers, and sister. Terrible affair. She certainly does not need to be reminded of the horrors of this country. Please be understanding and discrete."

Eventually Samiha shared her terrible experience with me. There was so little I could do.

Further hours were shared with my offering comfort and a desperate understanding of the unknown pains of a lonely tragic individual.

My graphic report of the Haifa exodus and tragedy was now complete.   I concealed the information from Samiha. Roger Standish examined the report with care, and made a number of notes.

" Life is getting dangerous!"

I had already advised Roger of my recent visit to As'Ad Kamal's apartment.

He continued and referred to the Zionist's Plan Dalet.

" That Plan Dadet formulated at the Red House is very much underway. Obviously their intention is to expel all Arabs from the Jewish State. And whilst Ben Gurion continues to claim the ever threatening presence of the Second Holocaust, the Zionists will continue to garner approval and sympathy from the rest of the World. And no doubt United Nations will not have the guts to refute these lies.

And whilst these lies are believed, the desire to expel the Arabs   will continue."

Roger leaned forward, elbows on the desk top, frowned in thought, and decided.

" Yes - I am sure that is their plan. And for them all is well provided the Truth is concealed from the West.   Now our latest reports in the U.K., the expulsion of tens of thousands, the murder, rape, looting, bombing, and the complete demolition of villages. All that is left is rubble and death. We have to accept that the Zionists will be very much aware of these adverse reports here and abroad. We will have to be very careful - no doubt the Jewish Security has been instructed to find those responsible for the reports"

I imagine that my face revealed some concern - I was the one preparing those reports.

Roger reassured me.

" Don' worry Paul. You are safe. You know nothing. All your reports have been sent out by Ibrahim's office, and there is no evidence that you are responsible. Your employment is through my invitation, and you are here to assist me. Now I want that state of affairs to remain unchanged. You know nothing. Truly you are not implicated - just an office stooge - let it remain like that. If you should ever be caught and questioned, they will realise that I am the individual that should be questioned. O.K.?"

" Is there anything I can assist this very moment?"

Roger shook his head.

" No Paul. You are doing a great job with your reports. Regarding your recent Haifa escapade, all is well. When they investigate the registration plate of the Volkswagen, they will not make any connection - the registered owner is a spook. "

He grinned imagining the frustrated faces of the Jewish Security.

" By the way, could I see your notes made in Haifa and a copy of your photograph. I would like to relate that information with your latest draft. "

I returned to my office and pulled out my pad from the project file. There was nothing on the pad, and examination of my other pads produced no evidence of my notes. I searched elsewhere with no success. It was puzzling but not particularly important - I would never forget those events.

I then retrieved my camera from my knapsack, called Samiha, and instructed her to take the camera to a local shop, and get a copy of the film printed. She returned later puzzled. The shop had opened the camera to retrieve the film, and discovered that there was no film!

I stared at my knapsack. My notes were missing, and the camera film no longer in the camera. There seemed to be only one explanation. That inspector and sergeant had stolen the items whilst I was being questioned by that judge.

" All that effort for nothing" I declared angrily

" Those thugs stole my notes and film, and made an absolute fool of me"

" Don't let it worry you" Roger comforted me

" This is an excellent reminder that we are dealing with some smart criminals. Pity about the film - however I will be getting other pictures. Now you and Samiha, please complete your work as soon as possible. I need to send off all our data for the month of April. "

Later that week I cheered up. My Ariel 500 motor cycle was delivered from the U.K.. It would be ideal for getting around villages and towns, and in particular the many narrow and crooked alleys and streets.

Conditions around Jaffa were deteriorating. Fifteen villages in the Jaffa district during April had been attacked, and 30,000 inhabitants expelled. The town of Jaffa with its 100,000 also attacked. Now in May more villages were threatened with attacks and expulsion.

I took the opportunity to drive around the district on my motorcycle, and record the destruction caused by the Haganah, Palmach, Irgun, and Stern gangs. Rapidly it was apparent that the inhabitants of neighboring Jewish settlements around Tel Aviv had also participated in the hostilities. In so many villages, there was little evidence of life and activity. The roads leading out of Jaffa full of refugees. There was no protection, no assistance, and no effort to stop the attacks.

And of course the district of Jaffa was not exceptional in April. Nearly 150 villages throughout Palestine had been attacked, and 150,000 expelled and fleeing to some unknown destination. Jaffa itself was relatively free of attacks, and we had the comfort of a 1,500 volunteer defense force.

There had to be relief from the   terrible news, however heartless it might appear. Man cannot dwell always on bad news.   Friday. Roger announced

"Let's have a party"

A few friends were invited. No alcohol was available in respect of our guests. But what a fantastic spread of national food, snacks., and coffee. A common Palestinian staple was rice, lamb *Samla*, yoghurt and dates *Thamra*. Another popular staple was olive oil, oregano (*Za'Atar)*, and bread. Grapes *Inab*,   Olives *Zitun*, Oranges *Burtuqal*, Butter *Zubda*, Honey *Asal*, Tomato *Tama Tim*, Mint *Na'Na*, and so much more.

Popular meals differed according to the District location. Thus in Galilee adjoining Lebanon a favorite was *Kibbee* comprising of Bulger, spice, and meat. In the mid districts of Palestine such as Jenin and Tulkarm the favorite was *Musakhan* (Roast chicken, oven *Taboon* bread *Khubz,* topped with fried sweet onions, sumac, allspice, and pine nuts). And in Gaza adjoining Egypt and the Mediterranean, fish *Samak* was extremely popular stuffed with Cilantro, garlic, red peppers, and cumin, with a marinated mix of coriander, red peppers, cumin, and chopped lemons.

The party was a great success. Dusk was rapidly approaching when the phone rang. I picked up the phone, and an urgent voice demanded .

" Roger please"

A few minutes later Roger returned with a urgent look. Quietly he advised everyone that we must leave the office building immediately, and that we should go to a apartment in a nearby street. Everyone stared at Roger with his unexpected news .Impatient he demanded.

" Hurry up everyone - this place is to be raided this evening"

" Are you sure?"

" Certain - quick everyone - get moving"

There was some confusion and a general commotion gathering our possessions, and we left by the back door. Within ten minutes we were entering the apartment two blocks away. Through all this unexpected excitement, I was unaware that Samiha was not with us. I looked around the apartment and enquired. No one had seen her.

Dark and silent, a jeep arrived and parked by the street curb opposite the office building. Inside the vehicle four soldiers were seated. Two men left the vehicle watched by their comrades, approached the entrance of a house, smashed down the door, and immediately sprayed the interior with gun fire.

There was a sharp crack of rifle fire from across the street. Momentarily one man stopped, and slumped to the sidewalk dying. The other, puzzled by this unexpected development, leant over to speak to the dying man. There was another rifle shot, and a second man lay slain on top of his comrade.

The driver Zvi and his companion, aghast at this unexpected retaliation, realized their danger, and quickly concealed themselves behind the jeep. Zvi whispered.

 " *There is someone in the upper floor of that office building. Tell you what. I will divert his attention, and you can get across the street, and deal with the bastard*"

Moshe nodded

" *Alright. Go ahead - distract his attention. I am ready*"

Zvi carefully placed his hat on the end of his rifle, and slowly exposed it above the Jeep hood. Immediately there was a bullet hole through that hat. The driver stared at that hole thoughtfully - that was great shooting in the dim street light.

Meanwhile Moshe had scurried across the street, stood by the office entrance, and signaled that he would enter the building. Zvi, rather excited about the success of his distraction, unwisely raised his head to watch Moshe enter the building. There was a sharp crack, and a bullet whined past his head.

It was clear that this sharp shooter was an excellent marksman. Moshe would need assistance. Zvi decided to crawl around the back of the jeep, and take a pot shot at the marksman. Grunting heavily and hugging the sidewalk, he slowly raised his rifle, and directed his line of fire at the assailant now appearing at the second floor window. As the driver fired, he in turn received a neat hole in his forehead, and abandoned all interest in further aggressive Zionist activities.

Zvi's bullet struck the marksman's left shoulder and shattered the bone. With blood running freely, the shoulder bone completely shattered, the sharp shooter slid down to the floor immediately beneath the window ledge. The injured body remained still, breathing heavily, conscious of agonizing pain and increasing weakness. The marksman strived to concentrate aware of someone ascending the main stairs and approaching the office entrance door.

With ever dimming eyes the marksman watched a Haganah trooper, large and heavy in physic, carefully enter the office with gun in hand. Moshe quickly assessed the situation. The marksman was hurt, and lay on the floor in the shadow of the window   with still eyes.

The trooper advanced with a leer.

" Well. Well my dear. You are just the kind of woman I like"

That cruel leering face remained unchanged as a rifle shot tore through Moshe's head, and he collapsed onto the floor.

Samiha, suffering intense agony, slowly rolled onto her right side to ease the pain in her injured shoulder. Her head lay hard against the floor, her teeth clenched, her eyes increasingly dim. She was feeling very weak, and her eyes partially glazed.

And then she saw her father and mother, her two brothers, and sister all anxiously beckoning. The room became dimmer and dimmer. The darkness of the Palestinian desert had arrived, and Samiha left to join her family free of the horrors of this inhuman world.

I did not sleep that night concerned about Samiha's absence. Despite the risk involved, I decided to check the office in the very early hours of the morning. Entering the back door, the building was dark, quiet, and deserted. Downstairs there was no evidence of Samiha. Wearily I climbed the stairs, and entered the front office. In my way lay the inert dead body of a Hagana trooper. And across the room close to the window lay Samiha.

I was too late. She had passed on to her parents. I grieved at the sight of her poor shattered body that I cherished. I grieved with the thought of her short unhappy life. I raised her into my arms and whispered to her *" Samiha. I wish you the happiness that you deserve. Happiness that was denied to you on Earth."*

Sadly I returned down the stairs carrying her light body. There was no difficulty conveying her to the apartment, and later that day I arranged for her burial. Samiha had departed, but would always be remembered.

The Desolation of Jaffa

Samiha's death devastated me. How I missed her sweet presence. I was unwilling to speak to anyone. How I hated the thugs responsible for her death, and the death of thousands of other innocent people. And how I despised the Zionists who supported these criminals, safe .and secure in their undeserved security in the USA and UK

Fortunately Samiha was now with her own people in peace free of these ghastly individuals. Mechanically I assisted Roger establish a new office in another part of Jaffa. The old office was a place to be avoided, and no doubt carefully watched by the Jewish Security.

And then our office suffered further. Roger fell sick. Initially it was assumed that he was just stressed and tired. But in fact it was Typhoid - possibly Roger picked up the germ in the town water supply. The medical authorities in Accra discovered that the city's water supply had been injected with Typhoid germs, and by the first week of May over 70 casualties had been reported, many of whom were British soldiers. In Gaza there was talk of both typhoid and dysentery virus in the water , and Jews had been apprehended infecting the water sources. There was now fear that the Jaffa water supply had been contaminated as well.

Roger passed away quietly. So tired, he wearily reminded me that the responsibility of all future reports and information was in my hands. Ibrahim would provide all necessary guidance. I held Roger's hand desperately hoping that he would survive, but it was not to be, and he passed on. There was little time to grieve.

Whilst attending to Roger, I received reports of Jewish troops marching through the streets of Tel Aviv celebrating the forthcoming Partition. It was a defiant open demonstration of aggressive strength with contempt of the UN declaration of a working economic partnership between Jews and Arabs.

On the 13th May 5,000 Irgun and Hagana troops attacked the city of Jaffa. Attacks had taken place well before this time but it had been assumed to be merely general hostility, and there had not been undue concern. There was a volunteer defense force of about 1,500. And of course the United Nation Referendum 181 declaration that Jaffa was to be shared equally by Arabs and Jews provided the people with a sense of confidence.

That confidence was rapidly shattered. The city was subjected to intense bombardment of 3" mortars, and barrel bombs consisting of drums of explosives and petrol, old vehicle tires fitted with detonating fuses rolled down from the surrounding hills that crashed and exploded into house walls and entrances.

Flames and explosions were accompanied by loudspeakers blaring out recordings of horror stricken souls, the agonizing shrieks, wails, moans of women, the whine of sirens and fire bells, and messages advising all Arabs to immediately flee for their lives. And these so called civilized thugs and criminals would repetitively send out messages reminding Arabs of the massacre of the 245 unfortunate inhabitants of Dayr Yasin in the Jerusalem District.

The city of Jaffa fell later in May, 50,000 were expelled, and despite British mediation, there were many scenes reminiscent of the Haifa exodus. Shelling, bombing, looting, and the firing of guns directed at the fleeing refugees took place. Loudspeakers with dreadful threats overwhelmed the demoralized people lacking organization and leadership. Wide eyed, haggard, panic stricken, the Arab population   fled.

I did not repeat my error in Haifa, and remained in the background unseen by the Jewish forces. Carefully I made notes and took photographs. May 14th, the State of Israel was declared, and within hours or possibly minutes Harry Truman President USA announced his country's recognition of the Israel State. Despite Washington's claim to fight for freedom and democracy, and despite so much trouble in the world,   there was space on Truman's desk to support a Terrorist State.

One of the last reports received was the attack and expulsion of Al-Tantura a village of about 1600, located on the coast about 20 miles south of Haifa. A Haganah Brigade, responsible for the attack, massacred 200 young men. Soon I realized that I also must flee. How fortunate I had the motor cycle. Rapidly I arranged the closing down of our new office, collected all my papers, records, and notes, packed my haversack, and planned my route to Jerusalem.

I decided that it would be far too dangerous to travel on the main highway from Jaffa to Jerusalem through the district of Al-Ramla, now under control of Jewish forces. I decided to take a circular route south of Jaffa to Al-Magdal, cross over east to Al-Falaja, Bayn Jibin, then Hebron, and finally north to Jerusalem. Once I was clear of the proposed Jewish State, I would travel over the hilly districts of the Arab State hopefully in relative safety.

Sadly my memories include hearing in the vicinity of the Hasan Bek Mosque the haunting calls of the minarets reminding all to pray. Now there was no one to pray - all had left. Grimly I started the Ariel, put it in gear, and commenced my exodus.

Ridng out of Jaffa, I saw much looting by Jewish settlers on city streets. Despite living in Jaffa a mere six months, that sight was extremely upsetting. I had become attached to a city reflected by Arab, Ottoman, and British civil development. My memories would always include a lovely boulevard which had the impressive colonial post office, the law courts, the many cafes and coffee houses. And always the huddles of Arabs busy discussing the day's news and scandals.

I passed by the Palace of Justice dynamited by the Irgun and Haganah, and grimly shook my head. Just imagine sixty young people under the care of the Social Services Department were killed by thugs that desired simply to terrorize innocent and defenseless people.

Extremely depressed, I traveled on, and never looked back.

Report - May 1948

Accra District	- *Villages expelled- (13,200) -AlBassa,KhirbatMa'Sub,* - *Al-Ghabisiyya, Al-Kabri, Al-Manshiyya, Al-Damum* - *Al-Nahr, Al-Sumayriyya, Altall, Umm Al-Farat, Al-Zib,* - - *Town expelled - Accra (10,000)*
Baysan District	- *Village expelled- (10,000) -At least 28 Villages* - *Town expelled - (4,000) -Baysan*
Beersheba District	- *Village expelled- (Number ?)-Al-Janmama*
Gaza District	- *Village attacked- (1,850) - Iraq Sunaydan, Julis* - *Village expelled- (19,000) -Arab Suqrir, Barqa,Al-Batani* - *Al-Batani al-Gharbi, Bayt Daras, Burayr, Al-Sharqiyya,* - *Huj, Hulayqat, Kawfakha, Kawkaba, Al-Sawafir al-Gharbiyya,* - *Al-Muharraqa, Najd, Al-Shamaliyya, Simsim, Bashshit,* -*Al-Sharqi*
Haifa District	- *Village attacked- (14,000) -Ayn Ghazai, Ayn Hawd, Ijzim, Jaba* - *Al-Mawara Khirbat, Al-Mansura Khirbat, Al-Tira, Wadi'ara* - *Village expelled- (5,000) -Khubbayza, Qannir, Umm Al-Zinat* - *Al-Sawamir, Al-Shuna Khirbat, Qumbaza Khirbat,* - *Al-Tantura* **(200),**
Hebron District	- *No Reports*
Jaffa District	- *Villages expelled- (13,500) -Al'Abasiyya, Abu Kishk, Fajja,* - *Al-Harrah, Al-Sawalima, Tall Al-Rish, Al-Shaykh Muwannis* - - *Town expelled - (70,000) - Jaffa* **(60)**
Jerusalem District	- *Villages attacked- (2,500)- Al-Maliha, Nitaf, Dayr Ayyub* - *Villages expelled- (2,650)- Bayt Mahsir*
Jinin District	- *Villages attacked- (2,200)- Nuris, Zir'n* - *Villages expelled - (Number ?)- AlJawfa Khirbat*
Nazareth District	- *Villages attacked- (4,775)- Saffuriyya* - *Villages expelled- (675) - Indur*

Report - May 1948

Al- Ramla District	*- Villages attacked- (8,300)- Bayt Nabala, Al-Latrun, Al-Qubab*
	- Al-Qubayba, Al-Tira
	- Villages expelled- (19,300)- Al-Shusha, Aqir, Bashshit, Bayt Jiz
	- Bayt Susin, Bir Salim, Dayr Ayyub, Bayt Dajan, Sarafand
	- Al-Maghar, Al Na'Ani.Qatra, Zarnuqa, - Al-Amar,
	- Sarafand al-Kharab, Zakariyya Khirbat
Safad District	*- Villages attacked- (2,000) - Kafr Bir'im, Salima*
	- Villages expelled- (29,500) -Abil Al-Qamh, Al'Abisiyya, Akbara,
	-Ammuqa, Aab Al-Shamalina, Biriyya, Al-Al-Shawka, Al-Tahta,
	*- Ayn Al-Zayjun **(70)**, Baysamun,Fir'im, Al-Shuna, Taytaba,*
	- Al-Butayha, Al-Buwayziyya, Dallata, Al-Urayfiyya, Yarda,
	- Al-Danwara, Al-Dirdara, Ghuraba, Al-Wayziyya, Al-Zahiriyya,
	- Al-Hamra, Harrawi, Hunin, Jahula, Al-Sanbariyya,
	- Al-Khisas, Khiyah Al-Walid, Lazzaza, Al-Tahta,
	- Mallaha, Al-Manshiyya, Al-Mansura, Al Zanghariyya, Al-Zawiya,
	- Marus, Mirun, Al-Muftakhira, Qadas, Al-Zuq
	- Mughr Al-Khayt, Al-Nabi Yusha, Al-Fawqani, Al-Zuq Al-Tahtani
	- Al-Na'Ima, Qabba'a, Qaddita, Qayjiyya,
	- Al-Qudayriyya, Al-Salihiyya, Al-Sammu'i,
	- Town expelled- (12,000) - Safad
Tiberias District	*- Villages expelled- (6,600)- Awlam, Al-Dalhamiyya, Hadatha,*
	- Ma'Dhar, Al-Mansura, Samakh, Yaquq,
	*- Al-Samakiyya, Al-Shajara **(2)**, Al Tabigha*
	- Town expelled - Tiberius (12,000)
Tulkarm District	*- Villages expelled- (4,000) Al-Talama, Kafr Saba, Qaqun,*
	- Qalqilya, Al-Zababida Khirbat
	* -*
	- Town expelled - Tulkarm (Number ?)

Villages attacked	*188*
Towns attacked	*6*
Inhabitants attacked	*279,000*
Inhabitants expelled	*243,400*

The Correspondent is Hunted

" Who is it?" demanded the watchman, secure behind the locked door within Ibrahim's house.

There was concern in the man's voice. And why should not he be concerned. During May over 220,000 people had been expelled in Palestine due to Jewish attacks. Admittedly only four villages at that time had been attacked and 2,000 expelled in the Jerusalem district. But in these days, any statistic, however trivial, provided little comfort.

I gave my Code number and Password, and was admitted within.

Ibrahim's servant grasped my hand warmly, and advised.

" Times are very troubling Master Paul "

The motor cycle was safely stored in the courtyard. When I re entered the house, a very anxious Ibrahim welcomed me. He had learnt of Roger's death and was very upset by the news. I described briefly the death of Samiha. Also the Jewish Security's awareness of our old Jaffa address. And finally the sad desolation of Jaffa, and the expulsion of its Arab population.

Ibrahim listened carefully absorbing all my information, and sighed.

"Well. Well. Well. It is wonderful seeing you again Paul. Your Reports have been excellent. The world will learn the Truth. You must be tired. Have a meal, and early to bed. We can speak tomorrow."

I collapsed in my bed - the stress never knowing if I might be subjected to a hostile attack or interrogation at a check point throughout my journey had worn me out. And of course throughout the day, I had been exposed to the extreme heat of the Summer sun.

At breakfast, Ibrahim smiled wryly.

" You are now our #1 Correspondent so your future information of these terrible events will be invaluable. At this moment the Jews have agreed to a U.N. truce - as you no doubt appreciate such an agreement is meaningless. They will continue to attack, kill, and destroy whenever they wish regardless of the so called truce.

My people are confronted with a terrible disaster. About 390,000 innocent people have been uprooted, expelled to foreign countries, and their property real and personal stolen. If those poor people were lined in single file, that line would be well over 80 miles. Just imagine. 80 miles of homeless, hungry individuals with many falling sick and dying during their tragic flight.

We must continue to feed our clients with the truth, and hopefully raise world concern."

His rather grim voice softened.

" By the way, a good friend will visit you this morning. So please do not go roaming around the city."

" A friend?" I was puzzled, and agreed to remain indoors.

Ibrahim was occupied with his business. I decided to examine the motor cycle which was leaking a little oil. The cause, I discovered, was the connecting nut attached to a short oil supply pipe. I had experienced a similar leak in England probably caused by engine vibration. Anyhow it did not take long to find the problem joint, disconnect, clean, and reinstal.

I started the engine, allowed it to run for a few minutes, and to my disgust the leak occurred again at the same joint. Again the joint was dismantled and reinstalled, and it continued to leak. I now suspected that the supply pipe was slightly off center. Finally the problem was resolved. Whilst contemplating my mechanical repair, there was a light tap by my side. I looked up. It was lovely Ghada.

She gave me a fond kiss on the cheek. I in turn a great hug. How wonderful to see her again. I followed her as she entered her father's house, and we sat talking until mid day.

" You are so much thinner" she declared with motherly concern

" You have not been eating properly"

Naturally I denied that was the cause. With a grin, I suggested that I was thin due to being chased all over the countryside by Jewish Security.

Ghada's face clouded.

" I have heard all about your visit to Haifa. You must stop exposing yourself to danger. Now you have that dangerous motor cycle."

She shook her head in disapproval.

The mid day meal was such a pleasure conversing with Ghada and her father. I felt very much a part of the family. Immediately afterwards Ghada returned to her home with the promise to return soon.

During the afternoon, I checked with Ibrahim to ensure that he had received all the May information and reports. Due to Roger's illness, I was uncertain what had been mailed to Jerusalem. My next itinerary also needed to be planned.

I decided that the districts of Tiberias and Safad should be surveyed. Ten villages had been attacked and the people expelled in the district of Tiberias. There had been a massacre at Al-Shajara , and according to reports 20 had been killed. Regarding the district of Safad, it seemed difficult to believe but 50 to 60 villages had suffered attacks, 29,500 inhabitants expelled, the town of Safad with 12,000 expelled, and the terrible massacre of 70 at Ayn Al-Zayjun.

Fortunately there was a reduction of attacks, presumably due to the truce, although one suspected that the truce was simply an opportunity for the Jewish troops to recover after over extending themselves. Regardless this seemed a good opportunity to investigate whilst the countryside remained relatively quiet.

Ibrahim listened to my proposed survey cautiously. He was of two minds. His clients in England were demanding more first hand reports - the Haifa report had been received favorably, and more of a similar caliber desired. The reverse side of the coin was exposing me to unnecessary danger.

" Let me think about your proposal. The risks of being apprehended are ever increasing. We will discuss your ideas tomorrow."

Ibrahim pondered and pondered. The latest first hand information was required. But the country was swarming with Jewish troops, settlers, spies, and informers. And Paul's disguise would not succeed under close examination. His correspondent was far too English in appearance.

Fortunately Paul was proposing visiting two districts with fairly small populations and few local Jews. Perhaps the survey was worth the risk.

Finally Ibrahim made his decision.

" I suggest Paul that your survey is confined to interviewing witnesses of the massacres at Ayn Al-Zayjun and Al-Shajara. Please make sure that your witnesses are reliable and not prone to exaggeration. Then regarding the rest of the villages, perhaps in general drive by all those who's inhabitants had been expelled. Get a general sense of the scene, take some photographs, but don't make unnecessary enquiries."

But his decision was not final . He was still uneasy.

" Let me see you in your proposed disguise mounted on your motorcycle"

He stared with extreme doubt at his transformed Correspondent - unfortunately far too English in appearance but perhaps might be adequate. The motorcycle clean and immaculate. He shook his head.

" Your motorcycle Paul. It must appear dirty and unwanted - no Arab vendor would bother to maintain his machine in its current condition. It is far too clean and bright."

" Did you say Arab vendor?"

Ibrahim explained.

" Under no circumstance will I permit you to go on your own. You are in a strange country, and your appearance puts you at risk. What I propose is that you will be a deaf and dumb vendor of dates and figs. My grandson Amin will be your guide and spokesman. He is acquainted with the Northern districts."

I protested..

" Ibrahim - I do not think it wise placing your grandson at risk."

He agreed.

" Certainly it is a risk, but not comparable to allowing you to travel around the districts on your own. And I think it important that Amin has a first hand experience of the sorrows of his fellow people."

A week later the Ariel 500 roared to life, battered and dirty, and conveyed a very deaf and dumb vendor, his handsome assistant Amin, and a supply of dates and figs towards to the north and Galilee.

It was agreed that they would visit the Safe Houses of Tiberias and Safad. The elderly proprietor and his daughter Ghada watched silently as we departed. They looked at each other with deep concern.

" You know my dear, I have my fears. There are so many treacherous individuals who without compunction will inform for money. That young man is rather innocent of such matters"

He held his daughter tightly. Life was becoming very difficult.

In the crowded London suburb of Clapham Common, and in particular within a small shabby terrace house, a meeting was held. The four men present were hard faced unscrupulous individuals. One of their group *Eliah* , holding in his hand a copy of the *Guardian*, a well respected newspaper that prided itself in accurate unbiased news, brought to their attention a front page headline that spoke volumes.

" Haifa Massacre - whole population 60,000 Arabs expelled, Unfortunate inhabitants, completely defenseless, were subjected to bombing, mortar shelling, machine gun attacks, and looting. Many killed in subsequent panic and fear "

The editorial discussed in depth the very vivid and horrifying description of these unfortunate panic stricken Arabs attacked as they fled trying to board overloaded boats in the harbor. It concluded that it was a damning account that completely contradicted the absurd Jewish claims that the Arabs were leaving Palestine voluntarily under their free will.

Eliah growled. " *Get a few more headlines and pictures, and all the sympathy that we Zionists desire in this country and America regarding the threat of a Second Holocaust will go up in smoke.*

He looked around at his companions, and stressed the obvious.

"All these reports have got to be stopped immediately. Any ideas how we can put a stop, and discover the source of all these reports?"

Harry, a particularly sly individual, thought it over, and volunteered a solution.

" *Should be easy. Contact some of those London newspaper reporters - they will know where that information is coming from. Mind you the information is probably confidential. However a drunken tongue has often been known to be reckless. "*

" *That seems a sound idea. Anyone else have any ideas?"*

For the rest of that evening the men discussed Harry's suggestion.

The " *Fox and Grapes"* located on St Paul's Quay off Fleet Street first opened in the 19th Century is little different to thousands of similar establishments throughout England. Those familiar of such establishments call them *" Pubs"*

Within the Pub the prevailing disgusting smell of stale beer and stale cigarettes dominates, a fact that is oblivious to the regular customers The scene is conventional with the usual dark wood counter and stools for the regulars, dark wood small tables and chairs for the formal businessman and the elderly, bottles and posters representing every conceivable drink, mirrors behind the counter that reflect the rather dim light and select products, a bored barman with his artificial tone of joviality who has heard everything repeated a thousand times, and finally his customers *the regulars.*

Why the pub's customers are *regulars* is a troublesome question, and probably an adequate answer would not be available. It is just the place that such individuals *constantly* visit day after day, week after week, month after month, year after year, and that feature alone would be considered an adequate explanation.

Why should there be any other reason? The solid bar man, the very solid bar counter, and the bar stools witness a constant flow of customers from late morning to late evening. Some sit at the small tables confidential in talk, but most stand in small groups earnest in discussion, quiet at the commencement, and often a lot louder later.

The subject of discussion might commence with some gravity and importance, but often becomes less serious in time and increasingly raucous. The ability of customers to stand vertical and think clearly tends to deteriorate as time goes by.

Regardless the *Fox and Grapes* has its *regulars* who would never consider going to a different pub. This was their second home - for some possibly their primary abode. Without thought, a regular would be assumed to turn up on a daily basis. However if one spoke to the pub owner Jack Jackson, we would be advised that there is a wide range of *regulars* , and many working for local firms would more likely turn up on a weekly basis. For example he would speak of a group of Reporters for the *Guardian,* very respectable people, with the world's affairs at their fingertips, always come in late Friday afternoon.

Funny how one remembers certain things. Jack Jackson scratched his head tackling that very tricky subject. of one's mind.

" I will always remember that Friday. You see the Guardian group normally have 2-3 drinks, and hang around for 1 to 2 hours, and then tool off for their home and dinner. But this Friday some of the group remained for 2-3 hours, and no doubt had 4-5 drinks, and were quite talkative. There was one guy, a stranger dark and swarthy, foreign type, who was the life and soul of the party buying round after round"

Now that is the recollection of the pub owner who obviously tends to connect everything from a commercial perspective. What of the Reporters of the *Guardian,* many of whom were severely chastised by their cross spouses and punished with cold dinners. As Reporters of a highly reputable newspaper, their memory should have been exemplary. And yet their memories were hazy dulled by excessive alcohol and cigarette smoke.

It was agreed that a foreign character joined their group because he bought a number of rounds. All assumed that he was a business acquaintance of someone in the group, but to whom he was acquainted remained a mystery. Someone had the impression that he worked for some Middle East Company, but all was vague.

Perkins remarked that this character was impressed with the reporting skills of the Guardian. Modestly everyone down played their great skills to which this guy pulled out a copy of their paper.

" Look at this great report on your front page - really first class reporting"

Having consumed four or more drinks, some reporters had difficulty focusing their eyes to identify this claimed masterpiece. Regardless of this difficulty, it was agreed that the title was *"Haifa Massacre"*

This foreign character now quite excited demanded.

" Now who of you was responsible for this excellent report? "

For a moment there was silence, then an awkward chuckle.

" Not us chum. Think that came from our special correspondent in Jerusalem"

The stranger interjected with excitement

" This is one bloody great report - your man is the best. I sure would like to make his acquaintance when I return - what a writer."

He looked around at the group, and asked.

" Anyone know how I can contact him? "

No one had any idea - apparently collecting reports from special correspondents was not in their field. However Perkins, eager to demonstrate his superior knowledge, blurted out

" This might help - his name is Ibrahim, and his office is in Jerusalem"

The foreign looking guy definitely bought another round that night. And it is believed that he declared.

" Here's to successful hunting "

But that ambiguous declaration was very hazily remembered.

It was quite warm, a reminder of the extreme heat of the Summer sun. Initially as we made our way north to Tiberias, Amin, unaccustomed to a motor cycle, held on to me very tightly. Slowly he relaxed as his confidence increased.

There was no urgency as we passed through the districts of Ramallah and Nablus on the main road adjoining River Jordan. Just as well because the road was packed with fleeing refugees.

I was conscious of being observed, and slowly realized my chosen route was a grave error. The level plains adjoining the River Jordan had been designated part of the Jewish State. No doubt many with that knowledge now viewed any Arab with curiosity and possible hostility.

I explained the situation to Amin, and proposed a fresh route.

" I think we will take the Nablus road through the hills "

Amin directed me to a country road that went through the hills to Ramallah, and from there we continued to Nablus and Jinen. When we approached the district of Baysan, I told Amin that we would visit the village of Al-Ashrafiyya about 2 ½ miles southwest of the town of Baysan.

The Golani Brigade attacked this village and some surrounding villages mid May, and expelled the inhabitants. Then the Haganah sent in sappers to blow up the village houses. I had expected an empty village, but did not anticipate the desolation and destruction. All houses had been bombed and demolished. Amin was mortified. He had not imagined such senseless destruction.

We gazed at the ruins so reminiscent of the London ruins caused by the German V2s. There was literally nothing but rubble - a few broken toys - cars with shattered windows, and silence. Occasionally the odd stray dog would be seen examining the remains no doubt bewildered like the villagers of this total lack of humanity - another major moral crime against all.

I called to an emaciated mongrel nosing around the ruins. The poor animal looked up and made a forlorn whine. There was something tied to its neck. I called again. At that very moment I heard a warning command .

" Don't"

Amin and I , unaware of others, turned. The individual a ragged Arab with a rifle. In a flash he stood in front of us facing the poor dog and fired. There was an instant explosion. The man turned, faced us, and spoke harshly.

" Take great care my friends - those bastards have placed booby traps and hidden mines in every village - stand well away or you will become another statistic"

We were shaken realizing the enormity of the crime, and our close brush with death. Both Amin and I thanked the man for saving our lives. He shrugged.

" It is our duty to ensure that as many of us as possible survive. All will have evidence of the terrible crimes of the Jewish people. Just imagine at this poor village - a few hundred innocent defenseless rural peasants who have never caused any harm - now expelled, killed, tortured, raped, their property looted and stolen. "

He was a Volunteer from Syria, thin, strong, and resolute.

" One day this scourge will be wiped off the Earth"

He ended his statement spitting forcibly.

It suddenly dawned on me - where did he suddenly appear from? I asked.

He smiled grimly.

" You will not live long if you do not keep well concealed. I was aware of your presence immediately. Take care my friends. Take great care."

And with an after thought, he advised.

" Keep to the hills - the designated Palestinian Arab State. It is safer than the Jewish State. And God keep you"

And within moments, so it appeared, he had melted into the landscape.

I had taken a photograph, and the memory of Al-Ashrafiyya would never be forgotten. I instructed Amin

" Let's get going Amin "

We took great care crossing the low valley of Mari Ibn'Amir, and passed by Nazareth and Mount Tabor as we swung east to Tiberias. Finally we descended the central hills, and entered the town of Tiberias. Fortunately Amin was well acquainted with the town, and he directed me to the Safe House. The sun was descending yet the temperature still very high. Both of us were exhausted as I advised the guardian of the entrance door of my number and password.

The owner had plenty to discuss. Over a dozen villages had been attacked, and 6.600 expelled during May. The town had also been attacked. The village of Hittin population about 1,200 had been attacked, their men repulsed the attackers who appeared to have come from the Jewish settlement of Mitzpa. Now Hitin and the two small villages of Lubya and Nimrin are subject to attacks by the Jewish Seventh Brigade.

But what was very much on the mind of all was the dreadful massacre of twenty at the village of Al-Shajara not far from Lubya. Everyone was dismayed and disheartened. Great caution had to be taken outside one's home. The British had already gone - not that they offered much security when they were there. And there was the ever increasing hostility of the Jewish people.

I explained the purpose of my survey - to visit villages that had suffered expulsion, and hopefully speak to a witness of the Al-Shajara massacre. I was advised to speak to Hajj Abd Allah who saw it all.

For   part of the week, I cautiously visited some of the villages expelled in May. The scene everywhere one of desolation and emptiness. It was so eerie and silent, the solitary rag waving in the wind , the rubble lying in excellent fertile land that had been farmed for generations, fertile land that was coveted by the local Jews.

Nasir Al-Din, a small village set 2 miles south of Tiberias suffered attacks and expulsion 11th and 12th April. Platoons of the Golani Brigade based in the Jewish Quarter of Tiberias entered the village of about 100. All the houses were destroyed, and at least ten men, women, and children were killed. No doubt this killing deeply demoralized the population in the town of Tiberias.. Now there is nothing but desolation.

By the end of the week, we had visited many attacked villages. Occasionally we were shot at by Jewish soldiers, warning shots assumed to intimidate us. It made little sense making a full survey with the risks involved. Next on my agenda was to interview the witness of the Al-Shajara massacre.

Al-Shajara, with a population of about 850 was located on the eastern slope facing Tiberias. In Arabic Al-Shajara meant *" The Tree"* . The village during the times of the Crusaders was known as Seiera. Crops included wheat, barley, olives and fruits. Within the orchards beehives, figs and olives. The stone built village comprised of clusters of homes and an elementary school.

The witness was a relative of a family that used to live in the village. According to him the first attacks by the Haganah took place in February and two houses were blown up. He, a very gaunt desperate looking man, had visited his relatives 6th May when the Haganah, the Golani Brigade, made a fierce major attack early dawn.

" Over twenty villagers were killed that day, and everyone else fled. " he claimed.

" A few of us tried to defend the houses - but it was hopeless for a few disorganized villagers attacked unexpectedly early morning in the dark. What could we do against a large number of ruthless thugs that suddenly attacked us?"

He paused to recollect his thoughts, and related his final recollections.

" They destroyed my relation's house, and many other buildings. I know the people in the nearby Jewish settlement wanted our land"

The unfortunate man shook his head in despair.

" How can God allow such greed and inhumanity?"

I had no answer.

The following morning we said goodby to our friends in the Safe House. They knew not what was their future, and simply hoped that they would be permitted to remain. We were warned to take great care and preferably keep to the hills. Amin and I mounted the faithful Ariel, slowly made our way to Al-Shajara, and took two photographs. Already wild vegetation was taking over amongst the ruins of the demolished houses.

We then entered the hills. Unknown to us, our presence had already been noted by Jews in the nearby settlements. Due to our circuitous route through the hills, our journey from Tiberias to Safad was about 40 miles. We had the whole day, and there was no obligation to hurry. The district of Safad, the most northern district of Palestine bordering Syria and Lebanon, had suffered many attacks during May. About 60 villages had been attacked and 30,000 inhabitants expelled. And it was claimed that the town of Safad had been attacked and people expelled.

Cautiously we approached a district within which perhaps 75% of the villages had been deserted.. Fortunately Amin was well acquainted with the district, and proved indispensable. He knew his way around Safad, and rapidly we arrived at the Safe House. Were our people still there? With some trepidation I knocked at the entrance door, quoted my password and number, and we were permitted within the security of its walls.

The family at the Safe House, rather like those at Tiberias, were despondent and in despair. The district of Safad was included in the proposed Jewish State, and already the Jews were determined to rid the district of all Arabs. Perhaps the western part of the district in the hills, being part of the Palestinian State, might be secure from attacks, but there was little confidence. Heads constantly shook with despondent thoughts - their fate seemed sealed.

I planned to make a general survey, similar to Tiberias, of the attacked villages. My hosts shook their heads with concern. It was too dangerous with Jewish troops and settlers everywhere. However when I mentioned that I would like to speak to a witness of the Ayn Al-Zaytun massacre, that was solved very simply. An individual staying at the Safe House had witnessed the massacre, and was able to provide me with a wealth of information.

He explained that the village of about 1,200 Muslims was set on the western slopes of Wadi Al-Dilb which adjoined the main highway leading into the city of Safad. Ayn Al-Zaytun *Spring of the Olives* was a stone constructed village surrounded with arable land, and had a school and a mosque. Olives, grapes, fruit, and grain was grown dependant on rainfall, whilst domestic water needs were met by a well half a   mile to the north.

" *Yes* " sighed the witness.

" *Zionist forces attacked the village early January, killed one villager, and bombed four houses. Then a major attack took place 1st May by the Palmach troops. They attacked 3.am in the morning with a barrage of mortar fire. There were many mortars. The troops entered the village, and rounded us all up. Just imagine our panic with this taking place in the early dark hours.*

The men were separated from the women and children. 37 Men were selected, and I understand were massacred in a group of 70 in a gulley nearby. I learnt afterwards that Moshe Kelman, commander of Palmach's Third Battalion, ordered the massacre. He had difficulty finding men to commit the atrocity, and finally it is claimed two men undertook the killing in cold blood. All the houses were burnt and blown up. This terrible disaster naturally frightened everyone living in Safad."

I had difficulty understanding the unfortunate man who broke down weeping - relatives had been murdered - and he was desolate. I shut my eyes momentarily - then tried to comfort the poor man. What can one say? I had not been brought up with experiences of such unbelievable cruelty. I lacked the education to countenance the misery and the ability to comfort. That is if it is possible to offer suitable comfort from such horrible memories.

We remained in Safad a week - cautiously we visited a few villages all empty and destroyed. During the survey, we approached the village of Ayn Al-Zaytun, the scene of the massacre. There was little to see other than rubble and the odd jagged wall pointing to the sky.

Seated with Amin at the Safe House, I pondered over our next survey. I examined the May reports for Accra District. About 12 villages had been attacked and the people expelled. And the City of Accra's population had been subjected to Typhoid   due to the intentional contamination of the water supply. I asked Amin.

" Are you prepared to visit the district of Accra before we return to Jerusalem?"

Amin grinned and nodded. It was a great adventure which would be remembered for ever.   So it was agreed, and the following day we said farewell to our hosts. They shook their heads learning of our plans which they thought most unwise. It was understood that Accra had been attacked and the people expelled. To visit the Safe House in Accra most unwise.

Despite the understood need to have first hand information, the head of the Safe House possessed a most solemn face, the risks considerable, and wished us God's Speed.

" Take great care young men - you are dealing with merciless killers "

In an austere office illuminated by bare electric bulbs, two men were huddled planning. Inspector Mendlesohn scowled as he jotted down some recent received reports. He looked up and asked Sergeant Gerber.

" My dear Sergeant - do you remember that slimy Englishman dressed in Arab clothing?"

" You mean the one we lost track of in Tulkarm?"

" Precisely Sergeant.   Precisely"

Mendlesohn leaned back with some satisfaction.

" This will interest you. I have reports from Baysan, Tiberia, and Safad of two young men on a motorcycle making surveys and taking photographs of numerous villages. Now they are heading for Accra today. Could you imagine who they are?"

Mendlesohn did not need an answer from his assistant to that question. He was certain that it was the same Englishman. This time there would be no mistake.

" Sergeant. Instruct Accra to report immediately these two are seen on a motorcycle. I plan to have a long quiet interrogation of that Paul Blackberry. That man, I am certain, is responsible for these unfavorable reports in the newspapers in England. This will be his last venture"

The villages attacked and expelled in May , eleven in number, were all located within 10-20 miles of Accra. I proposed to Amin that we should be able to survey the whole lot within a single day if we commenced early.

The village of Al-Damum was the first on the schedule, followed by Al-Manshiya, just outside Accra, and then Al-Sumayriyya. Soon after leaving Al-Sumayriyya, Amin tapped me on the shoulder, and spoke urgently into my ear.

" Paul. I think we are being followed"

I quickly glanced at the rear mirror. Amin was correct. I accelerated on the country road, and noted that the Mercedes had also accelerated. It remained on our tail. We were being followed.

I am not exactly a motorcycle ace, and speeds above 75   were above my prudent skill. Now we were rapidly approaching Umm Al-Jarat - I had to lose the following car. Abruptly I turned off, continued on some country roads., and passed through the villages of Al-Jall, Al-Namr, Al-Ghabisiyya, and Kuwaykat. Relentless the Mercedes followed.

Desperate, I realized that I would not shake off the pursuers remaining on paved country roads. Kuwaykat, a small village of about 1,100, was surrounded by extremely fertile land well stocked with dense orchards of Olives. Approaching the central market square, I quickly drove off down a very narrow alley - far too narrow for the Mercedes. Rapidly I drove out into the Olive orchards, and quickly we and the motorcycle were concealed. For the rest of the day we remained hidden. At one uncomfortable moment late afternoon, there was I imagine a search party driving around the neighborhood, but we managed to remain secure.

What would be our next move? I proposed to Amin that we take off early tomorrow morning before the whole neighborhood was subjected to intense searches. I now realized that two young men on a motorcycle would attract the immediate attention of many searching and aware of   that precise format.

" First I propose we walk about 2 miles out of this village - then drive to Al-Birwa, and then to Safad as fast as possible. If we start   before the sun rises, the distance of 25 miles should be covered within an hour or so. "

Amin agreed - my plan made sense. The Jewish Security hopefully would still be in bed early morning. There would be no need to turn on the motorcycle headlights once dawn approached. Provided we remained quiet walking between here and   Al- Birwa, and then continued around the outskirts of Al-Birwa, all should be well.

We could just identify the outline of the eastern hills that gave evidence of the early morning sun. Already we had commenced our trudge across fields pushing a heavy reluctant motorcycle. Fortunately it was still cool, and within 45 minutes we had arrived at a country road well away from curious ears. The engine was kick started, and we were off. Taking care and driving slowly 20-25 mph, the Ariel made little noise.

As we approached the outskirts of Al-Birwa, we carefully circumvented around the village. Unaware, we were observed by an early riser in a nearby Zionist settlement. That observer was well aware of an urgent search and general warning of   a couple of criminals on a motorcycle. Within 10 minutes Inspector Mendlesohn received a message - the motorcycle and riders had been seen at Al-Birwa!

The inspector gazed at a map. True it would not take long to get to Al-Birwa. But why not give their air force some target practice as well.

Within half an hour, we were riding rapidly along the Safad main highway, and approaching the narrow valley, hemmed in with high hills on   both sides, that led to Safad.

Initially we were oblivious of impending events. At that very moment Inspector Mendlesohn with Sergeant Gerber as driver was hurtling down the main highway 8 miles behind but rapidly catching up. And 5,000 feet above, an Israeli Spitfire was searching the highway for a solitary motorcycle.

As we entered the narrow winding valley, we suddenly realized that a Mercedes was catching up with us at a considerable speed. Immediately I increased the speed of the motorcycle - so much more adaptable to narrow acute bends than a large Mercedes. On both sides steep hills rising 1,500 to 2,000 feet above the road. What took us by surprise was the appearance of a fighter surveying the highway about 1,500 feet above which occasionally fired its guns to no avail.

We had no difficulty remaining well ahead of the Mercedes due to the nature of the winding road. However finally the valley opened out into the approaching plain, and now both the pursuing car and the fighter were in a better position to attack. Inspector Mendlesohn leaned out of the passenger front window, and opened fire at us.

The fighter now made an determined attack approaching us head on at low level with the intention of straffing the highway. I skidded off the road as the machine guns chattered, and bullets whined past us. The Mercedes lay in the path of the fighter attack, and was struck by many bullets. As we watched from the ditch, the car burst into flames. Sergeant Gerber lay dead, and Inspector injured and burnt.

We recovered from the road ditch, dirty, grazed, and bruised. Astride again the motor cycle, we rapidly departed. The Ariel climbed into the hills - both plane and car now lost - and within 20 minutes we were back in the Safad Safe House. As we entered I realized that I had blood on my clothing. I felt around. No. I was not hurt. I then turned to speak to Amin. At that moment he dropped to the floor. He was covered with blood.

Fortunately the bullet had struck his arm, the injury not serious, and now he was in safe hands. I decided to lay low - it was agreed that the motorcycle could no longer be used - it was too easy to be identified. For a further week I remained in the safety of Safad, and prepared my June Report. Finally it was arranged that I would be conveyed by a driver back to Jerusalem. Amin would need time to recuperate, and would remain secure in Safad.

Report - June 1948

Accra District	- *Villages expelled- (2,700) -Al Birwa. Kuwaykat*
Baysan District	- *No Reports*
Beersheba District	- *No Reports*
Gaza District	- *Villages attacked-(7,900) -Iraq Suwaydan,Bayt Tima,Ibde,Isded* - *Villages expelled- (6,000) Julis,Jusayr,Karatiyya,Yasur,Bashshi*
Haifa District	- *Villages attacked- (8,000) - Ayn Ghazal, Ijzim, Jaba, Al-Manara* - *Khirbat ,Al-Mansura Khirbat, Al-Mazar* - *Villages expelled- (4,100) - Sabbarin, Al-Sarkas Khirbat,* - *Umm Al-Shawf, Al-Sindiyana*
Hebron District	- *No Reports*
Jaffa District	- *No Reports*
Jerusalem	- *Village expelled - (50) Nirjaf, Dayr Ayyub*
Jinin District	- *Village expelled -(8,800) -Al-LajjunUmmAl-Fahm,Aqqaba,Zir'In* - *Ayn Ibrahim, Khirbat Al-Buwayshat, Murjafia, Mushayrifa,* - *Mismis, Mu'Awiya,, Al-Mazar, Nuris.* - *Town attacked - Jinin (Number ?)*
Nazareth District	- *Town attacked - Nazareth (Number ?)*
Al-Ramla Distric t	-*Villages attacked-(2,200) Innaba, Al-Latrun, Sajad, Al-Kunayyisa* -*Villages expelled-(12,200) -Al-Mansura, Al-Mukhayzin,* - *Al-Qubab, Al-Qubayba, Umm Kalkha, Yibna,Al-Nabirubin,* -
Safad District	-*Villages expelled- (600) - Al-Khisas*
Tiberias District	-*Villages attacked- (4,300) - Hittin, Lubya, Nimrin*
Tulkarm District	- *No Reports*

Villages attacked	*50*
Towns attacked	*2*
Inhabitants attacked	*82,000*
Inhabitants expelled	*34,500*

The Hunt is Intensified

Colonel Issar Harel, the dreaded shadowy leader of Jewish Intelligence, seated in his Tel-Aviv office frowned. His Department had specialized in collecting information about every Arab, his activities and possessions, in every town and village in Palestine. The fate of every Arab in 1948 was determined by his Department. It was responsible for some of the worst atrocities and also the dispossession of Arab property.

Life, death, probation, or freedom was determined by his Security Department. What villages should be destroyed, and who should be executed was its domain. Issar Harel was extremely thorough, and oversaw all interrogations and similar dreaded activities; a man highly instrumental for the oppression and the destruction of the Arab people.

At this moment, he is studying two reports. The first a strongly worded complaint from a Zionist group in England. Despite Ben Gurion's claim that his people in Palestine were in danger of a Second Holocaust and in dire peril of Arab attacks, newspaper reports in England were describing events that portrayed merciless Ethnic Cleansing, and the murder of thousands of defenseless Arabs. These news items were extremely damaging, contradicted Ben Gurion's propaganda claims, and must be stopped immediately.

Harel cursed and cursed. This criticism reflected very poorly on his Department.

He then examined again upsetting news from his Haifa district. Inspector Mendlesohn was badly injured, Sergeant Gerber killed, both involved in an abortive chase of two suspicious Arabs on a motor cycle. The Arabs had been seen and reported in Baysan, Tiberias, Safad, and Accra. Finally Mendlesohn was involved in a high speed chase on the Safad Highway that failed through a botched up arrangement with an air force fighter.

The Head of Security was no fool. He was certain that the Paul Blackberry apprehended by Inspector Mendlesohn in Haifa some time back was one of the individuals reported on this motor cycle. All the northern districts had reported seeing these two individuals and the motor cycle. He thought grimly

" A great pity Mendlesohn did not detain Blackberry last May."

Harel did not intend to waste any time. Immediately an advisory was sent out to all districts - apprehend these two men - if necessary shoot.

Ibrahim listened carefully, and made some notes, as I described my escape from Accra. He refrained from critiquing my decision to visit Accra. No where was safe to make surveys.

" Is Amin in good health?"

I nodded. Amin had been very fortunate. He had been struck by a bullet which inflicted a flesh wound to his right arm. We had been very lucky. The Israeli fighter had attacked, and by a miracle the Mercedes was destroyed, and we managed to escape.

" He is recuperating in Safad. Nothing to worry about. He will be well very soon"

" And what about your motor cycle?"

" I think it had better remain hidden for some time. I imagine that it is fairly famous in the Jewish Security files"

Ibrahim looked anxiously at me, and agreed.

" No more motor cycling for you young man. I am certain Jewish Security is very much aware of the significance of the motor cycle, its riders, and the current newspaper reports in England."

In case there might be any misunderstanding, Ibrahim stressed again very firmly.

" There will be no further motor cycle jaunts!"

Too much was happening in Ibrahim's world. He had an overload of worries - massacres in three villages in the district of Haifa. Enormous increase of attacks and expulsions throughout Palestine.

" Paul - you had better lay very low for the next few weeks. It is becoming far too dangerous. Remain indoors as much a possible at Ghada's. Now I need your June Report. Also your witness reports of massacres and photographs. Is your June summarized Report complete?"

I nodded

Ibrahim decided that he would visit his daughter this evening, and would collect the June Report. That evening Ghada complained to her father.

" You have got to stop wearing out Paul. He is becoming all skin and bones."

Her father acknowledged her concern, and capitulated. A woman's common sense has to be accepted. We sat at the heavy table - my summarized Reports for the past seven months spread out. He shook his head wearily.

" The situation is impossible - my poor people - my poor country. Over 400,000 have been expelled from their villages and towns. And no doubt 10,000 to 20,000 have died through the attacks and the subsequent fleeing for safety on the highways."

He shook his head in complete despair.

" My people are paying the penalty of being unwilling to live together and work for a common mutual cause. Just think Paul - our population is double that of the Jews - and yet we are helpless in the brutal hands of this criminal rabble.

And of course this unwillingness to work together is a common feature of all Arab people and countries throughout the Middle East."

Sadly he continued.

" Arab society is dominated by its tribal origins and their many highly disruptive entities. A political union of the Arab people seems impossible. And one has to recognise their varied life and conditions. Nomad life so different to that of cultivated areas, and that of cultivated areas to that of settled areas. Muslims may have a common religion, but there are so many groups that are completely unwilling to recognise and accept each other - thus any possible leadership and coordination of all for a common cause is most unlikely.

The only expectation of some form of unity is the responding to a duty to fight for God! That is about all that can be expected."

I pondered over Ibrahim's thoughts. It certainly explained the ease that a whole population was being expelled. And it was a grim reminder that due to the many tribal enmities, the exposure to deceit, informers, spies, and lack of loyalty, every time I made a survey I was treading through a mine field.

Ibrahim again reminded me, before he left, that I must lay low - very very low.

Whilst I was obliged to lie low, reports were coming in from the district of Al-Ramla. Numerous attacks occurred against over three dozen villages, and more than 31,000 had been expelled. There had been a number of massacres, the most appalling being at the town of Al-Lydd where 426 individuals were slain!

Al-Lydd located about midway between Jerusalem and Jaffa, was known as the city of Mosques. Famed mosques included the Big Mosque *Al-Umari* erected during the time of the Mamluks by Sultan Rukn al-Din Baybara. Another was the Dahamish Mosque with 800 worshippers.

July 10th the city of Al-Lydd was aerial bombed, and then a ground attack of the city center. There was a limited defense for a few hours by local men armed with some old rifles. Then the Jewish troops went on a rampage. 426 men, women, and children were slain! 176 were found in the Dahamish Mosque .Looting took place, and individuals robbed. About 50,000 were expelled and sent to the West Bank.

Close by the town of Ramla (17,000) was occupied immediately after Al-Lydd. The Jewish troop commander was Yitzhak Rabin. Ramla's people also were expelled. to the West Bank.

By late July, Issar Harel's sense of humor had deteriorated seriously. No one reported any evidence of the two motor cycle riders. Riders and machine had disappeared in thin air. Inspector Mendlesohn, seriously injured, was gradually recovering, but was unable to offer any further information of value.

Harel's humor was not improved with his Department being blamed for excessive massacres at Aya Ghazal, Ijzim, and Jaba. And to make matters worse, the Zionists in UK and the USA continued to complain bitterly about adverse newspaper reports.

With his usual thoroughness, he instructed every district department to again search and continue to search for the suspected reporters, and ensure that all check points on highways and railways thoroughly investigate everyone. Despite his instructions there was no success. There were such large numbers of fleeing refugees on the highways, it was extremely difficult to make any thorough search. Irregardless there were no reports of a chugging motor cycle anywhere.

Issar Harel visited his sick Inspector Mendlesohn. He now understood that Blackberry was a young Englishman, probably inexperienced according to the Inspector, and easily conned in the taking of his notes and films. The Inspector assured Harel that it would be a pleasure to get his hands on that miserable Blackberry - the cause of his many injuries, aches, and pains.

The head of Jewish Security returned to Tel-Aviv with some ideas. A few days later classified adverts in Palestinian newspapers were worded as follows

" Wanted. British motor cycle late vintage. Top price offered. Telephone 487.65568"

It was a good idea. However the owner of an Ariel 500 never read the advert. He had at last accepted the wisdom of not revealing himself in any form or fashion.

Best Quality Dates

Rapidly the month of July came to an end. The summarized Report for the month complete. The incessant attacks and expulsions continued. About 100 villages had been attacked, approximately 100,000 more villagers had been displaced, and now trudging the roads seeking safety, a home, and food.

Ibrahim studied the report silent and depressed. His fingers pressed firmly against his eyes. The situation was beyond his understanding. What would happen next? There was so little that he could do other than maintain recording the grim news, and keep the newspapers in England informed.

I was becoming very bored cooped up for weeks in Ghada's house.

" Why don't I make another survey - this time the Jerusalem district west of the Old City? "

Ibrahim ,very doubtful, shook his head.   The danger of being apprehended   too great.

I attempted to overcome his fears.

" I have been thinking about this survey - it should not be a problem. There are 15 to 20 villages that have been attacked and expelled - all within 15 miles of the city. I can survey all villages within ten miles by foot - the rest by bicycle. If I leave very early about dawn, and return at dusk, I should not risk raising any attention in this neighborhood. "

The elderly man pondered unwillingly with my proposal. It was such a risk, and yet he realized that a survey had to be made. Finally he capitulated.

" Alright. Now you must wear Arab clothing and carefully stain your face and exposed parts. You can use the old battered bicycle in the yard. And to complete your appearance you will take with you a sack of quality dates for sale.

I think it would be much wiser for you to stay at our Safe House in Al Walaja, and conduct all your surveys from there. Staying there will shorten and speed up your surveys "

So it was agreed. I would take the bicycle - a really beat up battered heap - commence my surveys from Al-Walaja, and operate from there for the next two weeks.

" Please be very careful Paul " demanded a very concerned Ghada.

Dusk was rapidly approaching, and yet dear Ghada had insisted that I have a fine dinner prior to my departure for Al-Wajala. I gave her a fond kiss and hug. Ghada, worried, watched me as I made my way down the alley complete with the old bicycle and my sack of dates.

From the surrounding neighborhood, the regular Muezzin call could be heard - a call that was so descriptive of Arab fatalism and spirituality.

> *" God is Great, God is Great.*
> *There is no God but God.*
> *And Mohammed is the Prophet of God.*
> *God is Great, God is Great"*

The Call. The foundation stone of Islam, offered a permanent peace which unhappily was forgotten so often due to hopeless enmities. And yet the Call provided a peaceful message, a reminder that offered peace , and always seemed so superior to the gloomy bells of the Christian churches of the West.

I was fortunate. A second Truce had been declared, whatever that might imply, and there was very little aggressive action throughout Palestine. But early August the people at the Al-Wajala Safe House were unaware of any lessening of attacks, and were very frightened due to the destruction and the expelling of so many inhabitants in the close villages of Al-Jura, Al-Lawz Khirbat, Al-Maliha, Ayn Karim, Sataf, Suba, and Aqqur.

I explained that I would walk very cautiously around some of the neighborhoods, and get a general impression. They shook their heads with disapproval - irresponsible and very very dangerous. It was madness. Most unwise.

These western district villages were set in the central hills of Palestine 1000 to 2000 feet above sea level. The village of Al-Jura was a typical example located on steep slopes overlooking a deep wadi, and connected to nearby villages such as Al-Karim with dirt paths. The population, about 450, were mainly Muslim. The village was known for its quality fruit. But that was before the Israeli troops bombarded and occupied the village 11th July. Now there was a deathly silence. Many buildings had been demolished, and there was a   general scene of desolation.

From Al-Jura, I trudged along a dirt path to Ayn Karim about 1 ½ miles distant. Al-Karim was a much larger village with a population of about 3,500. The Wadi Ahmad flowed through the village, and provided irrigation water for the nearby Olive orchards. It was attacked about the same time as Al- Jura. Despite a much larger population, there was no resistance. Now only ruins, the result of a severe bombardment, could be seen. The most striking feature of this stone built village was its complete silence and the absence of inhabitants.

Whilst walking to Al-Maliha, 2 miles distant from Ayn Karim, I was intercepted by two Israeli soldiers. One of them shouted at me to get off the path, and cursed calling me " Scum" With head bowed, I immediately obeyed, and scurried on my way.

Al-Maliha, population 2,100, was stone built on the hill slopes, with surrounding land planted in grain, vegetables, and fruit. It had initially been attacked in March, and in April many villagers fled due to the massacre at nearby Dayr Yasin. Finally it was attacked and occupied in July. Now it lay, deserted, with a number of damaged buildings evident of mortar shelling.

It was mid-day, and I sat down to eat my sandwiches. I had plenty of time. For the rest of the day I decided to visit Dayr Yasin. This unfortunate village had suffered with the death of 245 in April. The massacre was carried out by the Irgun and Stern gangs despite a signed non aggression truce with the Haganah. 120 Troops stormed the village, and intentionally killed men, women, and children.

Not satisfied with this horrific measure, the troops took some prisoners to Jerusalem, and paraded them as evidence of victorious might amidst the cheers of the Jewish crowds. These unfortunate prisoners were then carted back to the village and executed. The destroyed buildings demonstrated that the attackers had blown open house doors. and hurled hand grenades inside. Many buildings had been blown up. Now all was deserted and silent.

I imagine that all the dust and rubble, the deathly silence, and the temperature of the summer sun wore me out. Thankfully at dusk I returned to the coolness of the Safe House in Al-Wajala.

The following day I rested, wrote up my notes, and prepared for my next survey. This survey would include the villages of Al-Lawz Khirbat (500), Aqqur (50), Kasla (300), and Dayr Aban (2300)

The Har'el Brigade occupied Al-Lawz Khirbat 13th-14th July, and its inhabitants expelled. The village and land around cultivated for vineyards, olives, almonds, grain, and vegetables adjoining the Wadi Al-Sarah. Now silent and empty.

Aqqur two miles to the west was occupied at the same time as Al-Lawz Khirbat, and was now empty and desolate. Kasla three miles northwest of Aqqur had been subjected to severe mortar barrages and its inhabitants fled. All that remained were damaged houses, ruins, no inhabitants, and silence.

Finally I biked to Dayr Aban five miles distant. It had been a medium size village with about 2,300 population. It was located on a hillside, the west slope of a mountain, and possessed vineyards, olives, and cereal crops. It had suffered attacks by Jews in the nearby settlement of Hartuv in January and March. The people, mainly Muslim, still occupied the village.

I decided prudently not to enter the village which was located at a busy road junction that included the main road to Bayt Jibrin. On the far side I could see the Al-Umari Mosque which stood in the village center.

I peddled on heading for Al-Walaja, and approached a nearby   Jewish settlement. A couple of men blocked my path. One shouted .

" Get out of this district you "Farunkel"   (Pus)"

A very cowered Arab with head looking down stumbled around the two men with his old bicycle.

" Get out you damn "Cholera" (scum)"

Seething with rage, I wisely fled.

Ma'Zuz Al-Saftawi at the Safe House was angry, upset, and distressed to learn of my recent experiences. With flashing eyes, angrily he declared.

" My friend - your activities imperil our lives. You do not seem to understand. Do you realise that by May eight neighborhoods and thirty seven villages in the Greater Jerusalem have been attacked, the people killed and expelled, houses destroyed and looted, and every house of any consequence stolen and occupied by the Jews.

Now over 75% of all villages have been attacked and the people expelled. I have no doubt the rest of the villages including our Al-Walaja will soon be taken. There are tens of thousands of greedy Jewish settlers eyeing every property in this district, their intention to take everything, and get rid of all of us.

Any stranger such as yourself seen in the district is eyed as an enemy and to be expelled. Now here you are making surveys. Utter madness. I appreciate your good intentions my friend, but you endanger all of us. I must ask you to stop immediately or leave this house. One wrong move and we are all doomed."

The unhappy man was quite despondent. The future extremely bleak. My presence only worsened matters. With anger he stressed the dangerous futility of my presence.

" What good are your enquiries? You British meddle in our affairs, and never make any attempt to assist and protect us. All you people have done is sit back and watch rather than provide security, law, and order. In fact I understand that your British troops gave the Jews indispensable information that simplified their task of planning our expulsion and the theft of our property."

I was unable to satisfy Ma'Zuz Al-Saftawi. Obviously my activities could be prejudicial to his family. Yet for the sake of the Arab people, the truth of Al-Nakba *(The Catastrophe)* had to be recorded and revealed to the world, and the Zionist propaganda destroyed. I placed my hand on his shoulder, and assured him that I would take great care. Tomorrow would be my last survey, and I would return to the Old City.

Ma'Zuz listened, refused to be comforted, and shook his head with consternation and displeasure. I slept poorly that night. Ma'Zuz's world was rapidly being destroyed completely. The history of his people, his family, and the fate of his children obliterated by a very hostile and covetous strangers, recent immigrants to Palestine, supported by Zionist extremists in the USA and UK.

What kind of people would patently work to destroy others. To imagine that these Zionists included individuals inventing, designing, and making flame throwers, biological warfare products, and poisonous gasses designed to blind. And what kind of people honor these dreadful individuals and make them leaders such as Mordecha Maklet, future Israeli Army Chief Staff, who was the Operations Officer of the Carmel Brigade and instructed his troops when attacking defenseless and panic stricken people in Haifa.

" Kill any Arab you encounter, torch all inflammable objects, force open doors with explosives"

And what kind of people are these settlers who openly steal homes of the Arabs. And the many who rejoiced in Jerusalem the sight of unfortunate prisoners of Dayr Yassin who then were returned to the village, the scene of that infamous massacre, and finally executed.

It is thought provoking that these dreadful people were the very people whom Hitler did not execute a mere three to four years earlier! Thought provoking that these very people have committed aggressive conduct even worse than that committed by Hitler's forces!

Early well before dawn I pedaled to Dayr Rafat population of 475. The village was the site of a large monastery of the Latin Patriarchate, and had excellent agricultural land with orchards and springs. The population of Muslims fled when mortar shelled by the Har'r Brigade. Now it stood empty with ruined homes.

Sar'a about one mile distant suffered a similar attack, and stood desolate and empty. Another 1 ½ miles the village of Islin lay empty with its stone and mud buildings destroyed. And finally the village of Ishwa population about 700   close to Islin also silent and empty.

Seated under a tree by Ishwa's cemetery, I ate a sandwich, and planned my return to the Old City, It was strange. Although engrossed, I suddenly sensed that I was being observed. Cautiously I retired to the back side of the large tree, and was now aware of three men gesticulating and pointing towards me. I casually walked away from view, and then immediately pedaled furiously away intending to return through northerly villages and avoid the busy traffic of the Jaffa Jerusalem highway.

All of these villages had been taken and the people expelled last April. Perhaps that route was an error, because no doubt local Jews would be likely around, and would be quickly aware of an Arab furiously pedaling along dirt roads. That unhappy state of affairs proved correct. I was observed, and my journey was punctuated with shouts and a gun shot. As I circumvented the village of Qalunya riding as fast as possible, my heart sank. I was approaching some kind of check point, and had already been seen.

" What's the hurry Cholera?" sneered the security guard.

" Put your bike over there "   The guard pointed at a small shed.

" I want to see your identity and see what you have in that sack"

" Thanra" (Dates) " I explained pointing at the sack.

" Get over there Cholera, and be quick "

Fortunately guard Yitzhak Shawski was both bored and lazy, and idly watched me take the bicycle over to the shed wall, and lean it against the structure. I then took off my knapsack with the dates, and carefully laid it by the bicycle. I was rapidly approaching a sense of panic. A simple interrogation by that guard would reveal my identity. I knelt down pretending to tie a lace, noted in the corner of eye that the guard was relaxed just watching, and in a flash I bolted running hell for leather.. There were some shouts, and the firing of a rifle, and then I was gone.

Jerusalem Old City was about five miles distant. I had run about one mile and was totally exhausted. I lay hidden in an olive orchard trying to recover, and decided that it might be wise to lie low, and continue at dusk. But fifteen minutes later I heard the baying of dogs. Initially I gave it no thought - but the noise became louder, and suddenly fear struck my heart. I was being traced by a pack of dogs!

I fled through the orchard, and ran in the direction of the city. For one moment panting, I stopped , and looking back could see a group of men and some dogs following in my direction. Now very frightened I took off down dirt tracks heading for the village of Lifta which lost its population with tragic deaths last December and January. The path sloped down into the valley, and crossing my path was the Wadi Salman. Behind the baying insistent dogs.

My scent had to be lost. The busy roads with hostile residents would not resolve my problem. But the Wadi Salmon was a solution. Rapidly I clambered down the banks into the water, waded along the shallows for about a hundred yards, made my way across, and escaped up the far bank.

Very very cautiously I made my way back to Jerusalem. I had no doubt warnings had been broadcast of my presence. Thoroughly exhausted, muddy and filthy, I finally gasped my password and number at Ibrahim's house.

I was not the only one who suffered that day.

Guard Yitzhak Shawski, furious with my escape, investigated my abandoned bicycle and knapsack. His greedy eyes rejected the battered bicycle but lit up noting the contents of the knapsack. Already he decided to steal the knapsack.

At home he delivered the knapsack with the dates to his good wife Rivkah.

" I have a pleasant surprise gift for you my dear "

She looked at Yitzhak with suspicion, her mind   that dwelt on his numerous failings of the past.

" Perhaps he has changed" she decided, and went into the Kitchen.

Moments later she returned to her idiot of a husband.

" You damn fool - these dates are all mildew "

Unhappily Yitzhak's troubles continued, because he was then reprimanded by his chief for permitting the escape of an important spy.

Not everyone can succeed as   a responsible guard.

Report - July 1948

Accra District	- *Villages expelled- (10,500) -Amqa, Al Birwa, Al Damum,* - *Arab Suwayjaj, Al-Kabri, Kuwaykat, Jiddin* - *Al-Ruways, Shafa'Amr, Yanuk, Mi'Ar*
Baysan District	- *No Reports*
Beersheba District	- *Bedouins expelled- 11 Tribes commencing with the Jubarat* - *19 Tribes forced into reservations* - *Total number Bedouins 90,000 in 96 Tribes*
Gaza District	- *Villages attacked- (8,600) - Iraq Al-Manshiyya, Isdud* - *Iraq Suwaydan,* - *Villages expelled-(12,200)- Bayt'Affa, Bi'Lin, Hajja, Ibdis,* -*Karatiyya , Al-Masmiyya al-Kabira,Tal Al-Jermus, Summil,* - *Al-Jaladiyya, Jusayr, Qastina, Al-Masmiyya al Saghira,*
Haifa District	- *Villages expelled- (13,700) -Ayn Ghaza (30), Ayn Hawd,* - *Jaba (M), Kafr Lam, Al Manara Khirbat, Ijzim (M)* - *Al-Mansura Khirbat, Al-Mazar, Al-Tira, Al-Sarafand*
Hebron District	- *Villages expelled-(2,800) - Barqusya, Mughallis Zayta,* -*Tall Al-Safi,*
Jaffa District	- *Villages expelled- (7,000) -Al-Abbasiyya, Ranjiya*
Jerusalem District	- *Villages expelled- (9,500) - Aqqur, Artuf, Ayn Karim, Dayr Abani* - *Dayr Rafat, Ishwa, Islin, Al Jura,Kasla, Sar'a. Sataf, Suba* -*Ism Allah Khirbat, Al-Lawz Khirbat, Al-Malina,*
Jinin District	- *No Reports*
Nazareth District	- *Villages expelled- (7,900) - Shafa'Amr, Saffuriyya, Ma'Lul,* - *Al-Mujaydil* - *Town attacked - Nazareth (Number ?)*

Report - July 1948

Al Ramla District	*- Villages expelled-(31,000) - Abu Al-Fadl, Ajanjul, Barfiliya,*
	-Al-Barriyya, Bayt Far Khirbat, Al-Burt,
	- Bayt Nabala, Bayt Shanna, Bir Ma'In,
	- Bir Salim, Al-Buwayra Khirbat, Saniyal,
	- Dayr Abusalama, Dayr Jarif, Qazaza,
	- Al- Duhayriyya Khirbat, Al-Haditha,
	- Idnibba, Innaba, Jilya, Jimzu, Qula,
	-Kharruba, Al-Khayma, Al-Kunayyisa,
	- Al-Latrun, Majdal Yaba, Al-Musayri'a
	- Sajad, Salbit, Shilja, Al Tara,
	-Towns expelled - (67,000) - Al Ramla, Al-Lydd **(246)**
Safad District	*- Villages expelled- (Number ?) -Al Munjar Khirbat*
Tiberias District	*- Villages expelled- (6,300) - Hittin, Lubya, Nimrin, Al Na'ra,*
	- Al-Sanda Khirbat
Tulkarm District	*- No Reports*

Villages attacked	*102*
Towns attacked	*3*
Inhabitants attacked	*201,500*
Inhabitants expelled	*168,000*

The Cunning of the Ruthless

Ibrahim and Ahmad, briefed of my latest accounts and escapade, deliberated for some time. Finally Ibrahim made a decision.

" Paul. Your surveys will have to stop. It is far too risky for all of us to continue. Palestine is full of hostile observers and informers, and Jews are everywhere with evil intent.

You can still serve your purpose collecting the latest information from the various districts. But no surveys. As you can see in your August summarized Report, the current Truce is holding. With the exception of one attack in the district of Beersheba, and two attacks in the district of Gaza, everywhere is quiet. Hopefully the Zionists will honor the current Truce. "

I have to admit that I was relieved. The risk of apprehension was ever increasing and quite frightening. There was good news from Safad. Amin, Ibrahim's grandson, had fully recovered from his bullet wound, and now in good health.

It is very easy to criticise a solution, and ignore the complexity of a problem. However did that apply to Palestine and the United Nations. It is very difficult to refrain from venting criticism commencing with the deplorable recommendations of UNSCOP, and its subsequent acceptance by United Nations with Resolution 181. And then when the die was set November 1947, United Nation's inability to   oversee the terms of their Resolution.

UN failed dismally in that obligation. Agreed it had representatives in Palestine, but their presence was meaningless, and were no more than witnesses of the numerous atrocities that took place. The complete indifference of the Zionist forces to the terms of the Resolution was permitted to continue unabated.

Count Folke Bernadotte UN emissary was the exception. He arrived in Palestine May, realized the dangerous inequity of the situation, and proposed to re-divide Palestine in a more workable partition, and insisted that all Palestinian refugees be permitted to return. This demand was ignored during the First Truce. He repeated this demand in his final recommendation submitted to UN.

I received a batch of messages September from various sources. Most were of a similar nature. But one was totally unexpected and a shock. The source claimed that Count Folke Bernadotte had just been assassinated by Jewish terrorists in Jerusalem.

I called for Ibrahim, and advised him of the shocking news.

" I have some terrible news"

Ibrahim looked up from his desk, and no doubt wondered how any news could be more shocking than the events of the past six months.

" Count Folke Bernadotte has been assassinated!"

" Assassinated? How could that be possible?"

" Jewish terrorists in Jerusalem"

Ibrahim was shattered. His world was completely mad. It was a mere few months past that the Israeli government had agreed to Bernadotte's appointment as a UN mediator. His excellent reputation as president of the Swedish Red Cross, and its saving of many Jews during the Second World War, made him an ideal appointment.

The elderly man, tired and resigned, declared.

" Poor Bernadotte. Such an honest man. He tried so hard to protect the interests of the Arab Palestinians. The Jews never realized that an honest man would condemn the very people whom he had saved a few years earlier. He has now suffered the final penalty"

Late in September Ahmad visited Ibrahim's office, and I was asked to attend. As I sat, Ibrahim glanced at Ahmad, Ahmad nodded, and Ibrahim addressed the matter of concern.

" Paul. We have advise from a reliable source that the Zionist leadership is receiving ever increasing complaints from Britain and the USA about newspaper reports that are extremely damaging to their current propaganda. Israel's Mossad has been instructed to employ all their resources in crushing our organization.

Ahmad is convinced of our immediate danger if you continue to remain with us. He proposes that you stay at his place in Ramallah, and you can continue your work there. Hopefully this danger will ease."

Ibrahim suggestion seemed wise. I rapidly packed my possessions and papers, and later that day traveled to Ramallah with Ahmad.

Although the nature and character of many Zionists is extremely unpleasant , the nature of their wickedness varies according to their stupidity and greed. Thus London's Harry would tell his grand children around the fireplace in years to come of his remarkable skill and ingenuity discovering the source of the upsetting Palestinian information published in Britain's Guardian newspapers.

With considerable pride he would tell how he managed to get a Guardian reporter reveal that a certain *"Ibrahim of Jerusalem"* was the source of this disturbing information. In Harry's eyes, this investigative coop was a matter of considerable pride, demonstrating his skills and ingenuity.

He conveniently brushed aside subsequent criticism that there were thousands of *Ibrahims in Jerusalem*, and that his revelation was no better than advising that *Bill of London* was responsible for the latest British scam. Such criticism he considered was professional jealousy, and accordingly ignored. However, despite Harry's skill, there were authorities who continued to be extremely vexed searching for that elusive and obscure Ibrahim.

It was a late Autumn evening. The room dark, somber, and stark. The walls painted standard government cream and green, the starkness accented with a plain calendar and pin board. A bare worn desk, chairs, filing cabinets, and phones was illuminated by an exposed light bulb that revealed the room's two occupants in a very silent building.

Issah Harel head of Jewish Security, and his Haifa representative Inspector Mendlesohn, were there to discuss the latest events. Harel demonstrated his authority with a touch of sarcasm.

" So Inspector. Have you fully recovered from your latest botched chase?"

Few would know that Mendlesohn was Harel's subordinate. And fortunately few would know of that abortive pursuit of that criminal Paul Blackberry and his motorcycle. He and Sergeant Gerber had been so intent in catching up with that motorcycle through the winding hills, they had forgotten the dangerous instructions given to an Israeili air force fighter. At the very moment they thought they had snared their prey, that fighter had strafed the road, missed the motorcycle, and struck his car.

" Yes Sir. Fully recovered. That accident -   a miracle I survived."

Harel icily stared at the man, more concerned of the Inspector's screw up rather than the proclaimed miracle. He had a long memory, and had not forgotten the Inspector's failure to apprehend Blackberry in May.

" Quite so Inspector. But what concerns me is that these errors of judgment persist. You lost the man between Haifa and Jaffa in May, and you lost four men involved in that abortive raid of Blackberry's office in Jaffa. Now you had many reports of this man on a motorcycle in Baysan, Tiberias, Safad, and Accra in August, and here I have the latest report in Jerusalem that he was reported on a bicycle with a sack of dates, and yet lost at Qulam."

He glared with increasing anger at his unsuccessful man, reminded of increasing criticism from Zionist leaders who were extremely unhappy about adverse newspaper reports in Britain.

" What precisely is going on Inspector. The newspaper reports indicate that this Blackberry is covering the whole of Palestine with his distorted descriptions of current events.. And yet you are not competent to catch the man! What precisely is going on?"

Inspector Mendlesohn cursed within, and wisely kept his mouth closed. Harel was in a difficult mood, and no doubt these complaints from Zionist leaders truly upset him. Harel leaned back not expecting an excuse. The inspector had a good record, and little would be gained in upsetting the man. Harel stared at his desk in thought. Finally he raised his eyes, eyes that demanded the Inspector's attention.

" Inspector . This is our plan. Blackberry and his associates are to be eliminated. It is obvious that Blackberry is not the leader of this group that is collecting information. We have to find the leader.

Now as you know those idiots in London found a reporter for the Guardian who claimed that this mysterious leader is named Ibrahim, and that he is in Jerusalem. The obvious problem is that an Ibrahim in Jerusalem is as difficult to find as a Dick in London or a Harry in New York."

The Inspector agreed .

" We need more information "

" Correct Inspector - we need more information. You will fly to London as soon as possible, contact the Guardian staff, and get that information. I propose that you contact someone in Accounts, preferably some lonely spinster, share your amazing background and credentials with the good woman, and get the name and address of that Ibrahim. Is that understood Inspector?"

Mendlesohn left Harel's office late that night glum and thoughtful. He detested flying. And in his eyes London overly warm, muggy and dirty, or London overly cold., damp, foggy, and filthy was impossible. However Harel's proposal had merit. Already he imagined the pleasure of wringing that miserable reporter's neck, and he felt measurably better.

The D.C.6 droned on for ever throughout the night, and finally arrived at Heath Row Airport early morning After what seemed an endless walk along Concourse after Concourse, he finally arrived at the Terminal building. He wondered

" What kind of idiots are employed as architects in this crazy country ? "

Finally he passed through Customs and Immigration, collected his suitcase, and traveled by coach to London. Settled in the Savoy Hotel, Mendlesohn examined a map of London, ascertained the location of the *Guardian* reporters' favored pub, and planned his strategy. He had a couple of spare days, and decided that it might be productive if he could contact Blackberry's family. However an inspection of the British telephone book revealed that there were perhaps as many Blackberrys as there were Blackberry bushes. That idea was scrapped.

Finally Friday arrived, a taxi ordered, and the passenger experienced the impossible congestion of London streets. At the appointed destination, the taxi driver was paid, and the inspector entered the *Fox and Grapes*. Despite Harel' s sarcastic reprimand of his subordinate's lack of success, Mendlesohn was no fool, and was well prepared for this evening. He approached a very busy packed bar, ordered a drink, and introduced himself to the bar owner,

" I am seeking a group of reporters from the Guardian " he claimed.

The owner nodded, and pointed to a small group of individuals in a far corner.

" Over there chum "

An individual named   John Daviesohn introduced himself.

" Gentlemen - John Daviesohn Doctor Archaeology Jerusalem. Forgive me butting in but I am told that you reporters represent that excellent newspaper the Guardian. "

That opening address did not excite anyone. But that did not deter the Inspector who had a sound understanding of the human race. Here was a typical British group, no doubt prejudiced, and probably not attracted to an oily smooth talking Middle East character. But that kind of handicap is easily overcome with liberal drinks and a subject of mutual interest.

Very coolly Reginald Brown stared at this stranger, and responded

" So ? "

Already he had decided that he was looking at an unpleasant worm.

Mendlesohn   alias Daviesohn, aware of his handicap, was not deterred.

" I met a chap in Jaffa who claimed that your paper had considerable expertise and interest in the Middle East. Is that correct? "

Reginald demonstrated little enthusiasm, and his response unchanged.

" So?"

Surrounded by companions anxious to continue their latest scandal with half empty glasses, Mendlesohn responded in a very positive manner. With a hearty laugh, and a beaming smile he boldly addressed the group of six.

" Wonderful. Now I have another question. Your glasses need to be filled. May I have the pleasure of buying you a round.?"

It was a pleasure that was readily accepted. And what was more significant the presence of Mendlesohn became just a little bit more acceptable.. And for those who could remember, this archaeologist was quite generous, and ordered a number of rounds. He proved to be the life of the party reciting Middle East jokes, and his knowledge of Middle East Archaeology quite impressive. And everyone was pleased to learn of this stranger's admiration of the British.

" The British really created the Middle East. Remember T.E. Lawrence (Laurence of Arabia). Well I met him at a High Commission meeting with Arab Ministers in Bagdad. What a remarkable man - absolutely brilliant. And then there was Gertrude Bell known as the Queen of the Desert, I will never forget her - so knowledgeable and respected by every Arab leader in the Middle East."

Ed Perkins' attention was drawn to the inspector's claim.

" You were there?"

Very modestly Mendlesohn admitted that was so - as a very young assistant at that time.

" Bloody Hell - you are part of Middle East history!"

With the aid of a few more rounds, this gracious, modest, and very knowledgeable archaeologist was accepted. Just before the group broke up late that evening for home, Mendlesohn struck his head.

" I forgot to ask. Would your newspaper be interested in receiving reports from the Middle East?"

By then the coolness of the group had evaporated, and he was reassured.

" Speak to Accounts - mention us - they will set you up"

All good men departed for home, and the respected archaeologist retired to the Savoy presumably to discover relics of the past at that illustrious establishment.

The inspector had the whole weekend to plan his next move. He was well aware how stingy British firms are in the remuneration of their female staff, and this failing would be very advantageous.

Monday he introduced himself to the Guardian Accounts Department, and had a pleasant chat with an assistant. She in turn introduced this distinguished archaeologist to her office manager - a Miss Geraldine Browne.

Presumably British women differ little from those of other Nationalities. Most are married and we trust satisfied. The rest are not married, and in general extremely dissatisfied. There is a general lack of love, and more significant a lack of the good things in life!

Geraldine, now very much in the archaeologist's mind, was the ideal candidate deserving of some good things in life. He felt an obligation to improve her life for at least one evening. Already she was aware that this distinguished man was a leading archaeologist of the Middle East, that his family had a direct lineage of the Ottoman Emperors of the 14th Century, and was a individual who could speak volumes about any respectable subject.

And what a gentleman he proved to be. It was arranged - dinner at the Savoy - and he would collect her by taxi. And when the taxi arrived, the bashful archaeologist gave her a great bouquet of flowers and a large box of the finest chocolates. How could anyone not appreciate and remember such kindness.

How many of us have set foot in the Savoy? How many eaten at the Savoy? Certainly that excludes most of us. And certainly excluded Geraldine which reflects poorly on the hospitality of British men folk. Anyhow let us not be churlish, and let us demonstrate our gratitude that this famous Middle East archaeologist had fulfilled that desirable role with due humility and joy.

Geraldine, as she would so often stress many years hence, would stipulate that here was a gentleman, a direct descendant of the imperial line of the Ottoman Emperors of the 14th Century. A skilled professional archaeologist with such remarkable credentials, who had known T.E. Lawrence and Gertrude Ball. Assisted by an excellent education at Eton and Oxford University, he possessed such remarkable skills with a vivid interest of social and economic causes in Palestine. And he very shyly showed her his written reports of Palestine.

After two glasses of Champagne and two ample glasses of Cherry Brandy, Geraldine was only too happy to assist her admired companion. She explained in detail how he would be compensated for accepted contributions to the Guardian.

" Goodness" remarked her companion

" You are proposing just as fine an arrangement as my friend Ibrahim"

" Do you mean Ibrahim Shiqaqi who regularly sends us reports from Jerusalem Old City? "

He gazed at Geraldine with feigned surprise.

" Of course - what a fine gentleman - his reports are so accurate - you are very fortunate having his services "

It was understood that Geraldine had better return home at a reasonable hour because she had to be at the office 8.00am the following morning. A very understanding gentleman escorted her home by taxi, departed with a modest fond kiss on her cheek, and arranged another outing at the Savoy the following Tuesday.

Geraldine's visit to the Savoy, bless her, was one of her happiest memories in her rather dull life. It was a disappointment that her admired new acquaintance was obliged to phone explaining a change of plans due to important business matters in the Middle East. The urgent telegram necessitated his immediate return - a most remarkable archaeological discovery in one of his diggings of world wide dimensions. However he assured her that he would be returning as soon as possible. Sadly such assurances proved only assurances for all kinds of unexpected and important reasons. Geraldine continued to have faith in her new found friend who would slowly become a mere memory.

But not all is lost.. In future years, Geraldine will patiently describe to her children of this wondrous king of kings. Sometimes one suspects that she compares that king with her current husband Art Higgins. But one has to be fair, Art regularly returns home every night whilst her king of kings is inevitably delayed seated on his throne in the mysterious Middle East.

Meanwhile the Friday group of *Guardian* reporters noted that their new found acquaintance did not turn up as he had assured them.

" Typical - full of big talk "

But despite that opinion, they had been impressed with Daviesohn's connections - and continued to expect him to turn up - but like Geraldine, their expectations were never fulfilled.
Eventually Reginald Brown muttered

" Typical Gypo "

Reginald Brown's conclusion is further evidence that *we believe what we wish to believe*, and that the purchase of a few rounds of drinks cannot guarantee permanent admiration.

The date September 28th 1948. The time 5.00pm

A knock at the entrance door in the Arab Quarter resulted in the Janitor's query

" Who is it?"

There was no answer to the question, and the door remained   closed. Suddenly the solid entrance door was battered down by four strong thugs shooting out the lock and hinges. Immediately the heavily armed men stormed into the house. The owner and his daughter, quietly seated at the table, rose in alarm, and asked with fear.

" Who are you?"

Those few words were the last made by the distinguished Ibrahim Shiqaqi as a number of shots were fired. The force of the shots threw him back, his shattered chest covered with blood. As his daughter Ghada horrified rushed to cradle her dying father, she   also was shot to death. Finally two terrified servants who witnessed the attack were slain.

One cannot help wondering. Did it matter that these killers had no knowledge of the identity of those just murdered. They were simply instructed to kill. For such orders, knowledge of names and other information is merely an unnecessary distraction. It eliminates any possibility of association, guilt and remorse. Those killed are simply a statistic.-conventional day to day work.

An hour later Inspector Mendlesohn entered the Old City home. A meticulous search revealed very little. He cursed. The elusive Paul Blackberry was not there, and no evidence where he was. And despite a careful surveillance of this property for many weeks, no one ever visited the home of Ibrahim Shiqaqi except some sad relatives.

Report - August/September 1948

Accra District	*- No Reports*
Baysan District	*- No Reports*
Beersheba District	*- Villages expelled- (Number ?) - Al-Imara*
Gaza District	*- Villages attacked- (3,200) - Iraq Al-Manshiyya,* *-Iraq Suwaydan*
Haifa District	*- No Reports*
Hebron District	*- No Reports*
Jaffa District	*- No Reports*
Jerusalem District	*- No Reports*
Jinin District	*- No Reports*
Nazareth District	*- No Reports*
Al-Rama District	*- No Reports*
Safad District	*- No Reports*
Tiberias District	*- No Reports*
Tulkarm District	*- No Reports*

Coffee House Talk

Ramallah, like Jerusalem, is located in the hills, about 15 miles north of the capital. The district population 99% Arab, and according to United Nation Resolution 181 the district was within the Palestinian State.

The Second Truce had resulted in minimal aggression throughout Palestine during the months of August and September. Conditions in the district of Ramallah were relatively quiet. Ahmad provided me with a pleasant room, installed a table for my report writing, and made arrangements whereby district reports would now be sent to Ramallah.

But my sense of peace and security was shattered during the first week of October. Ahmad entered my room very distressed and advised.

" *Terrible news Paul. Ibrahim and Ghada were murdered by Jewish thugs. They burst into the house, and killed everyone. Fortunately I do not think they suffered - death was probably instantaneous.*"

Ahmad's news was a terrible shock. I just stared at him speechless frozen with horror and grief. Finally I forced out the obvious question.

" *Who was responsible?*"

" *Israeli Mossad* "

No doubt my face whitened with the shock - I would never see them again. With disbelief I groaned.

" *Are you sure?*"

He nodded.

" *Your old enemy Inspector Mendlesohn was seen sniffing around Ibrahim's house* "

" *How could he have found Ibrahim's address?*"

Ahmad had no immediate explanation.

" *Ibrahim was extremely efficient. I doubt very much that your Inspector has found any links with anyone. Every Safe House communicated with a special secure address that had no obvious connection with Ibrahim. All your reports for the past year went to that special address. Perhaps the weak link was Ibrahim's methodology and connection with Britain. Very difficult - one can only speculate.*"

I will now have to make further enquiries, and devise a new link to Britain. Ibrahim never advised me how he communicated with Britain - I think it is necessary to create our own method which will necessitate a special secure address here and in London. Then we do not have to worry about any possible connection with Ibrahim's system. "

For the rest of the month, I had difficulty concentrating on my work. Unhappily aggressive attacks commenced again all over Palestine. Fortunately Ahmad was quick arranging a secure address in Ramallah, and had advised all Safe Houses of the address. Now advise of all future attacks would be received through the new address.

Ahmad understood the nature of young people. Particularly young men anxious to be active. The necessity to be hidden in a house week after week would be very tiresome despite the grimness of the situation.

After a few days, he was aware of my boredom, and had a idea.

" Paul. There is a family coffee shop next door. Access is possible through the back door. If you are interested, I will introduce you to the owner Anwar Al-Masiri who is related to Ibrahim. He is a very reliable individual, and he will ensure your security when you visit his premises.

You probably would learn some interesting topics from Anwar and people that he knows. Perhaps some of their information could be incorporated in future paper reports. "

It sounded a great idea that would hopefully eliminate some of the tedium of being cooped within Ahmad's house .My face no doubt brightened.

" Gee - That sounds a great idea. When can you arrange a meeting with Anwar?"

The following day Ahmad led me out the back door of the house, and through the back door of the Coffee House. It was perfect .Both doors shared the same courtyard, and access was completely concealed from curious eyes.

Anwar Al-Masiri was an individual who inspired confidence. Although his appearance was very different to Ibrahim, it was interesting to observe that he had similar cautious eyes.

" I am told that you are a good friend of dear Ibrahim and Ghada. I welcome you to my house and coffee shop. My shop is quite secure, and only a select number of customers visit. I suggest that you and I have an understanding when you would like to visit, so that I can ensure your privacy and safety.

I have a number of interesting customers who regularly visit the Shop, and I am sure that some would be delighted to meet you, and perhaps discuss current events. "

He looked up at Ahmad, gave a brief smile, and nodded. It was agreed.

Ahmad decided that it would be advantageous to improve my Arab appearance. He shook his head appraising my ugly British face.

" What possibly can be done?"

Finally it was agreed that I must get in the habit of using my Kaffiyeh, and wrap it around my face exposing only my eyes. And even then Ahmad muttered in despair.

" Those British eyes!"

Two days later Ahmad announced that one of Anwar's customers would like to meet me 7.30pm that evening. So it was arranged that I would enter the coffee shop by the back entrance, and report first to Anwar.

I made my presence known to Anwar who advised me that Hikmat Al-Khatib had arrived. He led me to a back table that was very private, and introduced me to him.. Hikmat was a young man, 20 to 30 years of age, slight in build, with an intelligent and alert face. He smiled at me, stood, waited for me to sit, and then returned to his seat.

Hikmat seemed in my inexperienced eyes a typical Palestinian. Even his mother might refrain from considering him handsome although no doubt lovable. Bluntly some might consider his face a handicap. However it is the spirit and the mind that truly matters. For that reason alone Hikmat was a splendid fellow. There he sat with his Kaffiyeh, a conventional black and white head dress, possessing a beaming welcoming smile.

His most striking feature was his eyes - so bright, intelligent, and curious. He was a great character, a past student of London University, and now a reporter for *Al-Huuriyah "Freedom"*

Curiously he looked at me and asked

" Mr Blackberry. It is a great pleasure making your acquaintance. I understand that you are interested in current events in Palestine. "

I acknowledged that his understanding was correct.

" What is happening ?" questioned Hikmat.

I shrugged.

" Just the usual dismal attacks and expulsions. Just more and more depressing statistics. "

" Hmm " Hikmat accepted my explanation in silence.

We both sipped our coffee, and eyed each other rather solemnly. In the street buses, taxis, cyclists, donkeys, and vendors continued to make themselves heard. I decided I needed an explanation about his fellow people, and quietly asked.

" I do not wish to sound rude but I have a question that needs to be answered. Why have your people allowed these horrible thugs force them out of their country?. Why do they permit these terrible atrocities?. Why do they allow the theft of all their real and personal property? Why Hikmat? Why?"

The Arab reporter eyed me carefully. These were questions that reflected rather poorly on his people, and yet they were extremely important questions that demanded an honest appraisal. Carefully he prepared his answer.

" You have to understand that we are a fairly passive society, mainly rural in nature, and we had faith in the British for security, law and order. We have never approved Britain's declaration that the Jews should have their own State within our country. Why should we. We owned 95% of all the land, and we were very much in the majority in numbers.

Likewise we expected United Nations to recognise the rights of the indigenous people. Despite the complete inequity of its Partition proposals, we expected this authority as a world organization to protect our interests and lives.

One might say that we have been naïve and foolish placing faith in respected governments and institutions. But then were we naïve and foolish? For example if the Cockneys of London suddenly demanded to have their own State, talked the United Nations to declare a Partition Plan, and then seized all the London Counties as their own, would not the people demand justice and resolution by their government. Likewise if the Jews of New York inveigled the United Nations to partition the USA, and seized the State of New York, Connecticut, and Virginia, would not all the people of the USA rise protesting the inequity of the proposal.

He had made a significant point. And further he stressed.

" Read your history Paul - the Palestinian people have been shafted so many times over the past thirty years. "

Of course Hikmat was correct. It is difficult to imagine the enormous dishonesty, the lack of compassion and understanding, the intentional breach of British Mandate obligations that commenced with those biased rascals Churchill, Balfour, and Lloyd George.

But one has to accept that dishonesty, lack of compassion and understanding, and the breach of obligations is not some modern kind of phenomena. It is in fact common place in the history of man. Treachery has always. existed.

I decided to pursue my argument.

" Quite right Hikmat - you have been shafted for thirty years. But bear in mind that your people were shafted by the Ottomans for centuries before the British had the Mandate. Your people have had excellent training of the perfidy of mankind. And yet despite that experience you continue to allow others to manipulate your lives.

What puzzles me is that your people with education have become brilliant in their chosen professions - doctors, scientists, engineers, lawyers, accountants and the like. 40% of your people live in urban areas which should provide the necessary experience in administration, justice, and law if they do not adopt commercial employment. It just seems strange that despite the opportunities and skills, your people seem to lack the leadership and desire to control your own destiny "

The young Arab eyed me carefully and pursed his lips. He purposely avoided the issues just raised, and continued his line of argument.

" You have to understand that the British never treated us favorably - not as equals as would be expected under the terms of the Mandate. Bluntly we were considered third class citizens in their eyes, and   treated accordingly. During the 1920s and 1930s we were subject to acts of brutality and lack of consideration, and in 1936 our leaders were expelled from Palestine, and not permitted to return.

We are entitled to respect. The people of Mesopotamia have a remarkable record of scientific discoveries which were made many hundreds of years before Europe became aware of such knowledge. The Qur'an encouraged science " God will raise up in rank those of you who have been given knowledge:" - the importance of knowledge and reason and respect of learned persons was stressed.

Thus scientific enquiry commenced at the founding of Baghdad under the First Caliph Abbasid al-Mansur in 762. By the 10th Century Baghdad had a population of 800,000. When the Mongols sacked Baghdad 1258, it is claimed that the Muslim population was two million.

Consider the following:

Medical: Between the 8th and 14th Century enormous strides were made in medical discoveries. Hospitals of a substantial size with advanced facilities were built complete with research academies.   Many learned texts were published addressing numerous subjects.

Mathematics: Baghdad's Al-Khawaizmi invented algebra - solved lineal equations and sine algorithms in the 9th Century. Between the 8th and the 13th Centuries   Trigonometry, the *concept of tangents to facilitate geometrical calculations, and much else.*

Engineering: Enormous advances were made in Hydraulic Technology - underground channels, dams, water wheels, water lifting machines, intricate water clocks, pumps, and piston driven machinery - all this between the 8th and 13th Centuries. Paper Mills were constructed and were in operation in the 8th Century - by the 12th Century the Morocco capital of Fez had over 400 paper making workshops.

Astronomy: In the 10th Century Abu Sa'Id Al-Sizji declared that the Earth revolved on its own axis. There were observatories in Maragna (Iran), Samarkand, Istanbul. Inventions included astrolabes, sundials, celestial globes, and armillary spheres to track movements of planets and constellations. Planetary Theory were published in 200 to 300 Treatises.

13th Century Khorosan Al-Tusi persuaded the Mongol Hulagu Khan to build an observatory at Maragha (Persia). At that time he wrote over 100 works. A 3 storey observatory tower 156'0" diameter was built in Samarand 1432.

Optics: 10th Century Baghdad Ibn Sahl discovered refraction of light, 11th Century Alhasan Ibn Al-Haitham claimed that light traveled to the eye rather than the converse. 13th Century Kamal Al-Farisi discovered the visible spectrum of light by double refraction.

Chemistry: 8th Century Persian scientist Tabir Ibn Hayyan discovered Sulphuric Acid, Caustic Soda, and Nitric Acid.

Physics: 12th Century Persian scientist Abdur Rahman Al-Hazini invented a scale to measure density, buoyancy, and specific gravity of objects.

Evolutionary Theory: Tunisian Historiographer Ibn Khaldon declared his Theory of Evolution many centuries before Europe and Darwin ever gave the subject any thought.

Cartography: 8th Century Al- Khwarizmi drafted an elaborate map of the Nile River.
During the 9th Century accurate representations of Longitude and the Circumference of the World was created for the Caliph Al-Ma'Mum. And in the 12th Century Ydrisi prepared a world map.

Just imagine - there were scientific centers in Baghdad, Cairo, Damascus, Samarkand, Shiraz, Bukhara, Isfahan, Toledo, Cordeba, Granada, and Istanbul.

And perhaps most important was the realisation of the need of Peer Review and Citations to evaluate and confirm their source materials."

Our coffee cups had been empty for some time. I ordered some more coffee, requested some snacks, and then resumed our discussion.

" Sure. Sure. I agree with all that you say - your people has suffered some unfair handicaps. But what has to be faced is that whilst over the past thirty years your people never made much progress controlling your future, a small group, your neighbors and fellow inhabitants with determination conspired to determine their future, finally obtained financial and political support from sympathetic groups throughout the world, and that future has been purposely designed at the expense of your people.

I have to ask the question - why did not your people make successful arrangements with sympathetic groups in the Middle East such as within the Arab League over the past thirty years? Palestine is surrounded with Arab countries. Countries such as Egypt, Iraq, Jordan, Saudi Arabia, Iran, Libya. Syria, and Lebanon. Your interests could have been secure.

With reasonable mutual support, the end of the Mandate could have been demanded, and your people control its destiny."

Hikmat took a deep breath. I looked on expectantly - these questions had to be answered. He stared at his cup. He knew full well that the record of the Arab League was dismal, one of idle words, little or no action, and a total lack of coordination and leadership. His eyes hardened a little. The nature and character of the Palestinian was being questioned. Rather carefully he laid out his thoughts.

"Alright. The Arab League made a great mistake waiting for the British troops to leave at the end of the Mandate before intervening in Palestine. I assume that they did not relish the possible retaliation of 100,000 British troops.

On the other hand, and this is of no credit to the Arab League, it was well aware of the Zionist desire to undertake "Ethnic Cleansing" and rid Palestine of Arabs, and did nothing. By May, the Zionists had dealt a death blow expelling over 500,000 Palestinian Arabs, and had been permitted to create a military force of some considerable clout."

I interjected and rather brutally stressed.

" And when the Arab League finally intervened, what a pathetic half hearted gesture. Just a few thousand troop completely uncoordinated with poor leadership. Merely being indignant about the terrible happenings in Palestine without adequate training and arms is of no value. The League achieved nothing. "

Tonelessly he agreed *" You are correct - it was very disappointing."*

" But why the half hearted minimal intervention when it actually took place?   The Arab League's combined populations must be many hundreds of millions - and yet a paltry disorganized force of a few thousand!"

The Arab news reporter swallowed hard - there were so many reasons, and none of them palatable to admit.   The history of the Middle East for thousands of years has been high lighted by intrigue, treachery, lack of faith, deceit, religious persecution, tribal hostilities, family enmities, and other disagreeable factors.

Decisions,   policies, and actions   all so short term and   rarely based on honor and long term agreement. Much determined by short term immediate material gain. Thus Jordan's King Abdullah, despite part of the Arab League, treacherously made an arrangement with the Zionists whereby his army, one of the finest in the Middle East, would sit back and permit the Zionists take over Palestine with the understanding that he would get the West Bank.

The reporter remained silent, and did not respond. He rose, expressed the hope that I had learnt something of value, and departed.

I remained seated thinking over what had been said. One matter seemed obvious. A nation of people to succeed must work together as a team with a common purpose, preferably have similar interests and beliefs, and be honorable and loyal to each other.

The lack of retaliation and inability to plan and design a positive future reflected poorly on the Palestinian Arab. One is confronted with different religious and social beliefs, prejudice, extreme thinking verging on madness, subtle and deadly tribal and family hatreds, and so forth. In matters such as this, to typify the Middle East Arab can be unwise and   render defective conclusions.

I spoke briefly with Hikmat in the coffee shop a few days later, and remarked.

" I think the people of any nation have to work together for a common purpose. For a people to not have a common goal and remain passive spells doom. At one time your people worked together successfully with a goal in mind"

I could not help smiling at Hikmat's astute response, although it did not resolve the problems of his people.

" I suspect that the British have suffered in the past due to failings similar to my people - it explains the success of the Normans when they captured England in 1066 "

I thought it was so regrettable that the world continued to be so barbaric. The only hope of survival demanded strength, intelligence, and a common goal.

I had little to occupy myself, and made a habit of visiting the coffee shop. Cautiously I would always speak to Anwar, and ascertain the advisability of a visit. Normally Anwar's customers were all known locals, and my security understood. Regardless I would prudently choose a table in the early evening   where I would not be observed.

Friday was my birthday - I was determined to do something different. It was stifling hot despite the approach of Winter, and my room faced the afternoon sun. I pushed aside my papers, rose, and departed for the coolness of Anwar's coffee shop. The mid day crowd would have left, and I would have the place to myself and perhaps a few others.

Anwar shook his head - there were some customers whom he did not know. He suggested I visit later. Ahmad was aware of my rapid return from the coffee shop.

" What are you doing young man? "

" Just fancied a coffee but the place is crowded."

Ahmad identified my problem - boredom.

" I have an idea.   The city library is down the street. You will be pretty safe from being identified there. Let me check the street. If it is safe, I will escort you to the library. "

It seemed a great idea. Ahmad went outside into the street, surveyed the scene, and quickly came back.

" Right. Let us go immediately. You can return when it is dusk. Please take care"

Within two minutes we were outside the city library. I ascended the wide entrance steps, and entered a spacious foyer, and immediately appreciated the coolness within. I realized how fortunate wise societies are in possessing the thoughts of so many, now and in the past, in written records. The library is an oasis where one may read, study, and think free of the distraction and dishonesty of current day events.

I had already made a note that I should obtain information of a British Importer/Exporter of agricultural products. The business potential seemed considerable supplying modern implements for agriculture once peaceful conditions occurred again. And I imagined that a similar need would apply in neighboring Arab countries.

Ahmad had ordered the reservation of an Arab/English dictionary, and asked me to collect the book. I had no difficulty collecting the book although the librarian was aware that I was not a local resident. Ahmad's request was a request that should be complied.

I ascended the terrazzo stairs to the Second Floor, and entered a room that specialized in History and Genealogy. Although most books were in Arabic, there was the possibility of books addressing specialized subjects that might be written and published in English . Curiously I examined a couple of books that addressed the exploits of the Crusaders in the 1200s.

" What a scream if I found a Blackberry Crusader clothed in shining white armour!!"

It was a ridiculous search. I would have done better checking the names of servants who had the job of cleaning the gleaming white armour.

I turned, smiling to myself, and saw seated at a large solid wood table surrounded with books, an individual who eyed me curiously. It was Jenkins, Communications Officer of United Nations. We had crossed paths a few times at a number of receptions and conferences.

" And how is Mr Blackberry - I trust he is in excellent health?"

Jenkins was a Londoner, educated at Cambridge University, and currently stationed in Jerusalem. He grinned cheerfully. He was a pleasant individual who fortunately lacked any evidence of self importance.. Accordingly he did not take exception to my rather vague explanation of my activities.

I smiled back, confirmed that my health indeed was excellent, and responded with my question.

" And how is Mr Jenkins progressing in his task of uniting all nations?"

The Communications Officer's smile faded. Very thoughtfully he declared.

" Very very tricky. Yes. A very difficult question to answer Mr Blackberry. Indeed I must emphasise very very tricky, if you understand what I mean?"

I smiled at his dilemma, a problem not exactly assisted by his august world body employer.

He looked at me seriously, and with doubt spread all over his face, he quietly asked.

" What makes them tick Blackberry?"

I sat down at the library table, and looked around. - we were alone.

" You do understand Mr Jenkins that is a very obtuse question - who is them? Are you speaking of the British, The Zionists, The Palestinian Arabs, The Arab League, or Others?"

Jenkins drummed his fingers on the table top - I am uncertain whether or not he welcomed my introducing so many groups to enter the equation. Regardless he had much on his mind, and was clearly troubled. Palestine was a total disaster. Gloomily he responded.

" Probably the whole damn lot "

He was no doubt right - all could, or should, accept blame for the unhappy events of the past ten months. But there was another authority not yet mentioned that was also responsible.

" How about including United Nations? "

His face reddened a little - it was an unexpected criticism which was far too close to the truth.

" Not so loud old boy - that is not exactly a popular opinion. "

He was dead right. That opinion would not be welcome in his circle. But why should one respect feelings when half a million individuals had been attacked and expelled, all their property stolen, and possibly 10,000 to 20,000 killed.. One has to ask a very pertinent question. - *What the heck is the purpose of United Nations if it is unwilling and incapable of carrying out its charter and the terms of its resolutions?*

" Well I do not wish to embarrass you, but consider the following.

UNSCOP, your special committee in U.N for Palestine recommended the partition of Palestine into two States. No one ever bothered to get the approval of the indigenous Palestinian Arabs who at that time owned 95% of the country. No one considered the consequences if the Palestinian Arabs disapproved of this totally inequitable idea.

Finally 29th November 1947 U.N. passed General Assembly Resolution 181 which confirmed the recommendations of UNSCOP regardless of the inequity, but at least did stress that both entities must adhere to liberal democratic concepts.

Not only was Resolution 181 inequitable and a crime against the Palestinian Arabs, U.N. thereafter has made no effort to ensure the so called liberal democratic concepts demanded therein were adhered to.

Now less than a year later, half a million have been expelled, 500 to 600 villages destroyed, ten to twenty thousand died,   and all Palestinian property stolen from them. And to cap it all, often these terrible happenings were witnessed by U.N. observers. "

Jenkins squirmed uncomfortably - he had no acceptable explanation. Irritably he demanded.

" What the heck do you expect chum? We have no armed forced here. We can only watch these damn thugs "

What a lame excuse. I was pissed off, and tapped the table irritably.

" Look Jenkins - I'm sorry. You guys should have created utter hell last December, crushed those Zionist thugs, and caused one almighty uproar in New York."

Sarcastically I asked.

" Or is all this Ethnic cleansing your definition of liberal democratic concepts?"

The U.N representative no longer possessed an amiable disposition, and clearly found his fellow countryman a pain in the neck.

" Look chum - Folke Bernedotte negotiated two Truces, and got assassinated for his efforts. I'm just a low level officer. All I know is that U.N. in New York did absolutely nothing."

I stared hard and unhappily. I was not being particularly considerate of unfortunate Jenkins but I was mad.

" You people are dishonest. Just lots of words and no action. Those two Truces were a complete farce. Ask the hundred thousand or more who were attacked and expelled during your so called truces."

Angrily I left Jenkins. As I passed the library foyer, I knew that I was right to be indignant. We have a moral duty to be indignant when we perceive terrible harms caused to defenseless individuals permitted and caused by smug government and institution employees who simply wait for their monthly check.

We should fight Institutions such as U.N who are the cause of many inequities, do not carry out their mandate, and are no doubt bribed by lobbyists promoting Zionist interests.

It is incredible to understand that UNSCOP at Geneva 1947 favored a ten year period of probably British trusteeship after considerable deliberation, and yet permitted Zionist factions to change their decision to one of partition. To ignore their obligation to consider the welfare of all, and to favor an extreme religious group was an absolute disgrace.. And just as incredible the General Assembly voted for partition November 29th 1947. Correspondence suggests that Truman himself may have intervened at the last minute to ensure success for the partition. And at least two nations Haiti and Philippines had voted for partition having been subjected to unauthorized intervention of American citizens.

How unfortunate that United Nations is located in New York, subject to unfavorable pressures , US domestic politics and special interests, and not concerned about the real problems of the world.

The League that Never Was

Haidar Al-Safjawi. What can I say! He was the most impressive individual I ever met in Palestine. He possessed high cheeks, stood tall thin and erect - a born leader. He had an excellent understanding of the Arab scene which he constantly presented and defended, and very much aware of political antagonisms and adverse factions. One suspected that he was always on his own, independent in thought, proud, and not willing to accept other opinions and advise without careful consideration.

His appearance impressive - a born leader robed in white who wore the conventional white keffiyeh, I sensed the complete leader impervious to the detrimental thinking of weak supporters. No doubt the ideal leader on any battlefield. As a man, he had charm and humor - his failing, if a failing, perhaps the inability to trust anyone.

Haidar was of Syria. I assumed that he had been part of the disorganized force that entered Palestine after the departure of the British.

Anwar Al-Masiri invited Haidar to meet me at his coffee house. At the time I was still struggling to unravel the conflicting claims of the Zionists and of the Arab League. Anwar thought that Haidar was the ideal individual to explain what did and what did not take place earlier this year.

I thanked Anwar, introduced myself to Haidar, and explained my confusion. Ben Gurion, time after time, repeated the claim that the Zionist people were threatened with a Second Holocaust, the threat being the Palestinian Arabs and the Arab League.. And yet all my research revealed a singular lack of aggression by either the Palestinian Arabs or the Arab League. What was revealed was natural hostility to the U.N Partition Plan, the striking passivity of the local population, and an Arab League that blew " *Hot and Cold*" with their threats, and eventually postponed intervention into Palestine until May after the British troops had departed.

This Arab League intervention would take place many months after Ben Gurion's claims of a Second Holocaust. In the meantime there had been many months of severe Zionist aggression, and the expulsion of hundreds of thousands of Arabs. My hope was that Haidar could resolve the apparent contradiction. I posed my question.

"Was *Ben Gurion correct or were his claims simply propaganda lies?*

You are no doubt aware, it is a very important question because if a propaganda lie, it implies that all the Zionist attacks on many hundred villages and towns, the expulsion of about 500,000, the death of thousands, and the wholesale destruction of so many villages was vindictive, intentional, and inexcusable, and bluntly Ethnic Cleansing at its worst."

Haidar smiled bitterly - it was not a pleasant subject that would give him any pleasure. He shrugged and commenced.

" Let us consider Jordan first. Jordan , part of the Arab League, no doubt considered a major player.

King Abdullah was of the Hashemite Royal family of the Hejaz - the location of the holy Muslim cities of Mecca and Medina. Subsequent to the First World War, Abdullah, was given Jordan, arid desert east of the River Jordan.

Despite the poverty of his country, Abdullah possessed a powerful army trained and led by the British which was well respected by everyone including the Zionist settlers. In 1946, the Jewish Agency negotiated with Abdullah and arrived at an understanding whereby Abdullah would ensure that his army would not intervene with any Zionist attacks in Palestine involving its take over. In return it was agreed that Abdullah would be given the West Bank of Palestine.

Throughout the months of January to May and later, the Jordan army did nothing to assist the Palestinian Arabs. Abdullah, so treacherous to the Palestinian cause, met Golda Meier in Amman May 13th this year, played a double game appearing to aid the military aspirations of the Arab League, but in fact his only interest was possessing the West Bank.

So my friend - you can write off Jordan completely. That country never represented any threat in any form to the Zionists, and the Zionists were well aware of that."

Haidar sat back with arms crossed. I sipped my coffee, and responded.

" Well. You have successfully written off Jordan. Now. What about the rest of the League?"

Haidar eyes flashed momentarily, and his face flushed a little. Now he was approaching less simplistic explanations of the Arab League's involvement and its failure to defend the rights of the indigenous Palestinian Arabs. He chose his words carefully knowing full well that however he presented the record of the League, it would appear a dismal failure. Even his involvement gave him no satisfaction.

" We, in the Arab League Nations, demonstrated and shared the resentment of the Arab people of Palestine in regard to the inequity of the proposed partitions of the country.

UNSCOP - United Nations Special Commission on Palestine - proposed in its recommendations to the U.N. that the British Mandate of Palestine should be partitioned into two States. This recommendation was not only criminal, it was completely inequitable and unacceptable.

The recommendations not only totally ignored the rights of the indigenous Palestinians who owned 94% of all land, but rewarded the Zionists with all the finest level agricultural land and strategic features, that included the two only major ports on the Mediterranean, the main highways and railways and communication systems. The Palestinian State was given merely the central spine of hills and mountains that had no access to the sea, and the isolated southerly strip of Gaza.

Naturally when United Nations Resolution 181 was announced late November 1947 recommending this Partition, we totally rejected the Resolution. The Arab League was obliged to resolve this unfair Resolution, and it was obvious that this minority group of Zionists extremists must be prevented from undertaking this land grab.

I am ashamed to admit that although all Arab League Nations agreed that the rights of the Palestinian people must be protected, that it would necessitate the presence of a strong united Arab League military force, no nation contributed meaningfully and positively throughout this year.

And whilst the Arab League procrastinated with words rather than action, the Zionists developed their military force of about 30,000 troops and 20,000 auxiliaries, stockpiled enormous shiploads of arms, equipment, guns, armaments delivered by ship from the Communist Eastern Bloc, and possessed a secret Spitfire squadron in Montenegro.

Without any real desire to intervene, the Arab League decided that it would intervene after the departure of the British troops in May. By that time, the Zionists had undertaken about 500 aggressive attacks on villages and towns, the demolition of hundreds of villages, the death of thousands, and the expulsion of about 400,000 individuals from their homes and country."

Anwar brought us two fresh cups of coffee. I ordered some snacks. Haidar Al-Safjawi needed to relax after his lengthy discourse. I stared at my notes - I understood well Haidar's explanation of the unfortunate failure of the Arab League to intervene until May. But that explanation did not resolve Ben Gurion's claims of the impending Second Holocaust and the Arab attacks claimed to have taken place during the first five months of this year.

" But" I stressed

"There are claims   of Arab forces and their attacks during that first five months!"

Haidar did not dispute my claim.

" Correct. There were   a few attacks, but let me finish speaking of the Arab League and its failure to act in good faith.

My country Syria was the only nation prepared to intervene with a military force early this year. The rest of the nations just dragged their feet.

Saudi Arabia and Egypt offered small scale financial support.
Lebanon a few guns.
Iraq agreed to train and send some volunteers.
Jordan made no commitment.

Despite six months of Arab League talks and threats, member contribution in May after the departure of the British was half hearted and deplorable.

Syria in May entered the north of Palestine with a few thousand troops.
Iraq a few thousand troops that did nothing neutralized by an agreement with Jordan.
Egypt a few thousand disorganized volunteers in the south.

There was no co-ordination, no co-operation, lack of trained forces, lack of arms and equipment. Lack of national support, and a lack of leadership. By the middle of the year the so called intervention had fizzled. "

Haidar no doubt was not keen to continue the Arab League's dismal record.. I pondered over this description of events. It would appear that the Arab League nations had been dishonest, and avoided any active participation involving a military force worthy of taking on the Zionist forces. Each Arab League nation had hoped presumably that the other nations would carry the banner.

I posed a thought to Haidar.

" I wonder if most of the nations in the Arab League were unaware of King Abdullah's treacherous Jordan agreement with the Zionists, and had relied on Jordan's strong British led and trained troops to be the main intervening contender?"

It was an interesting point that had not occurred to Haidar.

" That is a possibility. I was unaware of Jordan's agreement to hold back their troops, and not retaliate against Zionist aggressive attacks   in Palestinians."

Regardless it still did not excuse the disgraceful lack of Arab League involvement despite all their rhetoric and threats.

Haidar was anxious to address the attacks that took place early in the year.

" Now allow me to address your important observation. You are correct. There were records of Arab forces and attacks during the first five months of this year.

December 1947, the Arab League, unable to arrive at any agreement regarding immediate intervention, met, and recommended the delivery of arms to the Palestinians, and also the formation of a volunteer force which was given the name of the Arab Liberation Army (ALA). A Syrian general was appointed   leader. Very small groups entered Palestine which were of no consequence.

January 1948 the ALA had a force of about 2000 Syrians led by Fawzi Al-Qawqji that entered Galilee. This force was far too small even to defend all the villages, and certainly was inadequate to undertake any offensive against the Zionist forces. There was also a small force of volunteers in Haifa as early as January 9th. A few Jewish convoys were attacked but no attacks were made against Jewish settlements.

According to Jewish information, the ALA never exceeded more than 3000 individuals, and the volunteer force was ill trained, lacked arms and rifles, and was really an uncoordinated disaster during the months of February and March. In general the ALA attacked Jewish convoys with the intention of isolating a few Jewish settlements, but their efforts were not a success.

During April and May, the ALA had a few isolated volunteer groups all of whom were ill trained, lacked arms and rifles which faced well disciplined and well armed Zionist forces two to three times greater in number.

In Tiberias there were 30 volunteers, in Haifa about 500 local and Lebanon volunteers, in Safad 400 volunteers, half of whom had no arms, and Jaffa 1500 volunteers.

* During April a force of 2000 troops of the Carmeli Brigade overwhelmed Haifa. Whilst at Safad a force of 1000 Palmach destroyed the Safad defence. Ihasn Qam Ulmaz Syrian leader was killed, and thereafter the ALA lost heart lacking leadership.*

Finally in May the Jaffa volunteer ALA force of 1500 faced 5000 Irgun and Haganah troops, survived for three weeks, and then surrendered.

Bluntly the ALA would appear to have been a cruel hoax encouraging naïve volunteers to participate in a campaign with completely inadequate numbers that should have been carried out by well planned organized military forces of the Arab League. Everything was against the ALA. In December 1947 the Haganah special units had already visited and scared villagers throughout Palestine of becoming ALA volunteers, and had threatened severe retaliation if any village co operated with the ALA. Any hope of the ALA getting support from the indigenous Arabs was minimized and destroyed."

Anwar refilled our cups. It was late. I decided to ask a pertinent question.

" I trust you will not mind my curiosity but what was your involvement during this time?"

His eyes indicated evidence of his contempt of all that had taken place. His nostrils flared.

" Mr Blackberry. My career is that of a professional soldier. What has taken place over the past year is the product and the interference of dishonest individuals and politicians. A soldier does not get involved in battles that cannot   possibly be won. It makes no sense.

Of course all that has happened is regrettable because Palestine should have had the full support of all Arab League Nations complete with well run strong military forces. That was not the case. All poor Palestine had was a small number of ill trained volunteers. "

It was now late, and Anwar wished to close. I needed Haidar's confirmation. of my understanding.

" So this so called threat of a Second Holocaust was merely a few thousand ill trained and poorly armed volunteers with no meaningful leadership. which was confronted by the enormous military force of the Haganah, Palmach, Irgun, Stern, hostile Jewish settlements, and the financial support of the Zionists in the USA and UK?"

Haidar nodded as he departed.

" Correct - the Zionist claims were terrible lies. The Arab League never existed as a meaningful force to protect the interests of the Palestinian Arabs. "

Report - October 1948

Accra District	- *Villagesexpelled-(10,500) Arab Al-Samaniyya, Dayr Al-Qasi,* - *Iqrit,-Al-Ghabisiyya, Iribbin Khirbat, Kafr Inan,* - *Al-Mansura, Summaja, Tarbikha. Tarshina*
Baysan District	- *No Reports*
Beersheba District	- *Villages expelled- (Number ?) - Al-Khalasa* - *Town expelled - Beersheba (Number ?)*
Gaza District	- *Villages attacked- (11,100) - Al-Faluja, Hiribya,* - *Iraq Al-Manshiyya, - Al-Jirja,* - *Villages expelled- (16,800) - Barbara, Al-Majdal, Bayt Jima,* -*Dimra Hamama, Hulayqat, Isdud, Al-Jura,, Kawkaba* - *Town attacked - Gaza (Number ?)*
Haifa District	- *No Reports*

Hebron District	- *Villages expelled- (19,500) -Ajjur, Khirbat Ammuriyya, Bayt*
	      *- Jibrin, Bayt Nattif, Al-Dawayima **(M)**, Kudna, Dayr Aban*
	- *Al-Qubayba, Ra'Na, Umm Burj Khirbat, Zakariyya, Zikrin,*
	                    -

Jaffa District	- *No Reports*
Jerusalem District	- *Villages expelled- (8,600) - Allar, Bayt'Itab, Bayt Umm Al-Mays,* - *Al Burayj, Dayr Abani, Dayr Al-Qabu, Al-Umur Khirbat* - *Ras Abu'Ammar, Sufla, Al-Walaja, Al-Jannur Khirbat,* -
Jinin District	- *No Reports*
Nazareth District	- *No Reports*
Al-Ramla District	- *No Reports*

Report - October 1948

Safad District	*- Villages attacked- (750) - Al-Farradiyya* *- Villages expelled- (8,000) Alma, Fara, Ghabbatiyya, Jish **(M)**,* *Al-Malikiyya,, Marus, Mirun, Al-Ras, Al-Ahmur, Sufla,* *- Sabalan, Safsaf **(80)**, Saliha **(94)**, Dayshum,- Al-Sammu'I,* *- Sa'Sa (M),*
	*- Town expelled - Safad **(M)** (Number ?)*
Tiberias District	*- Villages expelled- (5,000) - Al-Mansura, Mughar* *- Al-Wa'ra al-Sawda Khirbat **(15)***
Tulkarm District	*- No Reports*

Villages attacked	*71*
Towns attacked	*3*
Inhabitants attacked	*115,400*
Inhabitants expelled	*93,400*

Moshe Rabin - What actually Happened

I was always interested in the economic advantages and opportunities of market expansion. Simple economics- increase the demand and sale of a product, the cost of manufacture and distribution decreases, and theoretically business success and profit improves.

I imagined that the demand for agriculture products in Palestine would increase, and current farming practices would be improved with modern agricultural implements. My mind dwelt on Uncle Arthur's manufacturing plant in Kent. No doubt I would surprise and please him if he received some substantial orders from Palestine.

During my research in the Ramallah Library, I found the name of an Import/Export business in Ramallah named " *Middle East Company*" that possibly specialized in agricultural implements. The address was close by   about 2-3 blocks from Ahmad's address.

There was very little activity throughout Palestine November. I asked Ahmad.

" Do you think it wise if I visited this business, and ascertain if there is any demand for Uncle Arthur's agricultural implements?"

Ahmad reluctantly agreed that I could visit. But it was clear that he would have preferred that I remained safely indoors.

" Alright. If they ask where you are from, say you are a visitor from UK, and that you are staying with friends in Jerusalem. Under no circumstance mention this place"

The following day Tuesday, I visited the premises of the *Middle East Company*. Initially, not conversant with the economics of Import/Export companies, I was disappointed at the shabby and worn appearance of the business. Anyhow the young lady at reception was advised of the purpose of my visit.

" Do you think your company would be interested in importing agriculture implements from the U.K.?"

She gave me a bright friendly smile, and said she would ask Mr Rabin. She retired to a rear office, and for a few minutes communicated with her supervisor. Eventually she returned with Mr Rabin who appeared hard pressed, anxious, and a little frustrated having to deal with an unexpected visitor. He listened to me rather impatiently, and then cut me short.

" We do not import agricultural products, but we have customers who are accustomed to signing orders through our office for the purchase of such implements. Now I need to see brochures of your UK products and price list. I can then advise you if we are interested."

He abruptly left me standing, and returned to his office. The young lady handed me the man's business card .

" Moshe Rabin Manager, Middle East Company, Importers/Exporters "

I returned to Ahmad in two minds - I thought Mr Rabin was an unfriendly character - on the other hand if I intended to seek business, I would have to anticipate unfriendly characters. Ahmad stared at the business card, and thought .

" This is a Jewish firm - probably a hard business man - still only such people can normally succeed in the cut throat business of Import/Export. "

Ahmad warned me again

" Under no circumstance mention our local address. You are simply a nephew of your Uncle Arthur making some enquiries. "

Later the same week I visited the *Middle East Company* again. This time Moshe Rabin was more sociable, and invited me into his shabby office. I sensed commercial greed dominated his demeanor.

" Well. What have you to show me? "

I produced a number of brochures, photographs, and a price list - the price list of all products being FOB London Docks. He rapidly examined the information, and finally announced.

" We might be interested in that plough. Can you get confirmation of price and delivery date. Currently we are getting ploughs from a German manufacturer - excellent product but a bit pricey "

I was quite excited, thanked the Importer, and said I would return with the necessary information. Later that day I phoned Uncle Arthur who was surprised and pleased to hear from his nephew.

" Yes Paul - we would certainly like to have orders from Palestine. You can tell Mr Rabin that the price is FOB London Docks and that price schedule still applies. Of course if the price goes up, the old price will no longer apply. Now regarding delivery date, we should be able to deliver the ploughs probably in 1950. "

" Why 1950 Uncle? "

" Home deliveries take priority my boy. Just tell your Importer that we will be delighted to do business with him! "

I was quite excited, and visited Moshe Rabin the following morning, and relayed my news. He just burst out laughing,

" My dear chap. What kind of business is prepared to wait 1 - 2 years for an order to be delivered. You English are utterly crazy claiming that the home market takes priority."

He noted my disappointment, and shared another similar experience.

" A building contractor ordered 100 sanitary fixture sets - the total value considerable. The London manufacturer said he would be unable to meet the order for two years. That kind of attitude is totally unrealistic - I am getting orders met in Italy - immediate delivery - no delay"

Moshe was in a more sociable mood, and confided.

" Pity about the delivery delay of two years. The current price for that plough was competitive. But there again British products are poorly manufactured - no quality control - just one problem after another "

He sighed - there would be no commission sales for that Kent manufacturer. He handed over my documents, leaned back, and asked.

" Well young man - how do you like Palestine?"

" I think Palestine has great potential. It is a pity there is so much unrest"

The Importer Salesman lit a cigarette, puffed a cloud of smoke, and sighed.

" What can you do with these restless irresponsible people?"

I wondered *" Who is he talking about"* although I was pretty certain that this negative remark applied to the Palestinian Arabs. I pretended to not understand his comment and asked.

" What do you mean?"

" What do I mean?"   Moshe leaned back in another cloud of smoke.

" What I mean is that these shiftless useless Arabs are never satisfied, irresponsibly causing endless problems and hostility. Jewish settlers have suffered enormously because of them."

I decided nothing would be gained by refuting this character. Innocently I asked.

" How can this hostility be resolved.?"

" Simple. Expel every Arab. There is no other solution. They are all trouble makers, thieves, murderers. Really they are all scum. The quicker they leave the better. "

" What you say is very interesting. Are you aware that over 500,000 have been expelled over the past nine months. ? "

He frowned unaware of the number.

" As much as that? Did not know that. By the way they were not expelled - they all have left voluntarily. It was their decision to leave you know. "

I no longer had any cares about Moshe Rabin's feelings.

" Did you know that over 500 to 600 villages have been bombed and destroyed? I imagine that was a good reason why the half million Arabs have fled. "

He waved his right arm indicating that my claim was absurd.

" Ridiculous - Just evil rumors. I understand that a few houses left in a ruined condition were demolished by Jewish authorities after the Arabs voluntarily left"

I pretended to accept his explanation and continued.

" I am told that thousands have been killed in massacres and the like, and many have died fleeing the highways of Palestine. "

The importer was beginning to become excited.

" My dear man - that is utter rubbish - just typical Arab propaganda - such evil people. Do you realise these terrible people invited Arab military forces of the Arab League to enter this country and interfere with our peaceful activities. Do you realise that we have suffered the probability of a Second Holocaust for the past year. "

I sympathized.

" It must be a terrible experience for you. "

Rabin eyed me suspiciously. The nature of the current discussion was unwelcome. I presented him with another question.

" By the way perhaps you can solve a matter that has puzzled me for some time. United Nations has declared that all Arabs that have fled Palestine should be permitted to return and reclaim their properties. Why has that not happened? "

The Jewish Importer was now truly pissed off.

" Because my friend, if you truly understood what is going on, you would know that no Arab has returned to reclaim any property - that is if he ever owned any property. What is evident is that these evil people do not desire to be responsible citizens and return to this country."

I responded with feigned relief.

" Thank you for your explanation Mr Rabin. What still puzzles me is that the Arabs owned 94% of Palestine, and yet over 500,000 do not wish to return to claim their property.

Does that not appear rather strange Mr Rabin?"

The man glared furiously - it was time to leave.

It was very difficult but I engineered a bright smile, and thanked him for his time and interest.

 I now possessed further information, the understanding of Moshe Rabin, of what was really happening in Palestine.

I thought back to a discussion with a Jewish gentleman in Jerusalem.. I will always remember his claim.

" God has called us to be the World's Priests."

And he quoted the words.

" And you will be unto a kingdom of priests and a holy nation."

One sensed that in his opinion Israel was for the chosen, and it was a focus of God's intent.

I had then visited an area south of Old Jerusalem, the walls adjoined the deserted valley called Gehena *" Ge-Hinnah"* (Valley Son of Hinnah, Valley of Slaughter). What a depressing place filled with evil memories - overlooked by Peaks with names that spelled corruption.

On one side of the valley was *Mount Scandal* - on the other side *St James* (Christ's brother) where he was thrown to his martyrdom, and to the left *Mount Evil Counsel*. And there the tree which Judas hung himself. And the field purchased by the priests in blood money (30 shekels of silver) returned by Judas - they bought the field and named it *"Field of Blood"*

And I wondered, taking into consideration the current activities of the Zionists, what truly was God's intention.

Ahmad - Confidentially Unknown

Inspector Mendlesohn's Report lay on Issar Harel's desk.

The head of the Israeli Mossad had read the contents with care, and concluded.

. *" At last Mendlesohn was using his brain!"*

There appeared little argument that Ibrahim Shiqaqi was an active leader in the collection and distribution of information relating to Zionist activities in Palestine. But Harel was no fool. Mendlesohn had done a good job but obviously there had to be others.

"Where were they?"

Harel picked up his phone, and dialed for Inspector Mendlesohn's Haifa number. He did not bother to identify himself, and immediately addressed his concern.

" Good work Mendlesohn. With luck this will stop these troublesome reports in England. What have you done to catch the rest of these criminals?"

Mendlesohn already sensed that his chief's satisfaction was rapidly deteriorating, and with a rather wooden voice responded.

" The only information I found was a list of passwords and numbers. No indication what the passwords and numbers applied to."

" Why have you not resolved this all important information?"

" We searched the building from top to bottom and found nothing."

" He must have records somewhere"

" I checked his daughter's house. She was killed with her father by my men. There was absolutely nothing in her house."

" Well what are you doing now?"

Mendlesohn's feeling of well being sank, and glumly offered the obvious.- advise that he well knew would not satisfy his chief.

" Regret nothing this very moment. "

" What about that reporter Blackberry who keeps on eluding you?"

" I have a man keeping surveillance of Ibrahim Shiqaqi's premises that may produce results "

" Is that all Inspector? "

Harel's voice was both scornful and sarcastic. Mendlesohn wisely remained silent very much aware of Harel's dissatisfaction, and .listened carefully to his superior's instructions.

" Inspector. You are to leave Haifa immediately, and attend to far more important and obvious matters. You will return to Jerusalem, check every bank, and find the bank that has Shaqaqi's accounts. If you are not successful, or experience any bank refusing to respond to your important enquiry, phone me immediately and I will get that obstacle removed ."

The following morning the Inspector was trudging the streets of Jerusalem Old City visiting all the banks. Banks understand that their customers expect the utmost secrecy. Without such confidence they would have no customers. Accordingly Inspector Mendlesohn was obliged to make numerous explanations to doubtful bank managers, and in return the bank managers most loathe would finally admit that they did not have Ibrahim Shuqaqi as a customer.

Finally the stubborn inspector made some progress. Late the second day. The *Jerusalem and Hebron Bank* admitted that they indeed had a customer of that name. The bank quite rightly refused to divulge any further details without a court order.

Issar Harel was immediately appraised of this circumspect institution and its desire to protect the secrecies of its customer. The following morning the bank manager phoned Memdelsohn.. His voice seemed very strained and agitated.

" Inspector Mendlesohn. Ali Ashwani of Jerusalem and Hebron Bank speaking. If you visit my office, I will be able to address your queries regarding the account of Ibrahim Shaqaqi."

With some enthusiasm the Inspector entered the bank premises. However when he left, his bearing was heavy and depressed. The account transaction were quite easy to understand. Every month the account received a substantial sum from a London newspaper, the title of which Mendlesohn immediately identified. No other meaningful deposits were recorded. Monthly outgoings were conventional business expenses. There were no payments to individuals. What was significant was a substantial sum withdrawn in cash every month.

Mendlesohn was pretty confident that the cash withdrawal, in some form or fashion, represented payment to individuals involved in Ibrahim's business. But there was no evidence, and the manager assured him that there were no other accounts.

He reported his latest findings to Harel. The head of Intelligence, dissatisfied and impatient as usual, yelled at the man.

" Have you a list of the cash withdrawals? "

" No. Why make a list? "

" Because Inspector you are going to visit every conceivable institution that holds customer deposits. There is no doubt an account somewhere that will have deposits that include these monthly cash withdrawals. Find it and we will start to make some progress. "

So the unfortunate inspector continued to trudge the streets, and became an expert of the numerous institutions that specialise in looking after customer cash deposits.

Early November I had completed the October summarized Report, and I handed the document to Ahmad who arranged to send it to London. Ahmad was often absent, and I would be left to occupy myself with current affairs.

When I related my failed mission selling agricultural implements, Ahmad seemed withdrawn and anxious.

" It is not your fault Paul, but every Jew has to be considered a dangerous enemy, and your identification can be revealed through an unfavorable comment or report. Now I would like you to speak to witnesses of two massacres in the district of Safad. I plan to take you to the Safad Safe House which is fairly secure. Although the Arab and the Jew populations in Safad are about equal, their relationship is quite sound. The Jewish community are not admirers of the Zionist sect. "

So it was agreed mid November that we would drive to Safad, and I made preparations.

The night before we left, I sat down to speak to Ahmad.

" Is there anything I can do to assist you. You are always occupied and presumably rushing all over the countryside. What precisely are you doing? "

Ahmad smiled rather grimly, and then openly, and held my arm with warmth.

" Paul. In this horrible world that we are currently living in, and in particular the kind of work that we are undertaking, our success depends very much on all of us being as ignorant as possible about each other and our specific activities.

If you should ever get in the hands of Jewish Security, heaven forbid, and you suffer torture, it is far better for all of us if you have no knowledge at all. I am Ahmad Al-Husseini. I am a driver. I was responsible for meeting you at Beirut International Airport and driving you to Jerusalem, and then to Jaffa. When Roger Standish died, he requested that I should accommodate you.

Remember I am merely a driver. That is all you need to know - any further information can only imperil you and us."

" That information is not shattering. Both Roger and Ibrahim are dead"

" Precisely."

As we departed for Safad motoring through the central hills of Palestine, I had to tease Ahmad in reference to our brief talk the night before. There I was dressed in my Arab clothes, wearing the black and white keffiyeh, with only my British eyes peering out.

" You know Ahmad - you are the most remarkable driver I have met."

He laughed uproariously, and responded.

" To imagine that I be told that by the most British looking Arab I have ever met disguised as a Palestinian Correspondent."

Safsaf, a village of about 1,000, is located about 5 miles north west of the town of Safad, set on a low hill. The name Safsaf means *" Willow"* in Arabic. Close to the Tarshiha -Safad highway, it possessed a mosque, an elementary school, and a number of shops. Economic activity was mainly agricultural with fruits and olives irrigated from springs and rainfall.

The village had been the headquarters of the Arab Liberation Army (ALA) led by Adib Al-Shishakli who subsequently became president of Syria. On or about the 29th October, the village was attacked and occupied by Jewish troops after a brief battle.

The Safe House arranged for Ishaq, a witness of the Safsaf massacre, to meet me at their premises. Ishaq was a small wizened individual, who was clearly very frightened, and refused to divulge his family name.

I endeavored to make him feel secure, and gave him a cup of coffee. Eventually he was prepared to describe the terrible massacre which he witnessed.

" Initially we had the impression that the ALA would defend our village. However the intensity of the Jewish attack disturbed the volunteers from Syria, and they all fled to Lebanon.

Quite a number of villagers were killed or wounded during the attack. The Israeli soldiers entered Safsaf early morning at sunrise, and they ordered all of us to line up in a place in the northern part of the village. About seventy of our men were blindfolded and shot to death in front of us. One after one they were shot, and their bodies dumped in the village well.

Women pleaded for mercy and ignored. Four young women were told to accompany some Jewish soldiers to carry water. Instead the men took them to some empty houses, raped them, and then killed them.

The Israeli soldiers returned to our village a few days later, and told us that we should forget what had occurred, and that we could stay in our homes. But my people started to leave at night, and eventually Safsaf was empty of inhabitants."

Ishaq was very distressed being obliged to recite his horrible memories. I did not press him for further details - there was no necessity to imagine the dreadful scenes.

Saliha, a village of about 1,200, is located about 5 miles north of Safsaf, and stood at the edge of the steep Wadi Saliha in the Upper Galilee Mountains close to the border of Lebanon. Crops of cereals and orchards were irrigated.

The massacre at the village occurred 30th October during the Jewish Operation Hiram, and many atrocities took place committed by the Seventh Brigade.

Awni Majjaj was a witness of this massacre, and like Ishaq, was extremely nervous After listening to him, one could understand his current fear after hearing his description of the event.

" We had not been subjected to any specific attack that night, and I was not aware of any resistance by our men. It is my understanding that the Haganah Seventh Brigade had been ordered to proceed from the village of Sa'Sa and occupy the village of Al-Malikiyya. Perhaps some of our men were bitter about the attack at Sa'Sa and fired some shots at the troops.

Whatever the reason, I was woken by the noise of the entry of the Brigade into our village. I hid frightened but saw the soldiers herding about one hundred into a building which was blown up. The rest of us were expelled. "

Awni claimed that he lost some relatives. He was bewildered and could not understand why they had been subjected to this terrible massacre. I was unwilling to reveal my thoughts - thoughts that would do little to resolve the poor man's unhappiness.

Whilst waiting for Ahmad to return to Safad, I enquired about Ibrahim's grandson Amin. He was very fortunate last June. Inspector Mendlesohn's gun shot   that   struck   his arm proved to be just a flesh wound. He rapidly recovered at the Safe House.

He was instructed to remain at the Safad Safe House, and avoid any Jewish Security search. Finally in September he learnt of his grandfather Ibrahim and Aunt Ghada's death, and returned to Jerusalem. I was assured that he was in good health and spirits.

Ahmad returned to Safad at the end of the week. We then left taking the central hills route, and we arrived at Ramallah without incident.

I was able to prepare the summarized November Report quite quickly. There had not been a lot of aggressive activity. About 11,000 villagers had been expelled from eleven villages in the districts of Accra, Gaza, Hebron, and Safad. There were no reports from the rest of the districts.

I completed my work which included the witness reports of the two massacres in the Safad district.

Ahmad examined my report, remarked that November was very quiet compared to October, and indicated that all the information would be sent to London as soon as possible.

With obvious satisfaction. He declared.

" Very very good Mr Correspondent "

Later that day Ahmad had to leave, and advised that he would be back soon.

Report - November 1948

Accra District	*- Villages expelled-(2,200) - Al-Nabi Rubin, Suruh*
Baysan District	*- No Reports*
Beersheba District	*- No Reports*
Gaza District	*- Villages expelled- (7,000) - Hiribya, Iraq Suwaydan, Al-Jirra, - Al Jura, Al-Khisaas, Ni'Ilya, Hajja*
Haifa District	*- No Reports*
Hebron District	*- Villages expelled-(Number ?) - Al Majdal*
Jaffa District	*- No Reports*
Jerusalem District	*- No Reports*
Jijin District	*- No Reports*
Nazareth District	*- No Reports*
Al Ramla District	*- No Reports*
Safad District	*- Villages expelled - (400) - Kafr Bir'Im*
Tiberias District	*- No Reports*
Tulkarm District	*- No Reports*

Villages attacked	*11*
Towns attacked	*-*
Inhabitants attacked	*-*
Inhabitants expelled	*11,000*

The Noose is Tightened

I often wondered where and what Ahmad was doing. He wisely never told me, and I can only guess. Regardless he was very reliable, and returned as promised. However on this occasion his return was very alarming. With a very grim face, he advised me.

" Paul - it is time to leave - we are being hunted, and I suspect the hunters are very close. Now listen carefully. I have arranged your travel arrangements. Report to the Lebanese Air desk at Beirut International Airport - your air ticket will be handed to you.

Now I am giving you Three Hundred Pounds to cover your travel costs from here to Beirut via Damascus. Your costs should be absolutely minimal but you never know. From here to Damascus you will be in good hands and you will be secure.

Regarding your remuneration for your excellent services, it will be deposited into your UK bank account. The remuneration will include for the cost of your lost motor cycle.

Finally you will be contacted by a Mr Jessup in London who will arrange to collect from you your final reports for December."

He looked at me anxiously, and enquired.

" Is that in order?"

" But Ahmad I wish to stay - how will the reports continue without my presence.?"

He shook his head firmly.

" It would be wonderful to have you stay - but you and I are in grave danger. You must return to the safety of your country immediately."

" But ---------"

Ahmad was adamant.

" Sorry - There are no Buts ---------- if you wish to live!

Now listen very carefully because we have very little time. We are in immediate danger, and possibly this place is being observed. We will leave late this night, and will drive straight to the River Jordan. We are expected, and a boat will convey you across the river to Jordan. I am uncertain of the arrangements made for you from there to Damascus but I assure you that you are in very trustworthy hands.

Regarding your baggage - travel light - most important take copies of all your Reports and records."

Late in complete darkness we quietly left Ramallah. Ahmad very concerned and anxious, grimly drove around the narrow lanes of Ramallah until he was fully satisfied that he was not being followed. He then took off for Jericho and the river about 25 miles distant.

I was bursting with curiosity and asked.

" How did Jewish Security get onto our tracks?"

" I am advised that your old friend Inspector Mendlesohn has been sniffing around the banks in Jerusalem, and finally found Ibrahim's account. Fortunately Ibrahim was very discrete and there was no evidence in the bank account to link any of us. However that cunning bastard realized that Ibrahim must have had another account to distribute cash funds to all of us. I suspect he has found that account.

My informant was uncertain but was convinced that we are all in great danger, and time is rapidly running out."

We approached Jericho suburbs. Ahmad murmured quietly.

" We will have to take a chance and drive through Jericho."

I looked around apprehensively. Everywhere there seemed to be shadows that spelt danger. Every vehicle on the road a potential enemy.. The time was 2.30am. Although Jericho is within the district of Jerusalem and supposedly a part of the Palestinian State, one was very conscious of constant danger.

We were now about two miles from River Jordan, and approaching a small village. Grim faced Ahmad declared that we were being followed.

" Paul. I am going to lose our followers, and immediately park the car hopefully concealed. We will then make our way by foot to the river. We have to move fast and quiet. Understood?"

Ahmad was right as usual - our trackers had followed us relentlessly. Ahmad quickly drove around a number of twisting and confusing alleys, and finally it appeared that they had lost us.

" Come on quick Paul - follow me "

Part stumbling, part running, we made our way down slope in pitch dark to the river. The blood curdling baying of tracking dogs could be heard. The Mossad must have found our car, and now were tracking our scent. Fear exaggerates one's senses - the dog yapping seemed closer and more intense.

Finally we were confronted by a stone retaining wall partly lit by a street light close to the river bank. Ahmad held my arm, and immediately signaled with his torch three times. Immediately three flashes were returned.

" Go. There is your   boat - run as fast as your can - and God speed."

I ran, fell, recovered, stumbled, and ran into the helping hands of the boat crew. Within moments we were in mid stream.

Three men with two tracking dogs stood on the river edge breathless. The boat could no longer be seen. Inspector Mendlesohn cursed. His only hope now was the Jordan Army to apprehend the boat. He would have to be quick contacting the army. He stumbled back from the bank leaving his two men standing helpless with the dogs.

At that very moment Mendlesohn heard a very quiet and commanding voice.

" Inspector Mendlesohn."

Angrily he raised his head.

" What is it? "

As he spoke he was conscious of a shot, and   the shock of a hole through his head.

A few moments later there were two further shots.

Then all was quiet on the bank - over shadowed by the new moon   - and two lone sniffing dogs.

The Ships of the Desert

My memory of that night crossing the River Jordan, and being conveyed on the other side to the village of Zisa is vague and fragmented. I know I was frightened, confused, cold, worn out, and concerned about Ahmad's safety. I was assured by my escort that we were not being followed, and all was well.

We arrived at Zisa, located just south of Amman, at the break of dawn. The call from the local mosque advising all people that it was time to pray could be heard. My guides explained that we would travel via Amman to Irbid, Bosra, Dionysias, and finally Damascas - the journey over 150 miles - by camel!

" Camel!" I was full of misgiving. I had never ridden on a camel! In fact who had? Everything I had read and heard about the camel was not reassuring - bad tempered, stubborn, sometimes viscous, and other unfortunate and unfavorable habits.

My guides, escorts, and companions for this proposed journey comprised of four Syrian and Lebanon traders, and were familiar with this proposed route to Damascus. Faisal Abd Al-Qader the leader and Walid Al-Khatib his cousin, and the two other traders were a well organized, coordinated group, content, responsible, and cautious. Ahmad Al-Husseini's choice could not have been better.

I was instructed that riding a camel was presumably a *"Piece of Cake"* .I was ordered to act deaf and dumb, and to wear the keffiyeh wrapped around my face at all times. It would assist in eliminating curious thoughts.

With some apprehension, I seated myself on my camel, watched by two amused traders. They explained that my camel was very obedient, and should be treated gently. I should ride with only the halter that normally would be tied loosely to the peak of the saddle. A light tap of the camel switch to one side of the camel's neck advised the animal of the direction desired by the rider. With one's heels on the camel sides, the camel would understand the need to move forward.

I was pleasantly surprised to discover that instructing the camel to sit down was both simple and effective. One simply had to strike the camel's neck lightly a number of times, and at the same time call *" Kh", "Kh", "Kh", "Kh"*

Finally I began to understand why the camel is so often termed *"The Ship of the Desert"* Unlike the horse, the sensation of riding a camel is the roll of a boat, the large wide soft saddle one of comfort. The long comfy swing of the animal as it passed through the desert is an unique experience. One can rest, eat, and observe the passing landscape in complete relaxation.

And with that relaxing experience is the absolute silence of the Arabian deserts. At night the clear skies and the millions of stars glittering above. And to make life with the camel complete, every evening I assisted in the chore of feeding and cleaning of the animals. It passed the time, was of interest, and appreciated by my companions.

I was uncertain what I might expect to see in this arid desert.

My understanding of Arabia was a land of about 1.3 million square miles made up of uninhabitable deserts, some fertile valleys, and hostile mountains. The very scarce source of water an indispensable factor for survival.

The land of the Middle East ranged from the River Jordan , south to the Indian Ocean, from the Red Sea to the Persian Gulf, and to the borders of Persia (Iran) and Turkey in the north . This enormous area included Syria, Lebanon, Palestine, Jordan, Saudi Arabia, Iraq, and Yemen. It was significant that the reigning authority in many of these countries were tribal territories, regions, imamates, and sheikdoms with little concern of national law.

My general impression from what I had read was that the land in general was pretty wild with little administration, law, and justice. Bedouin sheiks did as they wished, defended their all important wells and sparse grazing land against all including their neighbors and rivals. The desert was a lawless place.

Historically Greeks, Egyptians, Persians, Armenians, and Assyrians, both Christian and Muslim, thrived on the camel borne trades between India, Europe, and Africa. And of course many benefited through the annual pilgrimages to Mecca and Medina.

I was already certain that this journey would be an unique experience and education. . Actually my education commenced well before we started out from Zisa. Faisal approached me, crouched down, and quietly asked.

" What gifts do you have?"

Puzzled I blurted out.

" Gifts?"

Faisal smiled, and   explained.

"Paul. We need gifts to present to every leader of every land, every tribal territory, every region, every imamate, and every Sheikdom we pass through. We are obliged to make our presence known."

I made the typical blunder through my ignorance.

" Do we have to make our presence known?"

Faisal looked at me with an incredulous expression.

" Everyone knows or will know of us throughout our journey. That is the way of the Bedouin world. You have to understand that a gift is a polite acknowledgment of the leader's authority. To not present a gift is considered an insult.

In return for the gift, he is obligated to make you welcome, offer security, and perhaps assist in the provision of a guide. Without that kind of understanding, most travelers would eventually perish left to their own limited resources.

The Islamic world complies to the 3rd Pillar of the Koran, "The duty of Zakat" - to provide help to the poor, needy, relief of debtors, liberate slaves, and in the desert the welfare to Wayfarers. Thus it is common for the local sheik to recommend a guide "Rafiq" to accompany the traveler through his territory

Did not Ahmad advise you?"

I shook my head.

" Ahmad was under enormous stress and pressure. He had little time. I guess he just forgot. What kind of gifts have you in mind?"

" Quite a wide range subject to the importance, wealth, and opinion of the local leader"

I was stumped by this problem. Then I remembered that Ahmad had given me three hundred pounds to cover unexpected costs.

" Would say one hundred and fifty pounds be adequate to purchase some gifts. That will leave me with about one hundred and fifty pounds for any other unexpected costs."

Faisal was relieved - the problem solved.

" That should be adequate - if we complete the journey, and some of the gifts are not used, I will return them to you."

So it was agreed. Quickly I realized the extreme importance of having a satisfactory relationship with the local leader. The extreme loneliness, the exposure of the elements, the lack of water and food, the possibility of losing the planned route, accidents, communication security needs and the like are some of the dangers   faced by the stranger.

I remember reading David Livingstone's diary traveling across the continent of Africa in the mid 1800s. He was reliant on the cooperation of the local negro chiefs normally achieved through an appropriate gift. Unfortunately his exploration involved journeys of many months, and eventually his stock of gifts was depleted. Life then became extremely difficult for the missionary.

Our first stage Zisa to Irbid was a distance of forty miles due north. Faisal announced that this stage would be accomplished in two days. Our camels calmly strode out into the arid desert without complaint, never faltered, and covered mile after mile without hesitation at a constant speed.

My ever lasting impression of the desert day by day was the absolute silence. I had never experienced such solitude and quiet. During the day, the blazing sun, the cool cutting wind, and the lash of flying sand. Rapidly I appreciated the value of being adequately clothed and protected from the elements,   and possessing sufficient food and water.

The weather continued to be cold, the wind from the West, and the occasional shower - typical December weather. By mid day it could become warm, by night quite cold. The loose flowing robes of the Arab and the indispensable keffiyeh offered excellent protection from the elements whilst the weather remained dry and not too cold, and in particular the constant beating of the flying sand.

Late in the afternoon we completed about twenty miles. Dusk was approaching. We were about midway to Irbid. Passing around a small hill we discovered a small encampment of black tents. The location was level and well protected   from the wind by a nearby hill.. Faisal announced that this would be our camp site.

I looked at this small ragged worn encampment so clearly poverty stricken, and thought .

" Would it not be better to camp elsewhere?"

Faisal approached the small encampment, exchanged courtesies, offered a gift that was accepted, requested permission to stay the night, and pass through his territory. The head of the small encampment insisted that we share his very poor supper of sour cream in a common bowl eaten with our fingers, and we shared a single cup of coffee that was passed from individual to individual. Faisal in turn offered some mutton which was readily consumed.

The next morning we prepared to depart for Irbid. It was then that I realized that the neighboring encampment had already left without a sound. I commented on their poverty to Walid.

" It is important to understand that we all can be poor. They are good people, and in our case they provided additional security throughout the night. "

The Jordan plain east of the River Jordan seemed endless, dead, arid, and cold. But I was told that in the Spring (March), the plain would be a mass of color with flowers of every kind growing 2'0" to 3'0" high. And large areas would have corn from seed sown by the Bedouin, which would be harvested later in the year when they returned.

Already I sensed that the life of the traveler of the desert was the rough track, the dawn, the sun, the wind, the rain, the dusk, the camp fire, the stars, and sleep. And it would be repeated day after day.

That evening we camped outside of Irbid. There was a large encampment of black tents and herds of camels. The people were of the Agail Tribe. Faisal performed the necessary formalities with the Agail Sheik. The small gift was courteously accepted, and Faisel returned to our camp. Whilst away, I assisted the other men with the feeding and tending of our camels. Everyone was tired, and my assistance, although unskilled, was appreciated.

Later after our evening meal, when coffee was served, a musician played his stringed instrument to the sheik and his attendants. Seated on cushions surrounding the sheik, we listened to his melancholy repetitive songs, each line of his song ending with a deep drop in sound rather akin to a groan. Occasionally a visitor would enter the open tent, greet the sheik with hand to his forehead. Then to the sheik attendants, the words *"Peace be upon you".* and they in turn would answer *" And upon you peace".*

Early morning, the sheik requested Faisal's attendance.

" We have heard of your Mr Blackberry - assure him that he will be perfectly safe with us. You are now approaching Bosra and the Jebel Druze. Take considerable care. I recommend Ma'Zuz to be your guide (Rafiq)"

Ma'Zuz proved to be a small dark individual, little more than a boy, who readily accepted payment from Faisal. We had planned to leave early. However I realized that my clothing was inadequate. I needed a heavy coat for warmth, a waterproof cloak to resist the rain, and a pair of stout high ankle boots. Faisal, being an astute trader, was well acquainted with the shops in the small town, recommended a sound establishment, and shortly I was well outfitted. Fortunately at the last moment, I wisely purchased a strong warm pair of gloves.

The weather rapidly deteriorated. The temperature dropped, the wind increased, and heavy rainfall persisted throughout the day. It was not good weather for traveling. However it was the ground which proved the greatest handicap. The dry soil loose or packed hard changed to soft clinging heavy mud. The unfortunate camels now slowed considerably having difficulty contending with the ever deepening ,adhering, and heavy mud.

Faisal shook his head in disgust - his planned schedule had allowed a single day for the 25 mile journey from Irbid to Bosra. Snow showers, sleet, and heavy cold rain made traveling uncomfortable, and by late afternoon we were only about half way to Bosra. Dusk was now approaching, and Faisal searched for a dry protected site for our encampment.

The country was a field of mud. Handicapped we attempted to set up camp, and had difficulty securing the tents. The camels were fed and clearly did not approve of their setting. Finally we sat huddled shivering in a tent, no fire,   and consumed a cold meal of mutton, figs, and dates.

I was curious about the Bedouin Druze. Walid explained.

" *The Druze are quite a fierce lot - a closed Muslim sect. Some people claim that they are subservient people and dangerous."*

" *I hope they will be friendly!"*

Faisal shrugged.

" *Probably."*

Early morning we broke camp - all of us damp, cold, and uncomfortable. Packing the tents and preparing the camels was a muddy and unhappy affair. Finally, already tired and cold, we expected a hard slog through deep mud to Bosra .I now realized another common feature of desert travel - I was absolutely filthy, and that condition was difficult to resolve.

Boswa, a small place, was a Roman city complete with a castle, located at the edge of the Druze Mountains. We entered the town, and Faisal accustomed to procedures, reported to the local Arab authority " *Musid"* and requested permission to enter the Druze territory. Permission was granted but we were warned that there was much unrest between the Druze and other tribes.

Apparently the Druze had taken part in a large raid, and stolen large numbers of sheep and tents. Now the Sakha and Howeitat were preparing to undertake their raid against the Druze. And as usual the Sharcrat had an axe to grind with the Sakha.

Despite the harshness of the country, it was interesting to note that many of the Bedouin were fine looking men, tall, many exceeding 6'0" It was understood that the Druze considered themselves valiant people, and a fine battle excited their thoughts.

" Praise be to God. We are a fighting race"

No doubt the other tribes in the area had similar opinions. Thus it was suspected that there was nothing better than a thrilling raid, the killing of the enemy, and the capture of spoils!

Our new guide (Rafiq) looked awfully scruffy ,wild, and of small stature . However As'Ad had been recommended, and was paid. The weather continued to worsen. The journey to Dionysias about fifty miles took a full five days. So slowly and wearily we trudged and trudged. During the second day we passed the dark ruins of the castle at Salkhad and the Jebel Druze. Suddenly a wild Druze appeared on horseback firing his rifle in a threatening manner. He approached one of the Traders, and demanded his possessions. The man shrugged, and threw his possessions on the ground.

At that very moment about a dozen fierce horsemen all armed with rifles appeared galloping and circling, firing indiscriminately and shouting wildly. . Some dismounted, approached us, and commenced to steal all our belongings. A particularly ugly individual with filthy matted long hair grabbed hold of my heavy coat.

At that very moment little As'Ad recognized the man who had been his family's guest three years past, and called out loudly. Immediately all the Druze stopped - one does not attack a friend - and all our possessions were returned to us. Within moments they all departed firing wildly into the sky!

The following two days were miserable. Howling winds, ice, bitterly cold fog, and sleet. And our encampments were equally miserable, cold, damp, no fire, and cold meals.

The last fifteen miles truly tested our strength and determination. Now we had to contend with deep snow drifts, howling winds, and the ever deep clinging mud. Wearily we led our camels towards a destination that seemed never to be reached. The camels clearly disapproved - just as well we could not read their thoughts.

Finally we arrived at Dionysias. We decided to remain in the town a day to recover, and rest our camels who looked decidedly unhappy and bedraggled. For the first time in four days, we had a hot meal of mutton. And then the hard task of recovering, the cleaning of clothes, equipment, and animals.

The rest stay at Dionysias did wonders. We were now well prepared to complete the forty mile route north to Damascus. The weather had improved, and provided the ground was firm, Faisal expected to be in Damascus within two days.

But there was an unexpected obstacle. Faisal had exchanged courtesies with the leading authority in Dionysias, and had requested permission to proceed. The mudir took the gift, but did not appear particularly grateful. Now, on the morning of our departure, a retainer came to our camp, and advised that we could not leave. The mudir demanded a gift in keeping with his importance.

We had disposed of all our gifts! I sat with the traders to decide what should be done. It was imperative that we leave immediately - we were days behind schedule. All I possessed was fifty pounds. Faisal shook his head - the mudir would not accept the money. As I withdrew the notes from Faisal, he noted my Rolex wristwatch - my only possession of real value.

Faisal eyes gleamed.

" I think he will accept your watch Paul "

Glumly I agreed, and handed over my treasured and valuable Rolex. One matter was certain - that watch would have little utility if its owner was stuck in Dionysias.

The Mudir accepted his new gift, and we were permitted to leave. The weather and ground conditions proved excellent. Everywhere on the road north were herds of camels. The camel owners were leading the animals to pasture, and eventually to either Syria or Iraq for the annual camel sales. Within two days we covered the forty miles, and entered the Syrian capital city of Damascus.

With regret I eventually thanked my guides and escort and bid them farewell. I had no doubt that they had been well compensated by Ahmad, but they still deserved my gratitude.

I gave Faisal my last fifty pounds, shook hands with everyone, and expressed the hope that I would meet them all again. They in turn wished me a safe journey and good health, and gave me a postal address for future communications.

For the first time in 18 months, I was accommodated in a fine hotel, enjoyed again the luxury of a hot bath, and quickly recovered from my long nerve racking trek across the desert.

From Damascus I traveled to Beirut by taxi, the capital city of Lebanon. Beirut at that time was known as the *Paris of the Mediterranean.*

Departure of my plane from Beirut International Airport was in the evening. I had been expected, my air ticket produced, and rapidly I was passing through Immigration and Customs.

The Muslim Immigration officer squinted, and examined my passport carefully. He then referred to his records, and invited me to his office.

" Mr Blackberry - you are from Palestine - Correct?"

" Yes "

" And you have just entered Lebanon from Syria - Correct?"

I nodded.

" Yet your passport does not indicate that you traveled to Syria?"

Without thought I explained

" Last month I decided to travel through the desert of Jordan by camel. I entered Syria by camel, and Immigration passed me through without objection."

The Immigration officer stroked his chin listening to my explanation. There was apparantly another problem.

" And you managed to travel 150 to 200 miles by camel safely?"

" I never fell off my camel."

" No. No. I am not referring to accidents like falling off.   There were no incidents? No attacks?"

I shook my head puzzled.

" Amazing. Absolutely amazing/ Mr Blackberry. I have a request from the Jewish Security head Issar Harel in Tel Aviv to have you arrested and returned to Israel.

Your crime the death of three of his men!"

I stared at him flabbergasted, and blurted out.

" I do not even own a gun or know how to operate a gun."

The Muslim Immigration officer stared at me for long time expressionless, and quietly remarked.

" I think you had better learn."

He stared at Harel's request for a few moments, and made a decision.

" Mr Blackberry. Your flight leaves in one hour. Tomorrow this request for your arrest will be recorded. This Issar Harel will be advised that his arrest warrant request arrived far too late.

I might add that my Palestinian friends are very appreciative of your fine work on their behalf over the past year.

Bon Voyage Monsieur Blackberry."

Within 12 hours I was back in London.

Two weeks later a Mr Jessup phoned, and a meeting was arranged to collect my December Reports. . My assignment in Palestine had ended.

Hot off the Press

I have risen, so often late at night, unable to sleep - my mind full of memories and thoughts.

Although sixty years have passed, that time in Palestine is still as vivid as I sit at this table writing.

And I am obliged to ask myself

" What value are these memories and thoughts?"

Understandably I desire that the Truth is commonly known, and that the Zionist lies and distortions still so prevalent in the USA stamped out. But as I write, I realise it is just as important to identify the major failing of the human race - its willingness to *" **Believe what it wishes to believe"*** irregardless of the Truth.

Consider the terrible damage caused to the World by permitting irresponsible and criminal politicians to mold and formulate major decisions affecting the future of foreign countries as well as their own. The advise and knowledge of experts completely ignored. Decisions so much the product of prejudice, corruption, and lack of compassion.

And understand the ease that modern communications brain wash the so called educated man. The failing of the individual to believe without critical analysis.

Palestine is a classic example. The year 1917. Prime Minister Lloyd George, the Liberal leader so admired by my Suffragette mother, Winston Churchill reckless and ignorant responsible for the death of millions during the First World War, and Lord Balfour Foreign Secretary all created a major tragedy, promoted by Zionist leader Chaim Weizmann. A major tragedy which still exists to this day - *the Declaration that a national home be established for the Jews in Palestine.*

The 1919 Paris Peace Conference perpetuated this conspiracy with the support, directly and indirectly, of USA's President Woodrow Wilson. And in later years both President Franklin Roosevelt and President Harry Truman supported the Zionist movement for a Jewish presence in Palestine - all three pressured by Zionists threatening an unfavorable outcome to domestic US politics without Zionist support..

Just imagine. The Muslim majority of that unfortunate Palestine, 80% to 90% of the population, owned 94% of the land, and yet were never consulted, their wish and natural rights for nationhood and independence totally ignored! It was an incredible state of affairs at that time which persisted another 30 years despite the Muslim majority demonstrating their unhappiness and resentment of this

Zionist conspiracy. It was deplorable that the thoughts of people who possessed expertise of Palestine, and understood the nature and character of the people involved in that irresponsible declaration of the Paris Peace Conference, were never consulted.

Gertrude Bell, possibly one of the Britain's greatest in political intelligence and understanding, was incensed that politicians and Zionists at the Paris Peace Conference would talk of Palestine as if the country was empty of people. She predicted at that time that the Arabs and the Jews could not live peaceably side by side. It was significant that she and the famous T.E.Lawrence and his considerable knowledge of the Middle East had no official standing at the Conference.

When she first heard of Britain's 1917 assurance of a Jewish State in Palestine, she wrote   January 1918 to Sir Gilbert Clayton, recent head Arab Bureau Cairo that Palestine for the Jews has always seemed to us to be an impossible proposition. I don't believe it can be carried out - personally I don't want it to be carried out, and I have said so on every possible occasion. *And she continued saying that to gratify Jewish sentiment you would have to override every conceivable political consideration, including the wishes of the large majority of the population.*

Jewish people of a wide range of social standing also voiced their opposition.

Sir Edwin Montagu, Secretary of State for India declared that Zionism was a mischievous political creed untenable to loyal citizens of the U.K.

Lord Rothschild had his doubts. Many Jewish leaders believed that to offer Palestine to the Jews would be a disservice to Jewry. And the Jews settled in Palestine of that time anticipated and dreaded the trouble that Zionism would cause to their future.

But the narrow and selfish interests of USA and British politicians backed by Zionists continued unabated for the next thirty years. Finally the 1947 United Nations Resolution 181 Partition of Palestine into two States was declared. Again the aspirations and the national rights of the Palestinian Arab was ignored.

The Muslim population was never consulted, and no consideration was ever given if the people rejected the terms of the Partition.

Again people with expertise and social understanding were ignored.

Mahatme Gandhi 1947 was very specific when addressing the proposed U.N Partition.

" *The Arabs could choose - not be forced, but choose - to give the Jews refuge, and it would have been a great generosity. **The Jews did not have a right to the lands; It was the Arabs' decision to make, and they chose not to give the Jews land.***

When Gandhi was asked what would be the most acceptable solution to the Palestine Problem, he declared:

" The abandonment wholly by the Jews of terrorism and other forms of violence"

The ignored experts were correct.

For the past sixty years criminal politicians in the USA and the UK have supported the illegal Zionist State of Israel in Palestine at the expense and the persecution of the Arab people, and have permitted and encouraged this horrific and illegal Terrorist State in the Middle East.

A debate at the House of Commons January 29th 1949, just after my return from Palestine, demonstrated the guilt of the political world in England and USA that had been manipulated like puppets by Zionists for the previous thirty years. The subject under discussion was *the half million or more Arabs who had been turned by the Jewish immigrants into homeless refugees without employment or resources.*

The corrupt Churchill claimed that the coming of the Jewish State had to be seen in the perspective of two or even three thousand years - he had not the least concern of the criminal inequity of the situation.

Ernest Bevin, at that time Foreign Secretary, was indignant that the Arab population which had occupied Palestine for more than twenty centuries, to be turned out of their land and homes to make way for another race was a profound injustice. He wondered how the British people would feel if obliged to give up a slice of Scotland, Wales, or Cornwall to another race!

The Foreign Secretary was astonished that the conscience of the world was so little stirred by the tragedy of the Arab refugees. And he blamed American interests as being one of the major determining factors of the prevailing situation. *It was disgraceful that the whole question of who should be elected to certain offices in the United States would be subject to the Zionists obtaining favorable policies regarding Palestine.*

What is so significant, and tragic, the brainwashed poverty stricken USA Taxpayer has been subsidizing this illegal Terrorist State the sum of over three billion dollars annually for many many years!

It is unbelievable that the most powerful democratic country on this planet denies its own poor adequate funds, and yet spends enormous sums on a   Terrorist State.. This money has been used to finance aggressive attacks against Arab nations, and the continued persecution and death of Palestinian Arabs.

The Taxpayer has financed a Terrorist State at the expense of the rights of all people in this World, and has caused enormous harm   to United Nations. Just consider these rights contained in the **1948 General Assembly Resolution 217A (III):**

Article 9: No one shall be subjected to arbitrary arrest, detention or exile.
Article 13/2: Everyone has the right to leave any country, including his own, and to return to his country.
Article 17/2: No one shall be arbitrarily deprived of his property.

Have these rights ever been respected? Ask the Palestinian people 60 years later if the hundreds of thousands forcibly expelled in 1948 have been permitted to return, to recover their stolen land and personal property, and been reimbursed for the hundreds of millions of pounds of stolen bank deposits.

The rights of all people of the USA have been contravened for many years subjected to illegal arrest and detention. *It could be you, the reader, this very moment.* Just ask Brandon Mayfield, a Portland lawyer, attacked, shackled, and illegally hauled away in front of his wife and three small children by the Portland Oregon FBI, and illegally imprisoned for two weeks without any evidence. His crime being a Muslim.

And it certainly applies to the denied rights of the unfortunate persecuted Palestinian Muslims over the past sixty years.

The Taxpayer has financed a Terrorist State at the expense of the Arab people with complete disregard of the terms of the 1948 United Nation Resolution 194 *which declared the unconditional right of the Palestinian refugees to return to their homes.*

For sixty years the Terrorist State of Israel has ignored Resolution 217A, Resolution 181, and Resolution 194. In 1948 the people of Israel demonstrated their contempt with the assassination of UN mediator Count Folke Bernadotte who had demanded compliance to the UN Resolutions.

I wonder if there is really much difference between American and Israeli policy and action. Both apply power and aggression rather than equitable discussion. Nothing changes. Late 2008 the Democratic Party has just replaced the Republican Party but the declared Washington foreign policies continue with the inequitable and ill thought declaration of support of the Terrorist State of Israel.

I examine the newspaper headlines - " *Israel is the Crime Capital of the Middle East. Chicago Mafia small fry in comparison."*

Am I surprised? How can I be surprised when criminals created Zionism and its seizure of Palestine - and unfortunately as we all know even criminals have children!

Someone is reading over my shoulder. It is David Ben-Gurion roaring from Hell.

" Issar Harel - you miserable inept head of Intelligence - Where are you? "

Another voice meekly responds.

" I'm here Prime Minister "

" What kind of Intelligence are you. I told you time and time again - get that Blackberry - and you failed."

" You did not mention Blackberry by name!"

" Excuses. Excuses. Just Excuses. What a mistake appointing you head. When I warned everyone of the impending Second Holocaust, all my people knew what to do without my mentioning names. Just wipe them all out and get rid of them. How I miss my comrades and their efficient massacres".

Ben-Gurion's voice drops sentimentally thinking of his faithful comrades. But it rises again as he addresses his Intelligence Chief.

" As for you - so often I complained of all those evil newspaper reports in England that contradicted our fine reports - and every time you failed the Zionist Cause.

Do you realise that nasty spiteful news reporter Blackberry for sixty years has complained about our Ethnic Cleansing. We all know that those people left Palestine voluntarily - all 800,000 or whatever. There is no sense of appreciation, no sense of pride, in the efficient way that we rid our country of those trouble makers. Our only failure you and your so called Intelligence."

Wisely, there is no response. David Ben-Gurion's temper deteriorates.

" If I could get my hands on you, I would send you back to my Terrorist State so that you can suffer the real Hell which I planned and created. As for that Blackberry wait until I get my hands on him."

Every night I wake in a cold sweat.

It is the same complaint, the same threats, and the same master criminal. Fortunately , as usual, Issar Harel. will deservedly suffer his master's dissatisfaction.

I then recollect the advise of my dear friend Ahmad Al-Husseini. My mysterious driver and respected adviser.

" You have to understand that the strength of any organization is, like a chain, subject to the failure of its weakest link. It applies to   my country, and equally to your country.

In the future you may be advised of the health and condition of a Palestinian tractor by our representative Mr Jessup if he considers it wise. In the meantime I am concerned about your future safety - please be prudent."

A few years later I received a letter from Mr Jessup regretting that a very fine tractor was no longer usable, and business was very disheartening..

Finally the reader should remember this is a novel, and its purpose to encourage you to ascertain the Truth.

 By all means study the content of this novel but remember the author is biased and prejudiced. Take with a grain of salt the opinions of the many characters in this novel because they also are biased and prejudiced. And most definitely critically examine the motives and decisions of the many criminal politicians in England and the USA. over the past hundred years.

You will realise the absolute necessity that you investigate and check the records throughout the past century because they exist.   Then you may realise the terrible injustice and persecution suffered by innocent people, and that the USA must stop financing a terrorist state with $3 billion or more annually that perpetuates this injustice and persecution.

I remind you again *"We believe what we wish to believe"*

For that reason your beliefs must be based on facts - not prejudice and hate.

www.ingramcontent.com/pod-product-compliance
Lightning Source LLC
Chambersburg PA
CBHW051955280526

45793CB00005B/734